Handbook of Interventions for Changing People and Communities

Handbook of Interventions for Changing People and Communities

Bernard Guerin
University of Waikato

CONTEXT PRESS
Reno, Nevada

Handbook of Interventions for Changing People and Communities

Paperback   pp. 245

Library of Congress Cataloging-in-Publication Data

Guerin, Bernard, 1957-
  Handbook of interventions for changing people and communities / Bernard Guerin.
        p. cm.
  Includes bibliographical references and index.
  ISBN 1-878978-53-5 (pbk.)
  1. Human services. 2. Counseling. 3. Intervention (Administrative procedure) 4. Change (Psychology) 5. Social change. I. Title.
  HV31.G84 2005
  361.3–dc22

                                                            2005013533

© 2005 CONTEXT PRESS
933 Gear Street, Reno, NV   89503-2729

Printed in the United States of America

Table of Contents

Preface

The philosophers have only interpreted the world in different ways; the point is to change it. Marx (1845)

…there are no rules for revolution any more than there are rules for love or rules for happiness, but *there are rules for radicals who want to change their world; there are certain central concepts of action in human politics that operate regardless of the scene or the time.* Alinsky, 1971, p. xviii

In Action Research practitioners envisage intervention as a cycle of formulation, planning, intervention and evaluation followed by the same again but even better. Meanwhile in Social Work, there is an approach called the Research Intervention Paradigm that formulates, plans, carries out an intervention, researches the results, and starts formulating again even better. The two have probably never talked to one another or read each other's work.

In carrying out interventions, reading about them and teaching about them, I have had this frustration that practitioners in different areas do the same thing under different names but have no idea that someone else is doing the same thing. There is another frustration that academics dress interventions up in fancy theories that appear to contradict one another, but meanwhile the interventions they devise from these fancy theories are identical. A further frustration is that some interventions are made to sound magical or extremely complex by the jargon or theories wrapped around them but when you pull apart what exactly is happening in concrete way— what the people are actually doing to one another—the components are very common ones and very simple ones.

My last book was aimed at getting all the social science approaches to practical analysis and finding a common way to talk about social behavior that encompassed all of them, or at least encompassed the findings that we know about social behavior. *The aim of this book you are holding is to find a way of pulling apart interventions, showing the basic things that are being done to people and communities to help them, and finding a way of talking about all this that synthesizes the different approaches with the least jargon.*

This book was not written to train people to carry out interventions, but to introduce people to interventions and produce better-rounded practitioners. To do this stuff you will need specialized study and practical experience under a supervisor, but this book is to let you know what is available at present and what you need to be able to do to implement an intervention. *By the end of the book you should be comfortable in planning interventions of all sorts and if you do not have the skills and experience yourself by that point you will at least know the sort of person you must hire to do it.*

There are three aspects of building this stripped-down approach to interventions that will be unfamiliar to most readers. These are spelt out in the text but I would like to forewarn you here so you can pay special attention to those parts.

1. A major idea is developed in Chapter 1 that is referred to throughout the rest of the book ("*Analyzing the Contexts is more important than Finding the Causes*"). It points out that there is much social influence in interventions that happens in a hidden way, but the "cause" for change is commonly attributed elsewhere (Guerin, 2001d). For example, just getting someone to attend therapy, however it is done, is probably half the influence already needed for change, in the same way as I will argue that just getting people to agree to go up on stage is most of the intervention already done for stage hypnotists. These events, however, are never used as the causes of change, and so that is attributed to the "magical" procedures used by the hypnotists. This will be an important point and many intervention studies will be criticized (nicely) for having effects but not letting us work out how they came about because not enough of the social and cultural context was documented, and that was probably where the real change was taking place. This will make more sense as you read, but I would like to alert you to this issue.

2. A major part of the framework is re-working the distinction between interventions with individuals and interventions with communities. While this may be a true and useful distinction for typically western people—what I called non-kin-based groups in Guerin (2004)—it is not true for kin-based groups. As we will see, interventions to change the behaviors or practices of a single individual in kin-based groups must be considered as community or family interventions, and must be approached this way to even come close to being effective. For close communities, interventions with an individual are automatically interventions with the community and need to be handled as such. This goes further than just involving the extended family, a topic for Chapter 2, and changes the very conception of what needs to change and how an intervention might be effective and maintain. Chapter 1 goes through this in more detail and presents a summary in Table 3 that is also referred to throughout the book. You might want to bookmark it.

3. The ideas of cognitive therapy, cognitive anthropology and cognitive psychology are reworked in a way that will be familiar to readers of Guerin (2004). All talking, conversation, and even talking to oneself are treated as social events that strategically do things to people—even self-talk. This seems strange at first (see Guerin, 2004, Chapter 5) but it allows us to make much more sense of interventions that involve changing how people talk about themselves and others. In short, there is a whole new theory of cognition in this book that comes about in Chapter 5 by translating "cognitive" events into talking, discursive or conversational events. Most importantly, it shows the truly social nature of thinking and "cognition" and translates individualistic events into social events.

This point relates closely to interventions for "mental health and illness" but I have included little of that in this book because we are dealing with this elsewhere as a special topic. There are hints here in Chapter 5 of how we can re-conceive "mental illness" as social but not the full picture yet. For the purpose of this book, mental illness can be viewed as arising from "normal" strategies of social life (Guerin, 2004), especially talking or cognitive strategies, but ones which either escalate too far for ordinary life, or which become chronic and develop social properties by virtue of being chronic (essentialistic attributions are made by others, they are spread across all social contexts in the person's life, inability to avoid them in any context, etc.). Whether escalation or chronicity, the social properties go too far and are not ordinarily present in everyday life so they look weird. The interventions therefore are also special.

So the main idea of the book is for you to learn the issues about running interventions, to learn about a large number of interventions, and to try and re-think some common ways of thinking about social behavior in a way that allows us to make more sense of interventions by pulling them apart into components. It also aims to teach you about interventions from all disciplines and approaches and how they might be fitted together into a truly interdisciplinary social science that can usefully change people and communities.

In reading and writing all this, I have been supported by many people and institutions. The University of Waikato and the Faculty of Arts and Social Sciences have, inadvertently this time I am sure, allowed me to go my own way and run all this material through graduate students over several years now, improving it all the time. Doing this has greatly changed and I hope improved the presentation. I have also been helped by Emma Wood who ran some of the "Intervention" classes for me. A special thanks to Wendy Gunthorpe for working with me on a proto-proto-interventions course many years ago now, and to Mike Innes for his early applied social psychology courses that first inspired me to think about interventions.

Most of the support though, has come from Pauline, who looked after Rhianna, Vincent, Giles and Gracie who would not otherwise have allowed me some small breaks in which to write. Thanks again, you guys! You still make living worthwhile.

I wish to thank Steve Hayes for having faith in what I write even when he might initially have had no idea what I was going to say. He supported my last two books, and this one, when other publishers could not see into the future. Like last time, Steve saw beyond that and I hope this also works out well for him. He has supported many other writers through the Context Press with his personal budget and sweat over many years now.

Emily Neilan at Context Press has been extremely helpful and friendly, and has done a great job setting up the Tables and things within chapters. Many thanks for your help on these jobs.

A lot of the ideas and integration of ideas has come from working on our large project *Strangers in Town: Enhancing Family and Community in a More Diverse New Zealand Society*. Many thanks to the Foundation for Science, Research and Technology in New Zealand for supporting this long-term project (UOWX0203) and Pauline, Richard, Elsie, Linda, Fatuma, Abdirizak, Asad and others for working as a great team in which I have learned so much more about communities and especially "kin-based-groups". I also have learned a lot about interventions with non-western communities in this way, and thanks to the Somali and Tūhoe communities for letting me learn from learning about them. I have also been supported through another project with interventions, *Solutions for Energy Efficiency at Work and at Home*. Many thanks again to the Foundation for Science, Research and Technology in New Zealand for supporting this long-term project (UOWX0302).

Many thanks to you all, and others I have forgotten.

For the Teacher

This book can be read without doing a course although the reader needs to be clear that this will not teach you the practical side of carrying out interventions. This book is to teach you about interventions and, for the first time, about interventions from all over the social sciences. To gain the practical experience you will need to work with professionals either in a specialized course or as an apprentice. The book, though, does teach you about the skills you are going to need to do these interventions. For those in more managerial positions, it will teach you about the skills needed in people you hire. So it can certainly guide you to know what you have to learn.

For those working within a course, this book will provide a normal course-length introduction to interventions that can then be supplemented with practical work or practicums, and even with practical work within the class (Gundy and I used to have students in class teach each other folk dances using the different methods from Chapter 3). You will need to emphasize the issues and ethics of interventions carefully, otherwise the course will end up teaching merely recipes that will not transfer beyond the class setting.

Like my last book, I envisaged this one as a flexible tool for the teacher to work around rather than a plan to follow mindlessly. Whether you are in psychology, social work, organizational studies, anthropology, etc., you will want to emphasize parts of this book more than others although I recommend you cover all the main areas in a little depth at least (to produce well-rounded, adaptable and *employable* students). So, for example, social anthropologists might gravitate more towards the latter parts of the book but I believe that in running numerous training programs for developing countries and other applied projects, the earlier chapters will be of direct use to at least some social anthropologists also.

Within this, I recommend that teachers use their own examples where possible to replace mine, since students can read my examples anyway. This will make the course fit better with other courses your students are doing at the same time. Again, though, make sure your students learn some examples beyond your own area so they can branch out later and be widely employable.

My other recommendation for teaching from this book is to teach it the first time using material that you are familiar with; examples and exercises from your own discipline or area. In the following year, read up more on some other areas and begin to include material from elsewhere (or read and use my examples). This will be beneficial to your own development as well as your teaching profile.

For example, if you are teaching within a health promotion framework then use health promotion materials extensively in your first year teaching from this book, but make a point during that year of reading more about applied anthropology methods and techniques of intervention they use in relation to health. In the following year you can then begin branching out. I did not start out miraculously knowing all this stuff but gradually included more and more, attended conferences in other areas, and talked to colleagues from remote parts of the social sciences. It works well for the course and helps your own development at the same time.

Chapter 1

The Basic Issues of Intervention

The foundation for this book is that social science interventions are adjustments in social contexts and relationships. To understand and successfully carry out interventions, you need to know something about social relationships: you cannot intervene in the same way with strangers in a western society as you might a close community of inter-related family members. You also cannot just add on a 'cultural' package to a strangers-in-a-western-society intervention and expect it to work. People have been trying for a long time to find interventions that are independent of the various social contexts and relationships, but success has been elusive.

For example, if we are intervening by introducing a new social policy then there are many political relationships that need negotiating both to have the policy accepted and to get it implemented. If, on the other hand, we are talking face-to-face with a person to change their behavior in some way they desire, then the relationship with that person needs to be developed (sometimes glossed over as "building rapport"). Even if we are intervening by giving a lecture to a group of school kids to change their risky behaviors, the social relationship between the class and the lecturer is vital. They might disregard the intervention merely because the lecturer seems 'uncool', and this is indicative of the social relationship or lack thereof. Or a big sports star might present an intervention on TV but the kids know (quite rightly) that the real relationship here is an *economic relationship* –the big star is only saying all those things because they are getting well paid for doing so–not because they care about the TV viewers.

Thinking about interventions in this way, as adjustments in social relationships, opens the field right up in several important ways. First, this means that we are conducting interventions all the time and they are not new or mysterious. Any time we ask a spouse or friend to do something for us, we are intervening. Obviously, this is not what the book is about, and further down I will be limiting interventions to planned and ethical interventions (although 'planned' does not mean they are as clean and well organized as the word sounds), carried out because there is a problem or issue that results in people getting hurt, or because someone has requested help with making a change.

What "interventions are adjustments in social contexts" also means is that the effectiveness and duration of influence is going to depend upon the context of the relationships. There are unlikely to be plug-in intervention packages that work for everyone at all times, in the way that aspirin works for most people at most times, since what happens in any intervention will depend upon the relationships between the intervention 'agent', the person undergoing change, and all the other people involved in the social context. The exceptions to this, we will see, are cases for which the form of social relationship is either so detached or so common that the social context can be duplicated across persons, and also where artificial relationships can be set up. This will make sense to you later.

Finally, what we are really talking about with interventions, then, is *what we can do to other people* (leaving aside self-interventions for another chapter), and this is about what we can do in our relationships with people (Guerin, 2004). We must face up to it that if we are going to intervene then we are changing people and doing something to them—and this leads to a lot of legal, ethical, political, and personal issues. *In a broad sense there are no benign interventions.*

To know what we might do to others to change them, we need to know what we can do with our relationships, whether that is a stranger relationship or a very close family relationship. For example, if you are completely and absolutely dependent on me then I can probably just tell you to change and you will, although there are still ethical questions about doing this at all. If we are family then I can make you change through family obligation but I need to know about the reciprocity of our relationship to know exactly what is going to happen in the long run. If you walk up to a stranger in the street there are strong limits on how you might change that person (Guerin, 2004). "*Hi. You don't know me but I want you to stop smoking right now. Okay!*"

We therefore have to understand the social contexts and relationships in order to understand and implement interventions. Every branch of the social sciences has its own set of words and ideas for discussing social contexts and social relationships, but I have previously attempted to bring these all together into a synthesis for analyzing social relationships of all kinds (Guerin, 2004). The framework for the present book will be loosely based on that because it encompasses most other approaches, but a thorough knowledge is not needed to understand this book. A little introduction will be given below, however.

The main point is that we need to know as much about the persons before intervening, and especially the *social, cultural, economic, environmental and historical contexts in which they are embedded.* If some western interventions can work even between strangers, such as happens with most education, therapy and psychiatry, it is because western social relationships normally involve strangers and people are used to it. But those very same "interventions from a stranger" might not work on people who are always involved with extended family members in their life.

First Steps in Intervention: Know Your Social Context!

The most important part of an intervention is the beginning. Like any analysis of behavior, you need to know the behaviors or activities with which you are dealing, the social contexts or situations in which they occur, and what the typical consequences have been in the past for those activities in those contexts (Guerin, 1994, 2004). The best way to do all that is from what I call *know your social context!* This applies to both human and non-human animals for any type of training or intervention—get to know the people, communities and the situations with which

---

Intervention Analysis 1. **Interventions as Changes in Social Contexts**

Making an intervention is changing a social relationship

Interventions across many people will only work if:

    Form of relationship is common
    Form of relationship is simple or detached from context

Where possible we need analyses of:

    Social contexts
    Economic contexts
    Cultural contexts
    Environmental contexts
    Historical contexts

---

you are dealing. Spend as much time as possible with them, participating in their life if possible. I recommend psychologists to spend more time with their subject matter—people—and use more participatory methods, because they are normally trained to spend very little time with people. They give out a questionnaire or spend a clinical hour talking in an office and learn everything about a person from what that person verbally reports.

You also need to spend time watching informally and not only talking to people who are experts, but also talking to people who are not academic experts but have spent a lot of time with the people involved. Practitioners and service providers often have a lot of important information and views to incorporate. Doing this will help you more than anything else probably. You do not have to believe at face value everything they tell you, just find out about it from them and integrate that into everything else.

If you *know your social context* properly, then the rest of the intervention is straightforward: define the activities to be intervened upon and either train new behaviors or change the contexts or consequences until the behavior changes. Sounds simple? Well it is not quite that simple.

Suppose you were concerned about the welfare of women who get battered by their spouses. Start by talking to the women themselves, or people who know the women well. The women themselves might not be able to tell you the official scientific causes of what is happening, nor why their spouses keep doing it, but at the least you will learn a lot about the contexts in which it occurs, the precursors to the abuse, and the consequences that maintain the abuse. Another good question is about what happens on nights when the spouse does not abuse his partner? How do they interact then? What is different in the context? All of that will be useful. Talk to people who work with battered women, people in shelters or refuges, social welfare personnel. Talk to the spouses themselves if you can about the conditions and consequences. They are obviously a most important link in this whole activity. *Remember that your goal in this is not to come up with the causes of spousal abuse, or a theory even, but to find the contexts and consequences within which it occurs.*

A good example of this was published by Conte, Wolf and Smith (1989). They interviewed 20 known sex offenders about how they selected children, recruited them and then maintained the abusive relationships. They even asked them to write something like a manual for how to abuse children. The interviews gave much information not otherwise easily available to help with preventive interventions for such people. Such information can then be used to develop interventions to train children to recognize and resist such attempts at selection and recruitment, and also to stop adults offending.

Having done this, you still might not be the wiser about the official scientific causes, but that is not a concern yet. Getting descriptions about what exactly is happening, the conditions (contexts) under which it occurs, and the consequences of it occurring and not occurring, will be as useful at this stage as reading about theoretical causes. Also try and find out about the incidence of such activities amongst "ordinary" people—the conditions and the consequences. What do "ordinary" people do if their spouse hits them or threatens to hit them that *prevents* it happening? How often are "ordinary" women battered but this is not reported?

Of course, you should also go to written accounts and past research. If someone has already done all the above, it is silly for you to re-invent the wheel and do it all again, unless there is reason to suppose that your case or context is different in some way. Look especially in reliable, published sources for previous interventions of the

---

***Intervention Analysis 2.* Key Questions for Intervention Analysis**

What do "ordinary" people do in this sort of situation?

What would happen if this situation *was* to change? (are the likely outcomes maintaining the situation?)

Who are all the audiences (social influences) in this situation?

What is the historical context of this situation?

What has been tried before (from both researchers and practitioners)?

same problem. What have people tried before under what conditions; what has worked and what has failed (often this latter does not get into the written accounts so you need to talk to people or EMail them to find out what interventions they have tried that failed).

The questions that arise following these steps are about the type of intervention. We will look at the major divisions or characteristics a bit further below, but remember that your first intervention analysis should be to get to know the situation and the people involved.

What is Included as an Intervention?

As mentioned earlier, thinking of interventions as adjustments in social relationships opens up the field of interventions but also allows the field to become too huge. Probably many interventions occur with little or no fuss: we ask someone close to us (with family obligations or social network obligations) to do something differently and they do it (*"Can you please stop leaving the milk on the bench and put it back in the fridge?"*). Such events happen frequently and with little comment unless it leads to a conflict. What we are really going to be focused on in this book are cases where things do not work out easily and there are problems with changes. Table 1, on the next page, lists a number of examples of these interventions.

These are all interventions we will be dealing with in this book, and the list hopefully will give you a feel for the range and types. We cannot deal with every intervention so more importantly, I will be trying to teach the main points you need to consider in planning any intervention, the ethical and practical issues involved, how to go about setting up the intervention, and some of the basic techniques people use.

The material for discussing interventions comes from all the social sciences and health sciences. There are interventions from social anthropology, psychology, geography, policy studies, sociology, health promotion, behavior analysis, family planning, clinical psychology, and sports coaching. Many of those doing these interventions do not know about the others, and might appear here for the first time together.

My real criterion for including an intervention is that it actually does intervene and change people. There is a lot of research under the rubric of "Applied Psychology," for example, that researches real world situations but does not tell us how to change things or attempt to change things. A typical study might show that two factors are associated with stress in parents but this does not tell us how to intervene. Indeed, many times we cannot change those 'factors' anyway to make a change, and moreover, showing that a factor is associated with an event does not mean that changing the factor will change the event. For example, stress is associated with working in modern organizations but we cannot just get the person to leave their job to reduce their stress. Stress is also associated with having large families but we cannot intervene and force people to leave their families in order to reduce stress. By the same logic, getting a divorce is very strongly associated with being married but not marrying is hardly the best solution to the increase in divorces!

Table 1. Examples of Interventions in this Book

✓ We would like people to cover up their skin at the sunny beach but they do not wear shirts and they do not use sun-block. How do we intervene to make this happen?

✓ People do not use protection during sex in many cases risking pregnancy or the transmission of diseases, so how do we get them to use protection?

✓ A basketballer keeps missing important shots so how does the sports psychologist intervene to improve their skills

✓ A community wants to reduce the use of drugs in all the kids in the neighborhood, so how could they go about this?

✓ A school sees too much bullying going on and wants to stop or reduce it; what might they do?

✓ A witness to a murder is having trouble remembering some details, so what can a forensic psychologist do to "get back" those memories?

✓ A government wants to reduce the number of deaths on the road, so how can they convince a whole country to slow down and drive better?

✓ A man is obsessing and thinking constantly that he is about to be killed by a mystery assassin, how can we help him if he requests help?

✓ Member countries of the United Nations were concerned at the number of small arms being sold around the world, so what did they do to begin curbing the proliferation of small arms and light weapons?

✓ A child with intellectual disabilities cannot eat with a spoon: how could you teach them when they have no language and little understanding of what you might show them?

✓ A rumor starts in an organization that the CEO is about to be sacked and the new bosses need to make 200 workers redundant. Should we ignore such rumors, deny them, punish anyone repeating them, or produce counter rumors denying this?

✓ Two neighbors keep having disputes about overhanging trees and noisy dogs, and they begin yelling at each other and making threats. How should we intervene if requested and negotiate a peaceful solution?

✓ A woman of a close ethnic community begins acting 'strange', and throws shoes on the road, lifts her skirt in public, and stops speaking to her family. What can we do?

The logic of these points means that a lot of the Applied Psychology literature will be left out here, although this is not to dismiss it. Studying those "factors" in intervention studies is the way to go, and learning about all those factors is certainly useful to sensitize you to building an intervention. It is part of the first intervention stage of *Know your social context!* So you should read such research diligently, but most of it will not be discussed here. This book is about carrying out interventions and is therefore based on actual interventions that have been tried. [A parallel discussion can be found about "Applied Anthropology" as well, which is usually contrasted with "Practicing Anthropology" (Gwynne, 2003; Nolan, 2003).]

Some Basic Features of Interventions that need Consideration

To start there are several characteristics of interventions to be considered. These will decide the people you work with, the ethics, the types of techniques used, and the measures of effectiveness and expected outcomes. *Intervention Analysis 3* has a list of these.

Intervention Analysis 3. **Some Basic Features of Interventions that need Consideration**

Working with *individuals* or *social groups*?

- Changing the behavior of *individuals* by changing the environment, teaching them skills, or by talking to them
- Changing the behavior of *social groups*, including families, neighborhoods, communities, societies and whole nations

People have *language skills* or *no language skills*?

- Working with people who can follow verbal instructions and have good fluency in a common language
- Working with people who cannot speak a language because of intellectual disabilities, age, or foreign upbringing

Teaching them to *do something* or to *say something*?

- Teaching people a skill in which they learn a new physical skill or stop doing something physical
- Teaching people how to say something, agree with something, follow instructions, give themselves instructions, or stop saying something out loud or to themselves

The *types of relationships* involved (see Table 3)

- Strangers
- Close friends and family
- Close communities and extended families

Working with Individuals or Social Groups

The first consideration is about how many people are being changed. Attempting to change the speeding of one person is very different from trying to stop a whole country of car drivers from speeding: different methods will be used, different ethical principles apply, and different outcomes will be expected.

There are advantages and disadvantages to both small and large interventions that you need to consider. Many psychology students believe that the only way to change someone is to work with them one-on-one, usually by intensive talking under the guise of therapy. While doing this could result in a useful change, only one person has been helped. If you were to see 30 clients you would still spend considerable time changing a small number of people, useful as that might be (in fact, 30 clients at once might burn you out).

Consider instead working in social policy, and spending the same amount of time bringing in a new social policy that covers thousands of people and is actually enforced or backed up institutionally by local authorities, police or military (depending upon the policy institution). In doing this you could make a beneficial difference to thousands of people instead of just 30.

So which is best? As usual, this is a non-question, and both have different uses and advantages. One problem with social policy, for example, is that it is very difficult to get it passed and enforced. People can spend huge amounts of time trying to get a policy approved only to have it thrown out, or the politics change and it gets left on a desk gathering dust. Working with individual clients can lead to observable changes but is limited in scope as was said above. Policies also usually have problems being implemented and enforced after being passed, but more on that later in the book.

With enough resources, of course, you can do a little of both and work from both ends. Changing car drivers' speed practices, for example, needs individual skill training and re-training, as well as government media promotions and policing campaigns. It does not have to be an either/or situation. My point here is for you to consider all options when first considering an intervention.

People with Language Skills or No Language Skills

Almost all interventions involve talking to people but there are cases in which the participants cannot speak or respond to instructions. In some cases this is because of intellectual disabilities, and special techniques are required. The next chapter has more on this. Similar interventions work with non-human animals although used very differently. This is not because people with intellectual disabilities are like animals but because they share two interrelated characteristics—lack of language ability and a lack of generalized reinforcement or generalized exchange operations (Guerin, 2004).

The techniques for these cases rely on using very salient and simple systems of motivation—they assume that the organism can be made to work for simple outcomes. Normal adult humans, however, live in systems of highly complex and generalized outcomes and any simple procedure usually has several effects on them rather than one (Guerin, 2004). In short, what people 'want' is very complicated and tied up with social and economic systems in a way that non-human animals are not. Any 'stimulus' presented would normally have several 'reinforcing' and 'punishing' effects at the same time if we are dealing with normal adult humans. Even something like chocolate (which has been used as an overly-simplistic 'reinforcer') is involved not just with taste but also with dieting, image management, status, stress, reputation, economic cost, social comparison to others, a long history of stories and conversations about chocolate eating, and a wealth of other social strategies. What all this really means is that we do not, and probably cannot, know the reinforcers and punishers for normal adults since they are not simple (Guerin, 2001a, b, 2004). In fact, anyone who puts their effort in for only a limited and simple range of 'wants' impresses one as being child-like.

Teaching People to Do Something or to Say Something

Another major distinction I would like to make that is not obvious at first is between intervening to make someone *do something* and intervening to make someone *say, believe, or think something* (Guerin, 2001c, 2003, 2004). While not different in principle–they are both just getting people to do things–the intervention methods and social properties are very different so they are usefully treated as distinct (Guerin, 2004).

To give you a feel for this distinction, if you look at Table 1, shown earlier, then the examples 1, 2, 3, 4, 7, 9, and 10 were primarily about getting people to do things, while examples 6, 8, and 11 were primarily about getting people to say or stop saying things. Examples 5, 12 and 13 probably had both involved–bullying is often about verbal teasing and name-calling and not just physical bullying, and the neighbors in example 12 want to stop the yelling and verbal threats but also wanted to do something less verbal about the trees and dogs (unless the trees and dogs were a pretext for verbal conflict).

Intervening in all these examples would probably involve the use of language except perhaps teaching a child with intellectual disabilities to eat with a spoon (example 10), but the distinction is about whether we want the talking to change (including talking to oneself) or the doing something to change. They can be very mixed, however. In getting someone to do something different, getting them to change the way they talk about that something is often important, but we must also then remember that just changing talk does not automatically change what people do. Most people can *tell* you the dangers of smoking or speeding and what is likely to happen to them, but they do not change their smoking or speeding. *Changing talk is useful but does not lead automatically to changing practices.*

This distinction will be especially important in Chapter 5, which is dedicated to synthesizing interventions that try to change the way people talk, believe, think, report feelings, or converse about topics. For example, therapies are not just about talking to people to have them do things differently, they are also (sometimes primarily) about getting people to think about themselves differently, talk to themselves about having a higher self-esteem, or report feeling better about things.

Types of Social Relationships

The next distinction separates social relationships into three types. This does not mean that every person is purely one or the other; it just means that the social properties of each type are different from the others and need separate consideration. There are different social properties of relationships between strangers in larger urban, western societies, immediate family, close friends and social network acquaintances, and very close and interdependent extended family and community members.

Table 2. Three Types of Social Relationships

1. Those exchanged between parties whose only connection is that they are members of a general society or community and they might not have any other ties whatsoever (non-kin-based)

2. Those involving exchanges between immediate family, friends or acquaintances—social networks (kin- or non-kin-based)

3. Very close family and communities, including remote and "traditional" communities and villages but also some groups within cities (kin-based)

The strategies for managing relationships and therefore interventions with strangers, with close family and friends, and with extended family circles are very different, and for this book the important point is that *how we influence someone to change is going to be very different for the different types of social relationships*. They can all be successful in the right circumstances, but the interventions strategies are going to be very different. Imagine trying to change your gambling problem by talking with someone, when that person is (1) a stranger paid to talk to you, (2) a close family member or close friend, or (3) someone who is part of your close and extended family and community network. Each might be effective but for very different reasons, and each might work best for different people and situations. For example, some people I know who live in strong, extended-family communities simply cannot understand how paying a stranger (such as a psychologist) to talk to you in their office for an hour a week could possibly ever change anything (Guerin, Guerin, Diiriye, & Yates, 2004)! But I also know westerners who would much rather pay a stranger to talk about problems than mention those problems to someone in their family or networks (who might talk about it to others). The latter want to buy the anonymity, the former believe you need community influence to make anything really change.

Table 3. Three Types of Social Relationships and their Main Social Properties Relevant to Interventions

Strangers:

Form of reciprocity: Exchange with a society of strangers is now done via ***money***

What you can get done is typically by paying someone and can be done at a distance, and ***in principle***: there are no other social relationships involved; there are no other social obligations; they do not usually impact on other areas of life

Personal influence will depend upon having economic (resource) status, often contextualized as a show of commodities

Monitoring: Will often not see them again, and others will not see each other

Accountability mainly through public rule following and policing, institutionalized

Avoidance and escape of consequences is easy especially if wealthy, and people can easily withdraw from social relationships. Secrecy and lying therefore are also easy.

Friends and Family Social Networks:

Form of reciprocity: specific supports that are returned

What you can get done depends upon your networks and the reciprocity you provide. The people are usually relevant in only a few other arenas of life

Personal influence will depend upon status within networks

Monitoring: Will see some of the people regularly, but not others. The others will not all see each other regularly, except if family

Accountability through public rules and policing, and through network members' contacts

Avoidance and escape of consequences is only easy if constantly changing networks or if high status within networks, or there are coalitions within networks (cliques).

Kin-Based Groups:

Form of reciprocity: taken for granted obligations

What you can get done depends upon the family social relationships. The same people will be relevant in most arenas of life

Personal influence will be important and depend upon status and reciprocity in the family and community networks. Time spent talking therefore rather than rule following.

Monitoring: Will see most of the people regularly, and others will see each other regularly

Accountability through complex family systems with historical context frequently utilized

Avoidance and escape of consequences is difficult and is limited mostly to secrecy and language strategies, or forming coalitions

Each of these is applicable for different social relationships, and Table 3 shows some of the general properties of the different social relationships–the ways they are managed and the strategies that often occur (Guerin, 2004). I will refer back to this table repeatedly through the book.

Most people have some of each of these occurring in different parts of their lives, and the differences are only true *in general*. On the whole, however, westerners do not interact much with their very extended families in everyday life, and close communities tend to deal mainly within their groups and have less to do with strangers. Indigenous peoples, as well as refugees and migrants from close communities and families who move to western countries, often have problems from the conflicts between these forms of relationships, or in many cases their children experience the clashes (Dingo, 1998; Guerin, Guerin, Diiriye & Abdi, 2004; Keen, 2004). They have lived in close extended family organizations but they are forced to settle in societies in which stranger relationships are most common and people do not understand how close family organization works.

A Word on Western Social Relationships and 'Culture'

Most books have a special section tucked away at the end on how things might differ for different cultures and social groups (where 'different' really means non-western). Instead, I want a section up-front about western social relationships. The reason for this is that most published "interventions" have been done in western countries and have assumed western-style social relationships (see Table 3). Such interventions probably do not work as well with non-western social relationships, which is one reason why many indigenous and non-western groups want to run their own interventions in their own ways. The published literature, on the other hand, tends to assume that published interventions will work for most people except that some minor adjustments might have to be made for those not completely westernized (hence the special 'cross-cultural' section tucked away at the end).

I want to reverse this order of precedence, and point out that the whole idea of a 'packaged' intervention that might work for a large number of people is in itself a model based on western-style relationships. The particular economies western countries live with, and their historical context, means that the norm in everyday life is to deal mostly with strangers (at least, non-family) through the medium of money (Guerin, 2004). We buy things and pay to get things done for us rather than rely on family obligations (services). This is the real basis for believing that all interventions can be pre-packaged to work on people and they just need to "do" the package and all will be well.

I am not claiming that such approaches are bad or wrong, or that they do not work. I am pointing out that they might not work with everyone, that they are not somehow morally superior to other interventions, and that you cannot export them by adding a little cultural module on the end to cater for 'different' people. If someone's life is thoroughly embedded in their extended family, then an intervention that does not involve that family will not work in the short or long term. The social relationships–the family or community relationships in this case–need to be part of the intervention design and not a cultural problem that needs to be addressed later. Interventions are adjustment to social relationships.

A Word on Kin- or Community-Based Social Relationships

In line with what I said in the last few paragraphs, there is a lot now starting to be written about intervening (and researching) with strong family- or community-based groups. This is particularly important for indigenous, oppressed, formerly colonized, migrant and refugee groups, although they each have differences (Guerin, 2004, Chapter 6).

The important point I want you to remember for these groups is that *interventions with individuals in strongly kin-based groups* **are** *community interventions*—whatever changes are made impact beyond the single individual, and this can work in your favor or against it. This is why such groups are demanding full participation and collaboration with interventions and research right from the very beginning, not just a quick briefing to say what is going to be done to them. My point in stressing that interventions are adjustment to social relationships is that having full participation and community collaboration is not just to be nice, or to get pass ethical approval guidelines, it is a necessary component because of how the social relationships are structured in everyday life for such groups.

In this sense, we westerners are the odd ones out, since changes in one part of our life usually have little impact on people in other parts of our lives. What I do at work only has little to do with my parents or in the gym, I can at least keep them separate or *compartmentalized* (Guerin, 2004) if I wish to in western countries. As is known to the social sciences, this ultimately falls back on the type of economy we live under, and how the economies structure our lives (Guerin, 2004; Keen, 2004). This also does not make such lifestyles bad or undesirable, just different. There are features of both that can help or hinder interventions. The important point we come back to is to analyze the social context first and work within that, utilizing whatever is useful to help.

The Ethics of Interventions: Some Issues

All interventions raise a lot of ethical issues (Banks, 2001). If you do not know what I mean by this then you should not be doing interventions. All interventions should be submitted through a local ethics committee, or at the very least run through a group of peers who are independent of the project and can give frank comments. I am not going to go through all the ethical aspects of every intervention program since there are too many. I will be assuming that no one will go ahead with any of the interventions in this book without going through an appropriate ethics committee.

The main point of ethics is that by intervening you are attempting to change someone's behavior and that is a very arrogant and presumptuous position to be in. How do you know that what you will do will help instead of making things more painful or worse for that person? What will you do if you do make things worse? Ethics committees are there to protect people from harm (including the intervention

---

Table 4. Ethics and Ethics Committees

✓ You should not do an intervention without ethical scrutiny and approval

✓ Ethics committees are there to:

    - protect people from harm (including the intervention agent)
    - put processes in place in case something bad does happen against all wisdom
    - point out the unobvious consequences which those initiating a program
      commonly cannot see ahead of time

✓ Ethics committees usually consist of:

    - *Peers* because they will be knowledgeable about the area of intervention and
      previous work
    - *Independent persons* since close colleagues or family members might just go
      along with whatever you propose
    - *Lay persons* who should be considered as the 'experts' on what is acceptable
      or not in everyday life

---

agent), to put processes in place in case something bad does happen against all wisdom, and to point out the unobvious consequences which those initiating a program commonly cannot see ahead of time. Try to think about ethics committees not as bodies that attempt to slow down your programs for a long as possible, but as a group that can protect both you and your participants from as much unintentional harm as possible and protect human rights.

Peers are required because they will be knowledgeable about the area of intervention and previous work. It is no use giving a drug rehab program to a person off the street to assess for ethics because they do not know what is commonly done and so you could nag them into agreeing quite easily.

Independent persons are required since close colleagues or family members might have too much owing and hence go along with whatever you propose just because they do not wish to be on your bad side.

Lay persons are required on ethics committees because they can be considered the 'experts' on what is acceptable or not in everyday life. Professional peers can also be tied up in the same little world view as the intervention agent and not see that such programs would be considered unacceptable to most 'normal' people. Lay persons can give a very refreshing perspective on any intervention. This is the same idea as having a jury made up of lay persons rather than experts.

"Doing" ethics gets easier the more you do, in working your way through the guidelines and application forms. This is not because you get smarter and learn to cheat the system but because you learn to plan your interventions in an ethically appropriate manner right from the very beginnings and so there is less to correct when considered by a properly structured ethics committee. You are less likely to develop your interventions in so much isolation that when you finally come to write it down you realize that what you 'need' for the intervention is for 300 homes in a town to have their electricity cut off for 3 days a week as a comparison to some intervention you are doing in other homes. Discussing this with a lay person could cut short these theoretical dreams and tell you that such a plan has no chance of happening and that there are all sorts of safety, insurance and others reasons why not! The lay persons on ethics committees are especially good for taking off your blinkers and showing you that the emperor has no clothes on.

So my message about the ethics of intervention is to always consult an appropriate committee and discuss what you intend to do widely beforehand with peers, independent workers in the same area, and lay persons. If you are unsure, do not intervene.

Should we be Doing Interventions at All?

An important issue you need to have thought about before starting is whether you should be doing interventions at all. [Incidentally, most of the arguments on this issue have counterparts in arguments about whether we should intervene in the economy or leave it all to market forces, and about whether a foreign power should intervene militarily or not in another country.]

Those who say *we should not intervene* argue: that we are adding forces to a situation that we never fully understand; that we are never sure that what we will do is not going to cause more harm; that it assumes we know better; that in doing so we impose how *we* think people *should* be behaving onto others; that interventions implicitly make everyone the same and this is not good; and that people and social systems always have their own ways of resolving problems so we just need to give them more time.

Those who say *we should intervene* argue: that people remain getting hurt unless we change something so it is unethical to do nothing; that both peer-reviewed research and ethics committee minimize the likelihood of increasing harm through the intervention; that we will never know what can work unless we try something; that people are always intervening in each others' lives anyway and we are just doing a more standardized version of this; that people and systems clearly do not eventually resolve any problems; and that we can always try to build diversity and creativity into interventions rather than conformity.

My view on this is that most interventions are harmless enough (if done through ethics committees) and that doing something about a painful and sometimes dangerous problem is better than doing nothing. However, what does need to be weighed is whether some specific intervention procedures should be done at all, including the use of punishment and aversive techniques, state-imposed interventions, interventions for which there is not informed consent, interventions which encourage everyone to be the same, interventions that are done only because they fit nicely with a 'theory' or idea, interventions for which there is little evidence, and interventions for which the intervention agent is making a lot of money. Hopefully these should all be weeded out and assessed by an ethics committee and peer review anyway.

Finally, the other category of intervention for which I sometimes have little patience and would like to see outlawed, are those interventions that make no attempt to assess whether they worked or not—however small and weak the assessment might be. It seems unethical to me to interfere and mess with people's lives and not even attempt to find out whether it was for the best. Apart from scams and hoodlums, the main source of these have tended to be government-initiated interventions which are not assessed because their real goal was just to spend money before the end of the financial year or to make a show that something is being done about the problem, without really trying to make something that works.

Analyzing the Contexts is more important than Finding the Causes

A point that will come up repeatedly in this book concerns causes and contexts. I will refer to this section a lot during the book.

A lot of talk and research is framed in terms of causes: what exactly causes domestic violence; why do kids bully, what are the causes; what causes hallucinations. I cannot go into the history and philosophy of this but many including myself have found it much more productive to think in terms of describing and analyzing contexts rather than searching for causes (Guerin, 2001b, c, d, 2004). It resembles ecology more than the physical sciences. "What are the conditions or contexts in which this tree will grow?", rather than, "what is the cause of this tree growing?" While this might sound like splitting hairs, the two frames lead to very different methods and conclusions. Describing contexts gives a long term observational stance to see how things work, whereas cause-seeking leads to short-term designs. Describing contexts leads to viewing whole systems whereas cause-seeking leads to looking for single causes.

However, the single major benefit I find from describing contexts rather than testing for causes is that many of what would be called necessary but not sufficient conditions of change are hidden in social science procedures and are never made salient in causal analyses (because they are hidden) even though they are crucial to anything working. We will see an example in the next section in which the researchers got girls recruited at health clinics to agree to watch an interactive STD video and come back for three more visits. The video was successful in a number of useful ways but we do not really know anything much about what it was that got the girls to agree to participate in the first place. My point is that those social conditions could be crucial to whether the intervention works, and that it might not work in other conditions.

A good case to consider in order to get your head around my subtle point is hypnosis, and especially stage hypnosis. The hypnotist gets people to come up on stage and then does the 'magic' intervention and lo and behold, the people do crazy stunts when instructed. The "causes" seem to reside in the words and procedures used by the hypnotist. You need to learn to ask, however, what were the conditions that got them up there in the first place? If I can somehow—and this is very much a set of very complex, hidden social influences—get you up there on the stage in the first place then the rest is easy. This is why when I later try the same magic hypnosis procedures (which are mostly arbitrary since the real work has already been done for the stage hypnotist) on my friends it fails miserably. Even professional hypnotists report that the 'hypnosis' part is somewhat irrelevant and is merely there to stop the person resisting or doing the opposite—all the 'hypnosis' procedure is doing is to make the person more receptive to following some simple verbal instructions (Haley, 1973).

Elsewhere I have pointed out similar problems with some key studies in social psychology: that they had 'hidden' social conditions and contexts not reported that probably were the most important manipulations of the whole process, and these led to the results rather than what the theory said caused the phenomena (see cognitive dissonance in Guerin, 2001d, for example). Put bluntly, in 'artificial' settings just *getting* people to cooperate and act 'as if' everything is normal may itself be a large part of what causes the results. For example, showing grief is said to be 'cathartic' and healing. What I suggest is that the whole process (almost entirely hidden social relationship adjustment) of getting someone to show grieving is what is really changing things in the situation, not the actual tears and wailing. The intervention really comes from how the conditions and context are developed and not from what seems to be the salient 'cause' (Guerin, 2001b, d. cf. Homans, 1941). As another example, self-disclosure to another person or telling them that something they do annoys you, are also said to be healing and useful interventions, but I am arguing that it is the skillful setting up of conditions that allow someone to do self-disclose without fearing the consequences (Guerin, 2004) that is really having the effect—not the talking or disclosure itself (Guerin, 2001d).

Note that in all the above cases I am not doubting that the interventions can be useful and have powerful effects on people lives. I am arguing instead that the reported causation of this is usually misguided and a full description of the social contexts that allow these to happen tells us more about what is going on in these interventions and allow us to adapt them to other situations better. For example, if you set up conditions for grieving that blatantly forces someone to grieve, rather than the usual subtle social conditions that are hidden, it is likely to backfire and not be 'cathartic'.

These are the reasons I urge you to spend time with the people involved in your interventions and carefully observe and analyze (Guerin 2004) the social contexts in the background (see *Intervention Analysis 1* above). So when you read an intervention in which a therapist reports that the best intervention is one in which he or she gets the spouse to go home and say out loud to their partner the ten worst, immoral and nastiest things they have ever done or thought about, before you start pondering theoretically on how saying bad things might lead to positive change (an ironic or paradoxical effect?), think carefully about how that therapist might have got someone into a condition in which they would even agree to do that in the first place! How would you go about getting someone to agree to do that? If you can actually set up those extreme conditions then that is probably the major ingredient for the intervention and what is exactly said might even be irrelevant. Setting up the context is probably what leads to the change or is a major part of it. Moreover, my point is that if you got someone to do the same thing (the very 'same' intervention supposedly) by using different methods to set those conditions up, perhaps by court order, then the intervention might mysteriously not work anymore.

This is a tricky point and is worth coming back to as you read more of this book. Better still, learn to not worry about finding the causes for change but spend your time systematically documenting the different contexts and situations for the practices and how they might change. Finding causes is not a waste of time but it is more difficult than most people think. So take your time experiencing and observing the situations you are trying to change—that will be more useful in the long-run.

How do We Know whether Interventions Work?

This is also a tricky issue, and a whole area has emerged called *evaluation research* which has the aim of finding out what works with interventions. Unfortunately there is no simple answer but instead there are some tradeoffs that need to be considered. I will go through some of these tradeoffs but urge you very strongly to study evaluation research separately (Becker, & Vanclay, 2003; Bingham & Felbinger, 2001; Campbell & Stanley, 1963; Patton, 2002; Tudiver, Bass, Dunn, Norton & Stewart, 1992).

There are many interventions done but most do not get measured for a variety of practical reasons. In many ways, if an intervention is not evaluated then it is a waste of time, since we cannot be sure anything worked and we cannot report to others what we tried and what happened. Very frequently people in an intervention report feeling good about the whole thing, and claim that great changes have occurred as a result of the intervention, but this can be very misleading: feeling good is not a good indicator of a program working; people often claim something worked when a good evaluation finds it did not; something might have changed but it was nothing to do with the intervention (something you will learn in evaluation research to discern); or a change might have occurred but it was so specific to the context (not measured) that it would be unlikely to work anywhere else in the universe. Even just carrying out a program known to be 'an intervention' might trigger people to claim they have been changed—something else a good evaluation takes into account (placebo effect).

So when I come across interventions that have not been evaluated properly I certainly read them and learn ideas from them, but I do not take them as useful until I see some sort of measurement of the context and what was going on.

The biggest tradeoff in evaluating interventions is between being 'natural' and being able to measure precisely. There is no simple answer to this tradeoff and both are needed. Most 'real' interventions are done in practical settings where there is little luxury of measuring everything that is going on: you are usually lucky to be doing the intervention at all. While we can overcome this by setting up more controlled artificial conditions in a more experimental setting, we then no longer know if those results would apply when tried out in a 'real' and uncontrolled setting. As I wrote in the last section, just arranging for those settings to be set up could "cause" the intervention to work.

Example. To give an example, Downs et al. (2004) did a nice study about reducing adolescent females' STD risk, in which they showed either a state-of-the-art interactive video, a book with the same material, or some pamphlets. It was found that those in the interactive video condition (randomly assigned) were more likely to be abstinent after 3 months, had less condom failures in the next 3 months, and after 6 months were less likely to report being diagnosed with an STD. This was a well-run study with important results and I do not wish to write it off because of what I am about to say. I hope the interactive video can be adapted to the problems I will raise in future interventions.

Let us consider this intervention from the point of view of "interventions are adjustments in social contexts and relationships", however. A key part of the context is how they got 300 volunteer girls to watch a video or read some information alone, and come back for more visits at 1, 3 and 6 months. They were paid a small amount for taking part but this was probably not known to them when they agreed (a common ethical procedure), and they were recruited from health clinics that were not specific to the populations we might want. These points were freely conceded by the authors (p. 1568) and some counters made to them.

My point is a more subtle one, however, reflecting what was said above about hidden social conditions. There were social conditions in place that led to these girls volunteering in the first place for a quite intensive series of sessions. While great control was possible over their performance because they were in an artificial set-up, we do not know the selection processes that were involved in getting these girls to agree, nor do we know the social influences that got them to agree—it could have been the nice experimenters or they could have ended up selecting only the most gullible girls.

What we really learn from this study then is that if we have these (hidden) persuasive conditions to get a set of girls to agree to do this task and do it alone, then watching the video has a positive effect. What we do not know is when and how these extra conditions apply in ordinary life or even how to arrange them. Without this extra description of the hidden social context we cannot know how to apply the intervention anywhere else: (1) We could take it to another health clinic without the same social influence necessary and find that no one uses the interactive video, (2) we could force people to do this intervention instead of using the hidden social influences from the original and not get the same results (perhaps a school gets the video and forces all the kids do it), or (3), in another setting it might be done with groups rather than quietly alone and this might make the whole thing fail.

Once again this is not to criticize the authors of this paper; what they set out to show they did very well. Rather, it is to show that the social context for everything that happened has not been fully understood or documented and this will limit the usefulness of the intervention. We at least still need to find out: (1) how well the interactive video intervention works when school kids are forced to watch it rather than volunteer, (2) what happens when another method of social influence is used to get girls to watch it (perhaps a close community gets all their girls to watch it rather than experimenters who are strangers to them), and (3) what happens when they watch it in different social settings (in groups, say) rather than quietly alone as happened.

Now while I have been using this example to criticize controlled studies for leaving out the effects of some added social context, this is not to imagine that 'naturalistic' studies of interventions are perfect. As evaluation research will show you, measuring real programs with real people with little control over what those people do and how they fill in your measurements (the bit I was criticizing controlled studies for not treating as part of the results) is often a complete mess and no firm interpretation of the results possible.

So here are the tradeoffs. (1) If I do not measure anything about my intervention then we cannot say that anything worked successfully. (2) If we try to 'just' measure the intervention as it is run 'naturally' then there are a host of practical and ethical problems. (3) If we try to take some control over how the measurements are made, how 'cleanly' the interventions are run, or over who the people are who participate, then we are never sure how much these processes play a role in the results and whether the interventions would still work elsewhere without this extra control being there.

So what are we to do with this tradeoff? The two best solutions are to: (1) run multiple studies, both controlled and 'natural', varying how they are run, and look at the robustness of the intervention that way, and (2), to spend more time on any intervention, not to do cross-sectional measurements (or multiple cross-sectional measurements disguised as longitudinal measurement), but to spend more time with the people and the intervention and to participate in what they are going through. This is more in line with the ethnography of social anthropologists and the participant observations of sociologists. I have elsewhere urged psychologists to begin this process (Guerin, 2001c, 2004).

For the Downs et al. (2004) study we could supplement the controlled approach with observing girls over time using the interactive video in more realistic settings—to see what they actually do with it and what they say about it. This will give us better knowledge of how much we can use the neat results from the original study. We could get schools to have girls watch it in groups and observe whatever goes on as a comparison.

What this also means is that for a large number of interventions we will never know if they were successful or know if the intervention itself is what led to the success rather than something else going on. This is regrettable, but in a realistic world there is probably not much else we can do apart from trying both types of studies whenever and wherever funds, ethics and practicalities allow us to do so.

Chapter 2

Who Should be Involved in Interventions?

Interventions with individuals and groups are not like interventions to repair a clock—there are always complex social contexts with other people involved. We have seen the ethical and cultural restraints placed on interventions both for reasons of principles and for reasons of success—an intervention forced on someone might work initially but is unlikely to last in the long-term.

Rather than battling other people to stop them interfering during an intervention, it is more productive, especially in the long-term, to utilize them as part of the intervention. While there is not room here to go into the full details, it can be argued that all human behaviors are social, even small ones and ones that we talk about as going on in our heads, and therefore other people are always part of the determinants of behavior. If our aim is to intervene to change what people do, or help them change in the ways they wish to, we must involve other people—it is actually not a choice (Guerin, 1997, 2001c). It is only western psychology and popular psychology that believe it is possible to "treat" an individual alone and talk it through with just that person so as to make everything better—as if the problem lay inside the person. But problems never belong to a single person.

To give the idea of involving other people in interventions, this chapter will discuss some common forms of this procedure: utilizing peers to help the intervention, utilizing parents and families, utilizing groups and communities, and utilizing larger social networks and whole countries. More recently, computers and the Internet have been used as "agents" for interventions. Examples will be given of each of these, drawn somewhat randomly from the published research reports. There are many variations and many different ways that other people can and should be involved in interventions. Using your imagination will produce more not thought of yet. The idea is not to give you an exhaustive list, but to get you using your imagination and collaboration skills to find ways to involve others productively in your interventions.

Who Should do the Intervention?

One of the questions that reappears throughout the reports of utilizing other people in interventions is that of whether the other persons should be similar or dissimilar to the target persons? In most cases this is taken for granted and the answer is assumed to be that a *similar* other will produce a better intervention—it surely must be better to have an Asian therapist counseling an Asian client.

This might not always be the case, however, and, as always, a closer examination of the social context will provide the answer (Cuco & Pierce, 1977, p. 51; Gatmon et al., 2001; Helms & Carter, 1991; Moon et al., 2000). Just to think of some simple reasons why dissimilar others might in some cases be more efficacious, many people do not do what similar others tell them to do, and someone dissimilar who is higher in reputation or status might be required (Andrade & Burnstein, 1973). Further, a similar person might view the problem in similar ways, and an outsider who is different is needed to bring a different view to bear on what is happening and how to change things.

By the same token, of course, an outsider can miss important facets that a similar other would notice. We also have to consider what is meant by 'similar', and in my example above, lumping 'Asians' together totally ignores the huge diversity of something like 2-3 billion people making up 'Asians'. Research interventions outlined below, for example, found that older children could help younger children in schoolwork; they were dissimilar in age but similar in the school and neighborhood from which they came. If language is a problem then we might expect similar ethnicity to help—even if English is used, for the slightly different accents and Creoles it is possibly better to have someone of a similar ethnicity. And finally, in most close communities knowledge can spread very quickly, so in some close communities people do not want a similar other to help them because they are likely to be a member of the same community and that is risky for gossip.

Examples. To give a few quick examples, Modra and Black (1999) set up two exercise classes for older women, one led by themselves (as peers) and one led by a professional exercise trainer. While their research design was inadequate to make a strong case, little or no difference was found between these two groups. Paton (1996) reports that for training relief workers to deal with disasters, having similar others might mean they are related. Trying to help survivors with anguish and stress when it might also be your own relatives who have been killed is not likely to work (cf. Tunnecliffe & Roy, 1993).

Women with breast cancer in another study reported that having a volunteer peer visit them was especially beneficial when the volunteers had similar experiences of breast cancer (Dunn, Steginga, Occhipinti & Wilson, 1999). There are probably a host of reasons why this might be so, including the visitors being sensitive to what is going on, the visitors being good models that the problems can be overcome, and that they had similar things to talk about besides the cancer. In this case, though, notice that the treatment was not the target of intervention so the similar others were not trying to get the target women to comply with doctors' instructionsso this could have helped their relationship. The intervention was about helping the women to avoid social isolation and to give them hope and an interest in getting well and carrying on life. Although there was no control condition for which women had dissimilar others visit, it is clear from the results that the visitations by similar others helped enormously.

Kim (1990; also De Andrade, 2000) pointed out some advantages and disadvantages of having anthropologists from the same culture working with a community. For example, same-culture anthropologists do not have to learn the language or the very basic customs. On the other hand, Kim reports occasions when as a Korean anthropologist in Korea he was placed under cultural constraints that a foreigner would not have had placed. A foreigner would have been taken to be ignorant of customs and the demands relaxed on them. Being same-culture and younger can also mean that elders do not take the intervention seriously.

Finally, Tom and Cronan (1998) had tutors take mothers through a literacy program to help educate their children. The mothers were trained in some Head Start techniques. Sixty-six percent of the tutee/tutor pairs were matched ethnically (primarily Latino American, African American and White). While the efficacy of the program was not reported, there were no differences between matched and unmatched tutee/tutor pairs; whether the people were similar or not ethnically, there was no measurable difference in the outcomes for the mothers or for the children.

So this mixed-bag of studies is a warning not to just assume that "similar is better." We still need to know a lot more about the social contexts that determine when and where similar and dissimilar others work or not. What dimensions of similarity/dissimilarity are important also need study. So the real take-home message is to look carefully at the social context to judge who is likely to help or not.

Who Should be Involved? Who Should be Told?

From the brief look at ethics in the last chapter it is not just who does the intervention that is important but also who is peripherally involved and who is kept informed. This could be kept to legal requirements, so that parents must be kept informed about all interventions with their children unless schools have some blanket agreement. But in many cases a lot of people will be affected by interventions and they need to be informed.

To think your way through this issue you will need to frame your intervention in terms of the different types of social relationships outlined in the last chapter. For interventions run by strangers in a westernized country where both parties are fully informed and are consenting, say a person paying to see a private therapist or consultant, then there is probably not much need to keep others informed unless specifically indicated (if it is about spouse abuse then the therapist might want to make arrangements to check that the spouse is ok, or there might be a legal requirement to notify the police). Indeed, in western countries such paid arrangements between strangers are usually considered to be totally confidential and the therapist is *not allowed* to reveal anything about the interactions, except perhaps in legal proceedings.

In most cases, however, there are people who will be greatly affected by an intervention and they usually need to be consulted or it needs to be arranged with the client to allow information to be passed on—you would not go and consult behind their back! This might be the immediate family for most people and for many communities this might also involve extended family, other community members, church leaders and mentors, or work colleagues if relevant. The point here is that you do not necessarily have to get these others involved in carrying out the intervention (see below), but they should be consulted if it will impact on them anyway. This requires some delicacy and knowledge of the context, however (which is another reason for these people to actually be involved in the intervention!). As an example of the delicacy needed, read or think about involving spouses in interventions for men who batter (Edleson & Tolman, 1992); such situations need a lot of thought and preparation, and there is no single answer as to whether it should be arranged or how it can be arranged.

Families and Close Communities as Intervention Agents

Spouses as the Intervention Agents

Utilizing a spouse to help with change is very common nowadays. Clinical psychologists and psychotherapists will normally try and interview both spouses if there are problems reported for one of them. Again, the perspective of this book is that this makes perfect sense because all human behavior involves other people and therefore problems will usually need to be sorted out around those different people involved.

The problem, however, is to not set up a new conflict situation in which one spouse is trying to carry out intervention instructions and the other refuses and this leads to conflict. For example, a nice idea for reducing speeding is to get spouses who are passengers to intervene and stop drivers when they speed. This makes sense in one way because spouses are frequently passengers, because they are not driving so they have time to observe speed signs, and because they also get killed or injured if the driver crashes. However, such an intervention could easily lead to nagging and fighting over who is allowed to tell whom what to do. It could also be used as an opportunity to make points about other arguments or conflicts going on. So overall, the idea is probably not a good one unless carefully controlled somehow.

Example 1. Mermelstein, Cohen, Lichtenstein, Baer and Kamarck (1986) looked at smoking cessation and tested whether spousal support helped. For half the people in the study, spouses attended the regular quit smoking sessions and were trained on how they could help as well as receiving some information. In the groups without spouse help the spouse neither attended nor was given any information about how to help. They found some evidence that spouse support helped smoking cessation.

Example 2. An interesting variation on spousal involvement is that of Al-Anon, the support groups for spouses of alcoholics attending Alcoholics Anonymous meetings. Al-Anon is not meant as an intervention to change the alcoholic's behaviors but to provide comfort and coping for their spouses. Miller, Meyers and Tonigan (1999), however, used Al-Anon as a control for their study that compared it to a family confrontation intervention (Johnson Institute intervention) and a community and family training intervention (CRAFT). They found, first, that the latter two led to the alcoholics attending their own sessions better, but mainly the CRAFT intervention. Second, all treatments helped the spouses cope and improve their overall well-being, even if their alcoholic partners did not engage in or maintain their treatment. In defense, however, it must be repeated that Al-Anon was not developed to engage the alcoholic partner in treatment, and that the CRAFT training had a large number of specific skills that were taught. As we will see, interventions with many components usually work better but we do not end up finding out what particular aspects help the most.

Example 3. Davies, Mitra and Schellstede (1987) found that for some countries, and developing countries in particular, husbands are the ones who obtain household supplies including female contraceptive pills. For family planning researchers, this makes the husbands important as the ones who obtain and maintain oral contraceptives. Targeting family planning interventions in such countries at women, as is often done, might miss the goal. Even if the women learn a lot about contraception, it will be up to the husband to obtain supplies, and with a husband as a gatekeeper (see below), his role needs to be considered.

Children as Intervention Agents

Most of the examples of children as intervention agents will be discussed below under peer interventions, because that is the most common example. While there are opportunities for children to carry out interventions within the family we again have to be careful about this setting up further conflicts over resources and control. We could train children to tell their parents to stop when they are smoking or driving too fast, but unwanted consequences are likely in these cases.

Example. I know of an intervention never written or published in which children were instructed how to monitor household waste and intervene through praise when members of the family recycled waste. Unlike smoking cessation or slowing down car drivers, this was probably innocuous enough not to cause too many family fights.

Parents as Intervention Agents

A big area of psychological intervention is that of parent training and intervention (Bogat, Sullivan & Grober, 1993; Forehand & Kotchick, 1996; Frankel & Simmons, 1992; Moore & Patterson, 2003; Peterson et al., 1997; Prinz & Miller, 1996). The idea is that instead of a stranger intervening with children, we should instead train parents better, or train them to handle the difficult situations. If this is done, the theory goes, we can overcome more problems than through therapist interventions. For this reason, there have been many examples of parent training attempted and studied.

Example 1. Dishion and Andrews (1995) looked at high-risk adolescents and devised programs that focused on the parents, on the teens, on both parents and teens, or on just materials to read ("self-directed change"). They found that engaging the parents had an immediate effect and helped with longer-term follow-up effects.

Example 2. An indirect intervention was reported by Perlman and Ross (1997), while they were looking at parents' natural interventions into arguments between children (2- to 4-years old). They made naturalistic observations and found that parents mostly intervened in the most heated arguments that had little signs of de-escalating. Comparing behaviors before and after fights that had parent intervention or not, they found that children used fewer power strategies and more sophisticated negotiation strategies when parents intervened. While not an intervention as such, these results suggest that teaching parents to intervene better would be beneficial.

The Wider Family as Intervention Agents

Most groups around the world, except for those in strongly western societies, embed life within a wider sense of family, the extended family or whanau. Clearly, it makes sense to involve this wider family in cases for which the changes involve actions spread across the whole family (Hogue & Liddle, 1999; Kirigin, 2001; Kumpfer, Molgaard & Spoth, 1996; McMahon, Slough, and the Conduct Problems Prevention Research Group, 1996; Tsey & Every, 2000; Valach, Young & Lynam, 1996; Webster-Stratton, 2001). Most of the reported interventions, however, focus on the nuclear family or on children and one parent only. There is a lot more that can be done to develop new ways to integrate traditional approaches for extended family interventions in family conflict with other techniques they might not have tried. For example, in many communities around the world the parents are not a major influence over children, who can be raised by grandparents, uncles or aunties, or "cousins". Instigating parent training programs might not be useful in such cases.

Example 1. Epstein et al. (1987; Epstein, 1996) reported an intervention aimed at reducing weight and obesity in children, that directly incorporated the parents in the intervention. Some participants were in conditions that targeted the child only, others in conditions that targeted both the parent and the child, and some in conditions that focused on neither specifically. Initially, all groups showed a reduction in obesity, including the parents, but over a longer time frame only the children in the child-focused intervention remained less obese.

Example 2. Behavioral family therapies are well researched in western contexts (Sanders, 1992). Techniques are many and varied, but include family forms of written advice, therapist contact, active training with rehearsal, role-playing, feedback, and instructions, and therapist interventions on specific parental problems such as marriage problems and anger management. Most behavior therapy textbooks have a good summary of methods. While often confined to nuclear families, these could be opened up to the wider family where the types of relationship indicate this would be fruitful (Table 3).

Example 3. Most close communities around the world have their own methods for intervening in family problems, usually involving the wider family but sometimes the whole community as well. My single example is taken from a discussion of how Maori whanau (the wider family) help during crises, but the anthropological and indigenous literatures are full of many other examples:

> Intervention often took the form of a relative coming or being sent, without waiting for a request, to stay in the home and help until the crisis was over. This was the particular role of unmarried and widowed aunts and grandmothers. Tui Netana's unmarried aunt regularly arrived when another

baby was expected in the family and stayed for several months. Matiu Waimea recalled how the tensions which built up between his sibling-set and his step-mother were periodically relieved when his father's mother came to stay and took over the daily supervision of the younger children.

Relatives also helped children cope with real or imagined problems at home by providing a temporary refuge and care. Epa Huritau had difficulty adjusting to his mother's re-marriage.

Because of the in-fighting between my step-father and me, I ran away, to my uncles or my grandmother. No questions were asked when I arrived. Then two or three weeks later my mother or one of my brothers would arrive and say, 'You are wanted at home.' Three weeks later the hurt had disappeared. I went home. My step-father, he always acted as if I had just been down the road.
(Metge, 1995, p. 259-260)

Example 4. Recent programs are aimed at strengthening families "in general," rather than targeting specific problem behaviors (Guyall, Spoth, Chao, Wickrama & Russell, 2004); Kumpfer, Molgaard & Spoth, 1996; Molgaard & Spoth, 2001). In one such intervention, Seitz, Rosenbaum and Apfel (1985) did a ten-year follow-up on impoverished mothers who had been given a "strengthening" program that involved pediatric care, home visitation, and day-care for the children. Each component was flexible and allowed for many other goals to be accomplished. For example, the pediatricians spent time with the mothers rather than rushing through a check-up, thus allowing the mother to observe behavioral control methods and to ask questions. After ten years the intervention mothers were more likely to be self-supporting, had more education, and smaller families, than did controls. The children had better school attendance, and the boys used less special services than children of control mothers.

Example 5. An interesting combination comes from a law in New Zealand under which for offending children there must be a Family Group Conference that includes not only the extended family, but also the victims, the one who offended, and relevant professionals. During the Family Group Conference they discuss healing (interventions) and plan and decide what happens next. While there are some good points about this, Levine (2000) also outlines some problems, especially when the offender's family and the victim's families are from different parts of Table 3 (Levine refers to "face-to-face groups"—close communities in my jargon—and "modern society groups" who are used to social network and stranger interactions). For example, one difference is that in close community groups everyone will know exactly what has happened and what is going on, whereas many family members in western groups will know nothing about the child and what is going on. The former will usually see some sort of community responsibility for the offending whereas the western families will see more responsibility as being the child's or the parents'. While the mixing of these differences can be seen as a problem for making the overall intervention work, we could also see it as a useful learning experiences when different types of relationships mix.

The Stress of Caregiving: A Warning

Family members have traditionally helped care for the sick and elderly (Bogat, Sullivan & Grober, 1993). More recently, the stress and strain put on such caregivers has been the subject of research and intervention (Biegel and Schulz, 1999). The use of family caregivers as intervention agents has been taken for granted, and most of the literature is concerned (rightly) with the strain put on them from intervening. This is exacerbated by western governments following a policy of trying to get family members to play a bigger role in helping the sick and elderly, instead, of course, the government paying for it all as welfare, and so the issues involved have become highly salient.

On the other hand, if the extended family is very close then they might relish to opportunity to be more involved with cousins, grandchildren or nieces and nephews, and it might not be seen as a "problem". In some ways, the 'problems' of family providing free care mostly arise in western societies (Table 3) for which the economy is such that people are very busy and the norm is to pay for services to be carried out rather than do them oneself (Guerin, 2003b). So this issue is very much tied up with the considerations of Table 3.

The upshot, however, is that family caregivers are there as an alternative for interventions, but care needs to be taken in making sure that the extra burden does not adversely affect the person used. Many of the tutoring programs involving family are probably fun, and evidence suggests that both tutees and tutors gain something from the experience. But if the family member is asked (or even paid) to take on onerous duties for an intervention then the issues need to be carefully examined. The bottom line is that whole books have been devoted to the problems and stress for caregivers of constant provision of services (see Biegel and Schulz, 1999).

Social Networks and Close Friends as Intervention Agents

The usual first choice for involving others is to choose people already within the social networks available (Bogat, Sullivan & Grober, 1993). This is not only a cost consideration, but also one aimed at better maintenance afterwards when the 'intervention' part finishes. Again, Table 3 suggests that this will apply more to those in western economies where the social networks are likely to be specific and cannot be assumed for everyone (what I call compartmentalized). So if someone has a problem with gambling we would not bring in their train-hobby network of friends to act as intervention agents.

Peers as Intervention Agents

There have been many interventions that utilize peers to help. Many of these have been with school children working to improve their social or academic behaviors, but there are also examples from all walks of life and all sorts of people. The ideas behind this usually revolve around peers as "motivators" for people, that is, peers normally influence each other to do things, and so utilizing peers can help the target person to change. There are some assumptions in this, however, that perhaps raise some doubts about the absolute benefit of peers as intervention agents. Their measured efficacy is still unclear, probably because the specific social contexts are important but not generally reported (Davidson, Chinman, Kloos, Weingarten Stayner, & Tebes, 1999).

First, if the peers are the ones already involved in the target person's behavior then their behavior will have to be changed also. For example, if peers are bullying a child and the child's grades are low, then utilizing peers to teach them maths might either make things worse if one of the bullies is chosen, or else, if a model student is chosen as the peer-intervener, then both of them might be bullied. What this is really saying is that, as always, the full social context of the child and peers need to be described and analyzed first, and just finding 'a peer' to help with the intervention is not always going to work automatically. How they interact is just as important (Barnard, 2002).

It also depends a lot on how the peers are trained. If no training is given the efficacy will depend upon the child's current ability and the nature of the behaviors. Having an older, good reader mentor a younger or poorer reader is straightforward, but having children act as peer mediator in conflicts might require crucial training to be successful (Humphries, 1999).

A second issue is that while peers do normally influence each other, this is not necessarily in a simple way. For adolescents, at least, there is good evidence that much of the "peer pressure" is about how they get selected into and out of groups, not about compliance to verbal instructions within the group (e. g., Bauman & Ennett, 1994). It is very difficult to get adolescents to join a new group by an adult mandating that this should happen, and worse things could eventuate if this was to be tried ("*Ok, I want you to mentor this child who has problems, no questions asked!*"). Moreover, even if the child was in a group willing to act as peer intervention agents, this is perhaps not how things normally occur and so other effects might occur. It could also change the social dynamics of that peer group and ruin the group for everyone in it. Dishion, McCord and Poulin (1999) have presented some evidence for one social context in which participation in peer groups inadvertently led to worse outcomes—retrospective reports of children who attended summer camps showed that these led to more bad outcomes.

All this is not meant to turn you off peer interventions, just make you cautious and vigilant about looking closely at the social context before jumping in. There are plenty of success stories around.

Example 1. Limbrick, McNaughton and Glynn (1985) did an interesting intervention in which underachieving 10- and 11-year olds became tutors for underachieving 6- to 8-year olds. The idea was that tutoring could help both the tutees and the tutors. Notice the danger, however, that using tutors who were underachieving is risky because they might not be able to explain to the younger ones what they do not know themselves. In the first part of the intervention (after baseline measurements), the researchers just got the two together to read their books but asked that the tutor help the tutee when they asked for help. This produced a little improvement but not much. In the main intervention, they taught the tutors how to help better, training them briefly in correct modeling, praising, repetition, discussion, and providing evaluations for the teacher (these techniques will be outlined in the next two chapters). This produced much better performance increases, and both tutee and tutor improved their academic performance.

Gumpel and Frank (1999) used a similar procedure in which older children who were socially isolated trained younger children (also social isolates) in social skills. Again, positive social interactions increased for both tutees and tutors. Kamps, Barbetta, Leonard and Delquadri (1994) used high-functioning autistic children as tutors for their peers and found both academic and social improvements for both as a result. Houghton and Glynn (1993) found that same-age pairs who were both less able academically improved when tutoring together.

Example 2. Biglan et al. (1996) conducted some large-scale interventions to encourage anti-tobacco messages to young people, and as a part of this multimethod intervention they utilized peers. They tried a wide variety of procedures (p. 321) to engage youth, such as posters, t-shirts, balloons, many of which could be traded for old ones bearing tobacco company slogans on them. Each community in the intervention necessarily had a slightly different set of activities, but all had some under the categories of academic, creative, policy, trade-ins, give-aways, games, planning and other. While it was difficult to separate the peer effects from the family interventions that were also used, at the end of two experiments the youth had a greater knowledge of anti-tobacco information and showed lower reported intentions to smoke when peers were involved.

Example 3. Black, Tobler and Sciacca (1998) reviewed 120 studies that looked at peer involvement in drug campaigns. Their discussion is useful for pointing out many of the complexities in forming conclusions too readily. They found evidence that the best peer-involved drug programs were effective. However, the contrast typically seems to be confounded between interactive programs that are peer-led and programs that have teachers or researchers talking to groups of peers. That is, the contrast is typically between a peer-led interactive program versus a teacher- or researcher-led non-interactive program, finding that the former is usually the better of the two. This is not surprising, perhaps, given that the latter really amount to lectures and passive presentation of information. It was not clear though whether having peers lead the sessions helped in and of itself. We do not know whether a peer-led but non-interactive program would be equally as effective (one where a peer lectured the other kids).

Example 4. Hull, Hasmi and Widyantoro (2004) were working with adolescent reproductive health projects to get information to an estimated 42 million Indonesian adolescents. They trained peer educators to run group information sessions in male/female pairs over ten districts, reaching over a thousand adolescents. They then had 20 teams of pairs run five sessions back in their own communities and reached nearly 4,000. The peers were slightly older than the adolescents and probably better skilled, authoritative and knowledgeable, but were still accepted well. Despite the large number reached, they concluded that other methods, especially through the media and internet, will be needed to reach the full population.

Example 5: A warning. As was mentioned at the beginning of this chapter, it is not always the case that similar peers will help more than dissimilar peers. Likewise, it will not always be the case that peer interventions will help more than interventions not involving peers. It is worth outlining one example to keep the reader cautious about accepting any intervention unthinkingly. As I emphasized at the start of this book, always examine the context in detail before starting.

Schwartz (1999) looked at how persons with multiple sclerosis (MS) were helped by two forms of intervention peer contact with non-directive support on the telephone, and a group course in coping skills for people with MS. Both were currently available treatments. With respect to the earlier discussion about similar and dissimilar peers, the peer contact persons were matched for levels of disability, age, and interests. Schwartz found that the coping skills training helped more for psychosocial role performance, coping behavior and many aspects of well-being, whereas the peer support only helped to give a more external locus of control for health (less blaming of themselves). For the aspects of MS involving depression and anxiety, the peer support helped more. So the message is that peer support was good for some aspects of the intervention but not for others.

Mentors and Buddies

Interventions in which a mentor or buddy is assigned overlap with peer interventions, and most of the problems and benefits are the same (Evans & Ave, 2000; Fo & O'Donnell, 1974; Humphries, 1999; May & West, 2000; Philip & Hendry, 2000). While for the most part the mentors and buddies are people loosely known or drawn from common social networks, there are few interventions that utilize close friends as the intervention agent. This is despite close friends being a strong part of the 'natural' support system that people have—people in western countries at least will often talk to a close friend before 'confronting' family members with a problem.

Once again there are a large number of issues with these interventions. A lot depends upon the starting point of the mentor and why they wish to mentor, and a lot depends upon the relationship between the two (Evans & Ave, 2000; May & West, 2000; Philip & Hendry, 2000). Most reviews that have been fairly made of this literature have come out as uncertain, since there are so many poorly controlled studies and prior training has varied so much that similar groups are not being compared. Most reviews, though, point out that some studies seem to show genuine positive benefits but we need to know more about the hidden social contexts for this occurring, and be clear about how much training has gone on (Evans & Ave, 2000; May & West, 2000).

Example 1. While mentors are most often thought of as friends, Blinn-Pike, Kuschel, McDaniel, Mingus and Mutti (1998) found that adult mentors of pregnant adolescents took on much more of a parental role than a friend role. They found they were welcome and helped with accessing services and resources, discussing interpersonal and infant issues, and being involved in many intimate aspects of life. The overall picture was of providing a "quasi-parent' more than a mentor as traditionally envisaged.

Example 2. One of the most widespread mentoring programs is the Big Brothers Big Sisters program, which links adult volunteers to at-risk youth, who meet 3 or 4 times a month. In general the outcomes have been very positive, but going back to what was written above, this program is very carefully monitored and supervised by professionals, and there is careful and thorough training of the mentor volunteers (DuBois & Neville, 1997; Grossman & Tierney, 1998; Parra, DuBois, Neville, Pugh-Lilly & Povinelli, 2002). So the success could come from these conditions rather than being mentored *per se*. Further, even when the outcomes are clearly beneficial, many collateral factors play a role such as improvement in parental relationships from having an adult mentor (Rhodes, Grossman & Resch, 2000).

Example 3. Cunningham and colleagues presented an interesting report of teaching students to use conflict resolution techniques for use in the playgrounds of their schools (Cunningham, Cunningham, Tran, Young, Zacharias & Martorelli, 1998). The aim was to measure aggression in the playgrounds and see whether teaching some students to mediate in conflicts could reduce it. The researchers got volunteer students (with parental permission) who were taken through a 15-hour training program on mediation. The training program used techniques covered elsewhere in this book: learning the concepts of mediation, modeling the steps of resolving conflict, and role-playing conflict resolutions to rehearse their skills. The results showed success, and simple training and implementation produced good reductions in aggression in children's play. [Note, this study repeats in Chapter 7.]

Gatekeepers

A gatekeeper is a person who controls access to a larger group of people or resources. In the literal meaning of the word, it is the person who operates the gate to a building or a house who determines who gets inside and who does not get inside. The people inside might be quite happy to have interventions done but if the gatekeeper does let the intervention agents inside, then the intervention does not even go ahead.

Example 1. We have already seen in Chapter 1 that for most interventions with "natural" communities there are appropriate channels to work through for interventions (or even just for research): this might be the leaders or elders; it might be a community committee. These people are natural gatekeepers or usually community-sanctioned gatekeepers. They can be community leaders (Capp, Deane & Lambert, 2001), advocates who become a gatekeeper, sometimes unwittingly

(Trinch, 2001), interpreters and translators (Davidson, 2000), or those involved in service provision and welfare (Forbat, 2000).

Example 2. Morrill, Buller, Buller and Larkey (1999) conducted a worksite campaign to increase eating of fresh fruit and vegetables (the 5-a-day plan). As part of this, they contacted and participated in a large number of organizations, of different sizes and shapes. Their report is an analysis of the gatekeepers in different organization and how one might identify those gatekeepers. Their first divisions were between individual gatekeepers and committees; between the locations around the organization (and this could vary widely); and between whether the rhetoric was about healthy workers being better workers or healthy workers producing a strong organizational culture.

The second round of distinctions made put all the forms into a two-fold cut. Gatekeepers were sourced according to whether the decision making routines were rational or political, and whether they were centralized or decentralized. Rationalized meant that there were rules to follow in the bureaucracy to make decisions, whereas political decision making meant that managers and others were seen as negotiators between factions or coalitions to come up with decisions. For example, in a rationalized and centralized organization there would be one top manager who would be the primary gatekeeper. In a rationalized and decentralized organization there would be many individual managers who would be the primary gatekeepers. In a political and centralized organization there would be a ruling or most powerful coalition who would be the primary gatekeeper whereas in a political and decentralized organization there would be multiple coalitions acting as the primary gatekeepers.

The point of this scheme by Morrill, Buller, Buller and Larkey (1999) is that different categories of organization present different problems to those trying to make contact, in our case, contact for intervention. For example, many indigenous groups do not have a single source of authority that decides what can and cannot be done; instead, there might be multiple coalitions. Getting in through being friendly or convincing one group that you can intervene might put many others offside for no other reason than your point of entry. In the example of such an organization given by Morrill, Buller, Buller and Larkey (1999), they were not successful in gaining entry to the organization. Going in naively expecting there to be a single rule that determines who should give you permission did not work.

School and Education Networks

Schools are becoming more frequently targeted as sites for interventions through the social networks developed around them. While some argue that this takes too much time away from the educational functions of schools, others argue that schools are about more than academic education, and interventions to improve life more generally for children should be required as part of a school's mission. However, some schools are just overloaded with requests for them to become the site of interventions. Examples are replete in the published literature, and any browsing of the typical journals in the reference list will find many more (Clayton,

Leukefeld, Harrington & Cattarello, 1996; Dumas, Prinz, Smith & Laughlin, 1999; McBride, Midford & Cameron, 1999; Orlandi, 1996).

Example 1. As part of developing a school-based program for obesity, Neumark-Sztainer, Martin and Story (2000) asked adolescents what should be in such a program. The main idea was to set up activities for staff, students, and targeted high-risk students. Focus groups with the students produced a long list of activities and other aspects for such a program, including consultations by nutritionists, special leaders, participation with others of matched fitness levels, and better availability of healthy food at schools. While the results came from some students who dominated the focus groups, the suggestions are mostly easily implementable.

Example 2. Dielman et al. (1986) developed an elementary school program for alcohol misuse. They conducted some experimental trials as part of this, with treatment, treatment plus booster, and control conditions. The program was given in four 45 minute sessions, that chiefly told students about the dangers of alcohol misuse and pressure to drink (discussions, films, fact sheets, crossword puzzles, and work sheets), talked about advertising pressures and ways of resisting this (discussions, slides of advertisements, posters and pamphlets, and work sheets), developing skills to resist alcohol pressure (discussion, film, role-playing, and stickers), and further practice in resistance (role-playing, video-taping the students, discussion, films and posters). As will be seen, most of the methods are basic ones to be discussed in the next two chapters.

The results showed some advantages of the program (compared to the controls) in verbal knowledge about alcohol. Little effects on reported drinking behavior were found but the authors point out that this was a preventive intervention, and longer term effects would be more likely outcomes rather than some immediate behavioral results.

Example 3. Yee and Lee (1977) were concerned about the conflict that Filipino students were going through after migration, for example, in statements such as the following: "I love and respect my parents, but they think we still live in the Philippines. At home I am required to be obedient and not ever question my parents. In school I am expected to speak my mind and raise questions. What should I do?" (p. 241). A full intervention would require involving the parents and counseling but these authors wanted to conduct a preventive intervention that would "provide a sense of self-awareness and positive consciousness," to clarify Filipino and Western values as a means of fostering a balance, of cultures, to help family communication skills, and to highlight the usefulness of social support groups.

They structured their program around a 6-month Filipino bilingual-bicultural course, as 10 sessions of 50 minutes. The main methods were discussions, listing of things important to them (verbal intervention), role-playing of communication and listening skills, verbal discussion games about identity, verbal discussions about differences between generations, role-playing job-seeking skills, and building a large cooperative poster (all methods from the next two chapters). As an interesting side-point, the authors were worried that if they evaluated the program they would get stereotyped positive responses, replying as "well-mannered Asians." Instead, they got eight of the students in the class to do the evaluation instead. Overall, the results were positive.

Workplace Interventions

It is becoming more and more common to run interventions at workplaces. In the same way that for western kids (at least) the school is a major social network of their life (more so than families for some), so in the western economy the workplace is a major part of life and therefore a good site for interventions for adults. Many spend the major part of five days a week there. These are not just interventions directly relevant to work and productivity of the organization, but others for general stress and wellbeing (some examples: Gebhardt & Crump, 1990; Glasgow & Terborg, 1988; Ivancevich, Matteson, Freedman & Phillips, 1990; Kaluza, 2000).

Example 1. Jason et al. (1995) ran three conditions for a smoking cessation program on a worksite. These were self-help manuals, manuals plus incentives, and support groups plus manuals. The latter group had better smoking cessation outcomes, however it needs to be recognized that much more was happening in these conditions. During the group sessions they did exercises that the others did not receive, and they also established a buddy system. Once again we usually get better outcomes from programs with many more components but we end up not knowing which bits actually worked.

Example 2. Kaluza (2000) reports on a worksite intervention to help workers cope with everyday stress. The actual intervention components were all standard and most were basic ones to be discussed in future chapters—assertiveness, cognitive restructuring, time management, relaxation, structuring of pleasant activities and physical activity. They found positive effects compared to no-intervention matched controls, but only for some aspects of coping and not all.

Bringing in Strangers for Interventions

In Table 3 we saw that people in western counties are used to dealing with strangers in their lives, although many social conditions of economy, anonymity, monitoring and accountability are needed to make things happen with stranger relationships (Guerin, 2004). I have already mentioned that there are people I know living in very close communities who find it weird that a person with a problem would even consider going to a stranger's office and sit and talk for an hour and hope that this would solve the problem—let alone paying $120 an hour for the privilege of doing this! Likewise, many of us in western countries would find it weird to go and talk to family members about our problems—we keep the problems quiet and solve them ourselves or with the help of a stranger.

Part of the reason why interventions often do not work for those living in close communities is because their interactions with strangers (their social relationships and the development of social relationships) are very different from those who first develop the intervention. [There are other reasons to do with collaboration, ownership, exploitation, etc. as well. See Chapter 6.] The commonly published interventions are designed for people who can build a particular relationship with strangers very quickly, and follow their instructions with strangers (under the special social conditions mentioned above, of course). If you do not relate in those ways with strangers then the interventions are not going to work as they stand. You need to substitute family or community members for the strangers, have family or community members participate, or design a whole new approach.

So my point is not that most interventions work only for westerners and are biased and there is probably a conspiracy going on, but that we have to check the social conditions and change or adapt the interventions designed for one group of people for another group. Table 3 can help with this along with a good prior description and analysis of the social context of the people you are working with (Guerin, 2004).

Co-opting Professionals

The west has bred a whole range of strangers who are professionals at changing people, and who can be utilized in interventions (Foucault; 1973, 1977, 1978; Miller & Rose, 1994; Rose, 1996, 1999). While some are direct in this, such as doctors, many others are co-opted to intervene with other problems. Because people see professionals for a certain problems, the professionals and their offices become useful sites for other interventions, in the same way that schools and workplaces become co-opted.

Like the section on family caregivers, a warning should be placed here. Professionals, and General Practitioners in particular, have a job to do and if too many people co-opt them for other purposes it defeats their job. Legislation in New Zealand, for example, requires that GPs give informal counseling on smoking, sedentary behavior, and make some basic mental health judgments (e.g., Baum, Kalucy, Lawless, Barton & Steven, 1998; McKinlay, Plumridge, McBain, McLeod, Pullon & Brown, 2004; Mullins, Livingstone & Borland, 1999; Richmond, Kehoe, Heather, Wodak & Webster, 1996). There is also talk of them counseling for gambling problems (Sullivan, Arroll, Coster, Abbott & Adams, 2000). All this is supposed to take place during the last five minutes of a consultation period that the client is paying for. This can easily become too much and the quality of counseling and advice will drop. On the other hand, if the GPs are concerned about the health and well-being of the whole person, not just the symptoms that brought them there this time, then these wider functions might actually appeal to GPs as a way of gaining better acceptance from clients. Similarly, if they are GPs to extended family or close communities, "family doctors" in the old sense, then they will not doing mind wider interventions and might see it as part of their role.

Example. Kambo et al. (1994) report some results in which traditional medical practitioners in India (Uttar Pradesh) were utilized to deliver family planning services. Their traditional roles were for homeopathy and indigenous medicines, but they were trained for 11 days in birth control knowledge and motivational counseling skills. Measures showed increased contraceptive use, especially in some categories, and increased knowledge by their clients.

Developing New Social Networks for Interventions

Rather than look to already existing social networks and sites in which strangers meet and influence each other, another approach is to develop or facilitate new social networking (Bogat, Sullivan & Grober, 1993). This is something that can be taught, and many community interventions implicitly or explicitly teach networking as a useful skill. Aside from its benefits for stress management, networking can lead to many resources and relationships that can help with unrelated problems or hassles.

Example 1. Fontaine (1986) discusses the benefits of developing social supports for people relocating overseas, whether this is for work or for migration. Of special note is the discussion on how social support networks can teach new arrivals about the cultural and social aspects of their new country. As well as reducing the stress from moving, such groups can be sites for intercultural training or gaining access to intercultural training.

Example 2. Levin (1993) provides an example of developing economic and entrepreneur networks to help the economy of a region of coastal Norway. In order for the economic networks to work, groups had to be formed and stabilized, so an action research approach was taken (see Chapter 6). The major interventions included a lot of meetings with relevant persons to discussion approaches and participation, leadership training programs, a conference of all interested, and a report of the activities. The groups included ones specifically directed at the production and marketing of fishing, but also groups aimed at fostering talk and community involvement.

Example 3. Another common form of setting up social networks is the development of self-help groups. These differ widely in style and function (Davison, Pennebaker & Dickerson, 2000). Paine et al. (1992), for example, show how some leader training facilitated two mutual-aid groups relevant to low-income women and persons with multiple sclerosis. The main components were sharing personal concerns, sharing similar experiences, empathy, problem-solving, and general information. They are not far removed, then, from the negotiation and mediation techniques given in a later chapter, except that more social support was given to the individuals involved and a longer-term approach was taken. But the main goals were to solve problems together by drawing on everyone's experience. Morgenstern et al. (1997) found that those who maintained contact with Alcoholics Anonymous after the intensive treatment had better outcomes after 1- and 6-month follow-ups.

Home Visitations

A common form of intervention in community settings is to have someone as the agent who visits people in their homes (Marcenko & Spence, 1994). This, of course, is exactly what many health care workers and social workers do all the time, although their services are often not considered interventions. Recently, more traditional forms of "intervention" in clinical areas have "discovered" home visits as a method of involving someone else in the intervention.

Example 1. Olds et al. (1998) present results of two trials of a home visitation program. Nurses visited mothers of prenatal children and infants, and made a variety of assessments. The results were wide-ranging, with prenatal mothers more likely to give up smoking and improve their diets, less child abuse and neglect, more visits to emergency and doctor services, fewer pregnancies afterwards, and more employment for the mothers (at least two years after the end of the study). The results between the two studies were not quite as clear cut as I have presented, but the overall findings are consistent with such changes. The results in many areas of life were very impressive compared to control groups.

Example 2. Grant, Ernst and Streissguth (1999; Ernst, Grant, Streissguth & Sampson, 1999) implemented the "Seattle model of paraprofessional advocacy" with high-risk alcohol and drug-abusing mothers. The idea was that high-risk mothers would have less contact with normal health services and so another source of home visitation would fill this gap. Their Table 1 present some of the activities that occurred, including photographing the babies with an office camera, a gift of a layette, reviewing special caregiving techniques for drug-exposed babies with the mothers, arranging public assistance, finding and encouraging appropriate rehabilitation facilities, and working through family planning options. Some advocates did not succeed and some interesting lessons were learned. Of particular interest, such an advocacy position is not a steady job with a routine, and advocates who could not cope with missed and late appointments, emergencies, and last minute changes, did not do so well. Grant et al. (1999) also present a summary of their training methods for advocates (see Chapter 6 also).

Example 3. An example that is given in more detail in Chapter 8 is that of Sunil, Pillai and Pandey (1999). They compared family planning programs in India that had a small cash incentive for women to use a contraceptive and a contact person (CP) who was trained to give information about contraception and visited the women. Their results showed that the cash bonus had no effect whereas the visitations from the CP had a very strong effect on past and present use of contraceptive, 3 to 4 years after the campaign. Similar results were found by Arends-Juenning, Hossain and Barkat-e-Khuda (1999) and Simmons, Baqee, Koenig and Phillips (1988), who found that home visits by family planning workers were extremely important in making the intervention work.

Consultants

A lot of interventions in organizations and communities are done by outside consultants, persons who are hired or paid a fee to carry out the intervention. With a bit of thought it is easy to see some advantages and disadvantages of consultants, and the relative advantages of having consultants internal to an organization or hiring an external, independent consultant.

Internal consultants probably know what is going on in an organization better than someone who is brought in from outside, but internal consultants might also know "too much" and therefore either be biased in how they see things or have access to only one version of what is happening. External consultants might be more independent in judgment but they need time to learn about the organization and how it functions. They can often miss something important that is going on altogether. Internal consultants are in the organization for longer than external consultants, and so they probably have advantages in looking after the maintenance or implementation of any changes or in fine-tuning the changes over time. On the other hand, internal consultants probably cost more to an organization because they are likely to be on a full-time wage. Finally, external consultants probably get a chance to view many different organizations and therefore learn new methods, new ideas, and new interventions.

As always, then, there are tradeoffs for each option, and each case will be different and need thinking about.

Example 1. Pinto and Noah (1980) asked consultants to organizations about their roles, background, and clients, and then compared internal and external consultants. They found that external consultants were more likely to have a PhD, but otherwise their backgrounds were very similar (mostly white males). External consultants made more money, had been in training and development for longer, and were not likely to have worked with the organization for more than 10 years. External consultants worked with smaller firms, which probably indicates that only the very large firms could afford to hire people permanently for training and development, and they tended to deal directly with top-level management.

Example 2. While anthropologists have traditionally been seen as "working in the field" in remote places, their role has changed considerably in the last twenty or thirty years. More and more they are being employed as consultants for short- or long-term projects, in their "traditional" domains or even in corporate organizations (Gwynne, 2003; Laabs, 1992; Nolan, 2003; Van Willigen & Finan, 1991; Wilson, 1998). Some examples of this sort of consultancy will be seen in Chapter 7, when discussing the conflict resolution by Parker and King (1987). Parker was doing fieldwork among the Truk and King (Parker's husband) was appointed to the Trust Territory to work on preserving the culturally significant sites. They helped with negotiations while one was a consultant and one was doing fieldwork, and helped facilitate some changes.

The Ombudsman as Intervention Agent

A report by Wolkon and Moriwaki (1977) pointed out how the Swedish ombudsman could be viewed as an intervention agent. Appointed to give citizens an avenue to complain about bureaucratic procedures, and address wrong bureaucratic decisions, they argued that the ombudsman was really a preventive resource for reducing potential mental risks. To find out more about ombudsmen, they focused on the case of a radio station in Los Angeles (KABC Radio) that established itself as an ombudsman after California could not pass a bill to establish such a position.

KABC receive about 60,000 complaints (in 1977), and the authors analyzed a sample of 200 letters received. Only 2% of the letters seemed to be from persons with psychiatric problems. The main complaints were against helping and service organizations (46%) and business and commercial enterprises (37%). Most complaints were about material or employment difficulties (85%). As Wolkon and Moriwaki point out, these are somewhat everyday problems but they are major precipitating factors for more serious problems that would require more serious help. That the radio station helped people out and followed these problems through, placed them as a major intervention agent to reduce life-stress problems.

Relief Workers

When natural or unnatural disasters occur, helpers from networks are usually needed.

Example 1. Paton (1996; also Tunnecliffe & Roy, 1993) has outlined some guidelines for training helpers before relief work is necessary. This entails a multitude of problems, primarily because the help required after a disaster is unpredictable, varied, and requires many resources and skills.

The primary components of the help training cover all levels. Organizations need training in leadership and management during times of disasters. Plans for operations need preparation and clear communication lines established. At a group level, team building and peer support are the primary components, so the members work together and have trust in each others' capabilities and organization.

For individuals, stress inoculation in primary concern, involving knowledge of stress reactions and what might be expected, survivor reactions, support strategies, and religious and cultural factors that are likely to be important. In Paton's work this involves film and video recordings, sharing of experiences in discussions, and simulations. Specific skills are also taught, for example, for medical and rescue teams they are required to know about body handling and identification, scene preservation, aguish of relatives, grieving, and their own effects from exposure to the pain and suffering of others.

Example 2. Another useful discussion of issues for relief workers is given by Bakewell (2000). In analyzing relief work for Angolans in Zambia he illustrates how the division between refugees and hosts was not at all clear, and that even defining the situation as an "emergency" or "disaster" was misleading. He argued that using this categorization implies certain ways of dealing with the situation which were not useful. Instead, he recommended that for interventions one should stand back from the present difficulties and look at the "normal" ways of life that existed, and base the relief intervention around that instead (just as I suggested in Chapter 1 to examine the normal contexts!). This means, for example, that there is no clear division between the refugees and the "normal" people living in the area, they are now all going about their lives although each needs resources of different sorts. It means that locals can be involved more in the relief, with some training, and that longer-term implementation can proceed better.

The pattern of migration, for example, of refugees from the war in Angola into Zambia, had been a migration route for over a century, and it was not a case of some people fleeing into an unknown place along an unknown route. It also meant that repatriation was not necessarily the main objective. The external aid-relief workers had a policy of moving the "refugees" inland about 300 km because they thought they needed housing and jobs. However, they found that both the refugees and the hosts resisted this because most refugees had family ties that had been artificially cut by the border in the first place and they were staying with relatives already. The main message for relief interventions, from this case-study, is to get help from the local communities and let them tell you what the situation is about, and collaborate with them in planning the relief, rather than arriving from the outside with a master plan of what needs to be done.

The Computer as an Intervention Agent

We will see in Chapter 5 that research on bibliotherapy—reading books about a problem—appears to work just as well as contact with a therapist, at least for some categories of problems. This has been taken further and applied to the use of the Internet or computers as the basis for intervention. A lot of people now use the internet either instead of a GP or as a backup to check what GPs say. We should assume that the same will become more and more frequent for other interventions (Andrewes, O'Connor, Mulder, McLennan, Derham, Weigall & Say, 1996). Training can also be delivered by computer, although the benefits of this are unclear (Brown, 2001). There are many problems still with this, especially finding out whether you are reaching the target audience through the internet. Cotton and Gupta (2004) found that people utilizing the internet for health information were different from others on key factors, including income and education.

Example 1. Dunham et al. (1998) gave 42 single mothers who had infants access to a computer network, on which they could exchange messages, send Emails, and teleconference with up to 8 others. The themes had to do with parenting issues, and operated for 6 months, 24 hours a day. While not strictly an intervention, some follow-up measures were taken that show what happened.

Over the 6 months, the 42 mothers accessed the network over 16,000 times, amounting to about 2 accesses per day per mother. There was clearly a big impact of providing the service. Those who had less (physical) peer contact accessed the computer more. Most of the replies to postings were supportive, and in order of frequency were categorized as emotional, informational, and tangible support. Finally, mothers who participated frequently on the computer were more likely to report a decrease in parenting stress, although there might be some confounds with measuring stress since mothers who had more time to access the computer might have had less stress to begin with. Further research should be illuminating (cf. Tardy & Hale, 1998)

Example 2. While not an intervention, an older example of the use of computers is that of Salmon (1981). Salmon had farmers play with a computer farm game (the Central Tablelands Farm Management Game) to produce constructs of farming and farmers. The farmers had to make "monthly" decisions about economics and pastures and other aspects of farm management. From the playing of the game Salmon could provide constructs of farming. These were used in later interventions to guide the farmers' understanding about how they made decisions and how to use new technology to help with such decision making.

Example 3. Page et al. (2000) give details about how a support group was set up on the Internet, using a chat-room software program. They discuss details of choosing leaders on the Internet, selection of members, and training. There was no discussion of efficacy or usage, but the planning details will be of interest to anyone wishing to set up web-based support groups.

Example 4. Paul, Johnson and Cranston (2000) set up a videoconferencing satellite program to help rural caregivers with nutritional information for care-givers of dementia patients. While part of this was just giving information, the high-tech setup allowed interaction and questions, which made this much more successful than just sending information to participants.

Providing Community Models who are not Family

In some ways, communities should always be involved in interventions. Most indigenous groups ask that they be consulted about or run their own interventions; most neighborhoods like to find out what is going on if new events appear; governments usually have several groups lobbying when law changes are suggested to change what people do. These cases can be viewed in one way as having others as the agents of intervention, but because each of these has a chapter all of its own in this book, I will leave them out here. Instead, I will concentrate on persons in communities who might serve as models for behavior change but who are not family members, so that others in the community might follow suit.

Example 1. Winett et al. (1997) studied swimming pools for the skin-protective behaviors of both patrons and the pool lifeguards. The lifeguards should be good role models for others, and especially for children. The main intervention consisted of components we have already dealt with: posters displayed with facts, posters with feedback about current behaviors, lottery tickets for patrons wearing hats, shirts and glasses or sitting in the shade, and clothes with a displayed message for lifeguards to wear. Of interest here is that one pool required its lifeguards to participate fully and that pool had the best increase in skin-protective behaviors for both the pool lifeguards and the patrons. It suggests that good (almost perfect) modeling by the lifeguards led to the better increases in skin-protective behaviors by the public. Further to this, Dobbinson, Borland and Anderson (1999) found that sponsorship of surf lifeguards (ones at the beach) seemed to increase their skin-protective behaviors, although the data were not experimental. Thus sponsorship of lifeguards might also help the skin-protective behaviors of the public.

Example 2. Ludwig and Geller (1999) conducted a novel intervention in which pizza deliverers joined in a community seat-belt campaign. The pizzas had reminder cards on them that could earn a free pizza, patrons could remind the deliverers to put on their seat belts when ordering and get a discount, as well as local media coverage. While the authors were measuring community responses to this campaign, they also looked at the effects on the pizza deliverers themselves. Over the period, those who delivered wore a seat belt 32% more than baseline, and also used their turn signal 41% more than baseline, even though this change was not targeted. These changes were maintained up to 24 weeks afterwards. The campaign was successful in the community and the agents of the change also improved.

Example 3. A generic example of community models is the prevalence on television and mass media campaigns of media "stars": sports personalities, film stars, community leaders, and the like (Chapter 6). There is no good data on whether the presence of such people actually helps an intervention, but advertising and marketing "experts" seem convinced. I tend to take heed of what such people say because they usually have a lot of money resting on such campaigns and presumably do not do that lightly (billions of dollars, in fact). However, even if there is such an effect, we do not have any idea how direct the effect might be. For example, it could be that having "stars" on media campaigns serves to get viewers' attention, and whether or not anything more happens then depends upon the quality of the campaign itself. A later chapter has more on this.

Such social marketing campaigns can also be defeated because as much as we market for teens to reduce drinking alcohol, for example, the alcohol companies are putting in billions of dollars promoting their wares.

Chapter 3

Making Basic Changes with Individuals

The basic techniques of intervention are aimed at three outcomes: intervening to get a new behavior for people to use; intervening to strengthen or increase an activity; and intervening to reduce a problem activity. Each of these obviously depends upon the task involved and the persons being trained—training someone to use a computer will be very different from training someone to brush their teeth; and training someone to brush their teeth more regularly, increasing the strength or frequency of the activity, will be different again. We will look at more specific and complex skills in the next chapter, but there are some common techniques that occur in any of these situations, whether training to brush teeth or use a computer. You need to learn these common techniques for any type of intervention, even community interventions.

Changing the Environmental Contexts

How people behave depends upon the environment in which they live, not only the physical context and constraints, but also the social context and constraints placed upon them by their social groups (Guerin, 2004). Many times, behaviors can be altered by changing this environment, without doing anything to the persons themselves. Such interventions are often overlooked because trainers are focused upon the person or a group of people and tend to explain what is going on in terms of the people (Close & Horner, 1999; Levine & Perkins, 1997; Mair & Mair, 2003). For example, one of the best ways of stopping people from smoking tobacco would be to prevent there being any tobacco in the whole country: change the environment completely. With none available at all, people would have to stop smoking. Of course, there are other problems with trying this draconian solution, which is why it has never been done. But similar methods have been used for child pornography, illegal drugs, and sundry other activities (with varying success).

Most cases of altering the environment impact on other people not directly connected with the intervention, and therefore require community or government policy changes. For example, a local community cannot just declare a lower speed limit to reduce speeding and hence accidents and deaths in the area. Such a change would have to go through city councils or government channels, and possibly involve a change of law (Chapter 6). Changes of law require a lot of lobbying and getting support, which are usually difficult tasks.

Altering the Environment

Ergonomics or human factors is about changing the environment to fit people better or redesigning objects and environment to make less problems (Karwowski,

---

Intervention Analysis 4. **Changing the Environmental Contexts**

Alter the Environment
  Use ergonomic knowledge to build better environments
  Redesign objects to enhance behaviors within environments

Changing Objects in the Environment
  Providing New Objects
  Removing Objects

Changing Laws and Policies (Change the Social Environment)

Moving People into a New Environment

2001; O'Brien & Charleton, 1996). How can we best build the environment to make it safer and more productive for people? Used extensively in industry and government engineering projects, it is useful to read these interventions to give ideas for your own interventions. Often redesigning simple objects can overcome large problems. As is well known, specially designed objects for older people and for persons with handicaps have drastically altered the constraints on those people. Even the simple redesign of spoons and forks has helped older persons eat, and at least one couple I know have also used these same spoons and forks for their children's safety.

Changing Objects in the Environment

Providing new objects. A good question to ask before any intervention is whether there is any object you could provide that would change what is currently going on? This should be part of the "*Know your social context*" phase of intervention. If people are using cars to drive to work and polluting the air, what objects could be provided to stop the use of cars? Providing a better bus or train schedule might be all that is needed, and costly and lengthy changes in social policy could be avoided. Providing computers to access on-line information about health can help mothers who stay at home (Tardy & Hale, 1998). Providing solid rubbish bins can help people recycle.

Removing objects. Similarly, sometimes an intervention can remove objects to change the behavior of individuals or groups. An extreme example of this was the American alcohol prohibition in the early part of the twentieth century. Removing sharp objects is a common intervention with parents to stop young children having accidents. Not keeping chocolate in the house is used as a weight intervention (with varying success!).

The point here is that before any intervention, and especially before you start training new behaviors or reducing old ones, ask yourself whether there is anything you could take away from the situation to make an improvement.

Changing Laws and Policies (the Social Environment)

Sometimes just removing objects is not enough, or it impacts on other people too much to carry it out ethically. In such cases, a wider community needs to be approached for approval, and laws or by-laws need to be changed. Changing policy as an intervention will be dealt with in Chapter 6. It amounts to changing the social environment, changing the constraints put (socially) upon all the people policed under that jurisdiction.

Most examples of social policy changes are examples of changing the social environment within which people live and work. The areas of safety, child protection, illegal and violent activities, racism and prejudice, and health all provide examples of rules and laws changing the consequences of social activities. For example, changing the law so that people had to smoke outside of buildings, including work buildings, was shown in one study to lead to a decrease in smoking both at work and in the home, even though it was only aimed at the former (Borland, Chapman, Owen & Hill, 1990).

Moving People into a New Environment

Another strategy is to move people into a new environment to change their behavior, although this is not often done (Murrell, 1973, "individual relocation"). At the extreme this can amount to forced immigration, and the ethics of this needs to be considered carefully. It resembles ethnic cleansing and other short-sighted "solutions" of dictatorships. Any such interventions need to be thought through and discussed with others carefully.

One application that seemed ethical was the individual interventions conducted by Milton Erickson (e. g., Haley, 1973). For example, with some adolescents entwined in peer fighting and poor relations with teachers and other adults, he suggested to the families that they just move to a new city or state and establish themselves again. He first made sure that the adolescent had the skills to change so that the probability of the same problems occurring was minimized. Likewise, he sometimes recommended that an adolescent move out of home and into an apartment of their own, as an intervention for family problems with adolescents. The idea is that all the talk in the world was not going to change either the parents or the adolescent and they would be moving out sooner or later anyway—peacefully or not.

A strategy related to moving people to a new environment is to partition a social environment for separate use. The most common form of this is the "restraining order," as they are known in my country. A person is prohibited from approaching or talking to another person. This is usually used in abuse cases, for which the husband is restrained by law from approaching his wife, and with children in danger from a parent, in which the children are protected in custody by the other parent or by a legal guardian. New Zealand police have even used restraining orders recently for a bike gang, to try and stop their illegal activities being planned. All members of the gang were restrained for talking to any of the others for a set period, and could be arrested if found in the presence of each other.

This strategy is also in principle what is done when organizations restructure their management or move people side-wards into other jobs. A job unit is not working together well so some members are moved to another part of the organization as a solution, rather than training them to work together better (using techniques later in this chapter and the next).

All these strategies of moving people or restraining them are usually for extreme cases, where nothing else can be done or the situation is too serious to even try lesser solutions first. As mentioned above, they often do not solve anything but provide a delay, and the ethics of them should be carefully thought through before attempting them. While the solutions of Erickson seem gung-ho and fascinating, Erickson would have taken into account many aspects of the social context and used his very long experience before making a judgment. He also saw that a lot of training was done so the person was ready for their new environment. That sort of process gets lost in the write-ups of his work, and should be taken seriously before trying to use what he did like a recipe book.

Problems with Altering the Environment

At least three major problems face those altering the environment as an intervention strategy. First, thinking of the alterations or being able to carry them out are major difficulties. For example, if someone has delusions that the CIA is following them, how could you alter the environment to change this? Not all interventions have this solution, and many of the solutions turn out to be costly or not feasible. [If you put them in a new environment they will just imagine that the CIA followed them.] Second, many interventions that change the environment require changes in laws, because alterations typically impact on others, so the welfare of those others must be taken into account. The problem here, as we will see later in this book, is that law changes are difficult to accomplish. Thirdly, there are usually side-effects of altering the environment. Unforeseen collateral changes are likely and must either be guessed or carefully monitored after the environment is altered. For example, roads can be improved to reduce accidents by making them better at gripping car tires or giving them better corners. But the safer the roads are made the more they also facilitate driving very fast and hence even more accidents. If roads are made to be safe for speed X then people will start to drive at speed X+1.

Training New Behaviors

A common intervention is to train someone to have a new behavior—get them to do something they have never done before. There are several ways of doing this, although they are not always made clear during interventions. For example, a trainer might report that they just told the people how to work the computer, we do not know the details of what exactly they did for the intervention. Perhaps there was nothing—

the trainer told them just to use it and walked away, but usually there are simple processes glossed over. *Intervention Analysis 5* gives the names of the basic techniques, noting especially their problems and limitations.

Shaping by Successive Approximations

Shaping is commonly used only with nonhuman animals or with people with little functional speech (Ferguson, 2003). It is done by first selecting behaviors of the person or animal that *approximate* the one you wish to train. If you want a dog to stand on its back legs, for example, you would initially select any behavior the dog already does that has it raise its front paws, even just slightly. If there is nothing the dog does like that then you might select just lifting the head up. If you wanted

---

Intervention Analysis 5. **Basic Techniques to Train New Activities**

Shaping
      Basis: Successive approximations using activities already learned
    Problems: Takes long time and is a luxury for training normal adults

Physical Guidance
      Basis: Physically put person's body into the correct positions
    Problem: The behavior can become dependent upon the touch

Imitation or Modeling
      Basis: Get a model's behavior to control the person's behavior
    Problems: Must teach modeling itself first
           Person can imitate other undesirable behaviors, especially with
              generalized imitation
           Generalization and maintenance not guaranteed

Simple Verbal Instructions or Prompting
      Basis: Tell the person what to do
    Problems: Need to teach instruction-following first
           Need to have instructional control over the person
           Instructor can control behavior but then no generalization
           For non-verbal skills rehearsal or practice also needed anyway

Graduated Prompts
      Basis: Try verbal instructions first; if that fails then use modeling; if that
              fails then use physical guidance
    Problems: Similar problems to above if not done quickly

Role-Playing and Simulation
      Basis: Act out the behaviors required without the usual consequences,
              or simulate the entire situation
    Problems: If not realistic then generalization might be weak

to teach a severely disabled person to point to a picture board, you might begin with just a slight movement of the hand or of a finger and work from there.

Once the approximate behavior is selected, the trick is to make a reinforcer contingent upon the approximate behavior until it occurs more frequently. Following this, the process is to restrict the contingent reinforcer to some behavior closer to the desired behavior than the current one, and just as importantly, when a closer approximation is achieved then stop reinforcing the earlier approximations.

To go through our example, when the dog is lifts its head, give it a treat. When it begins doing this more frequently, then only give a treat when its head is really high. If the dog only lifts it head a little, do not give the reinforcer. Gradually the dog will lift higher and higher and start jumping up. At this point make the treat contingent upon lifting the front legs. It is important to remember to stop reinforcing the earlier approximations at this point. No longer give a treat for just raising the head—only for raising the front legs.

There are some obvious practical problems with this, although just the method I have outlined is surprisingly effective when done cleanly and with careful observations. One problem is that the dog will soon get full and not want more treats. To overcome this, you can, for instance, use a clicker that has always been clicked when the dog has been given treats before. The dog might have to accomplish ten clicks before getting a treat. Very similar sorts of (simple) methods can be use to train animals easily and effectively (Pryor, 1984). Each different species requires special conditions and methods, the best tricks with a dog are not the best tricks for training a dolphin. Karen Pryor's book (and her Websites) gives a lot of tips for those interested.

The major problem and limitation with shaping is that it can take a long time, and it is just easier to use verbal instructions with most activities done by normal adults. If I were to train every component behavior for using a computer by successively approximating the real one, it would take forever. It is far easier to say, "Press the big, red button to start the computer." Shaping you to move your hand towards the big, red button would be a waste, even though there are other problems with the use of verbal instructions (see below).

Shaping is used in a sort of way with some other nonverbal skills that are hard to put into words. An example of this might be teaching someone to start a car moving. You can verbally instruct them, sort of, by saying, "Well, once the engine is running, sort of take your foot off the clutch while pushing on the accelerator, but not too fast but not too slow either. You'll sort of know when to do it." But it is the sound of the engine, and the crunching noises of the gear box, that successively shape a learner driver to change feet at the right moment, and we have difficulty saying in words exactly what we are doing. Likewise, learning to ride a bicycle and fly an aircraft are similar nonverbal skills that are difficult to instruct verbally.

Problems. The main problems with shaping are the time it takes for any complex behaviors and the limitations when used with humans. Most human behaviors can be trained more quickly using verbal instructions. But for work in training animals shaping by successive approximations is the best, easiest and longest lasting technique. All zoos and animal trainers for television use it.

Physical Guidance

Physical guidance means that the person's body is placed so as they can carry out the behavior (Holding, 1970a). This is usually only used for clients with disabilities, so they can accurately perform the action until they can do it alone. There are examples, however, of adult human behaviors trained in this way. Golfing coaches, for example, often hold onto the golf club with the person being trained, or push their body into the correct position before they swing the golf club.

Physical guidance is useful because it get the person accurately into the movement and does not need as much compliance as later techniques. If the person is relaxed with their trainer they can be taught very quickly this way. The best advice for physical guidance, however, is to use as little physical contact as possible or do the touching as lightly as possible. If done clumsily, the person will rely upon the touching to shape their movement, which is not the aim of physical guidance. The aim is to get them correctly doing the action and stop guiding them as soon as possible. Touch is a very noticeable sensation and can easily become an essential part of someone performing properly. So the touch needs to be done once only, or else faded quickly, perhaps to verbal control ("Do it exactly like I just showed you").

Example. Horner and Keilitz (1975) were teaching persons with intellectual disabilities to brush their teeth. They broke the actions down into 15 separate steps needed to brush teeth and proceeded to teach them all and put them together. For some of the steps, the clients were difficult to teach so they used physical guidance (actually concurrent with verbal instructions): "The training method for this procedure consisted of the trainer instructing as well as holding, guiding, or otherwise physically assisting the subject in initiating the desired behavior, but allowing the subject to complete it on his own" (p. 137).

Problems. The main problem has been given. Touch can become a condition for correct actions and the client will rely upon the guidance. It is also slow, and clumsy for very complex behavior.

Imitation and Modeling

A common method for teaching humans, both children and adults, is to use imitation (Goldstein & Sorcher, 1974; Naugle & Maher, 2003). The client watches the trainer or a video of the trainer and does the same thing. The problem that is usually overlooked here is that imitation and modeling do not happen automatically but need to be taught or made to happen. Kids often imitate spontaneously (I think they actually have a long history of social reinforcement for imitation that is difficult to see so it is not really 'spontaneous', but that does not matter here) and so these can be great interventions for them, especially if the behavior modeled is a fun one.

Often, however, imitation is not so automatic and needs to be trained first. What we want is that there is a situation in which your behavior controls what they do, that they try and imitate your modeling. That cannot be taken for granted, and in fact, it is often the hardest part of the exercise. The problem is that if the "motivation" for imitating you dissipates then the client's behavior might stop unless there is another source of maintenance for it. So the method of getting compliance with your modeling is most important. As was mentioned in Chapter 1, the hidden conditions of getting someone to imitate are the major part of this intervention. Think about getting you boss to stand on his or her head by walking up, saying, "Do this!", and standing on your head. Getting the boss into a context in which he or she will actually imitate what you are doing is the hardest part of the intervention in this case. It is like the example from Chapter 1, that getting a person up on the stage for stage hypnosis is the main part of the intervention and doing that almost guarantees what comes next.

One method for getting imitation used with children and persons with disabilities is that of generalized imitation. In this method, the client is taught first to imitate a range of behaviors rather than just the specific one at that moment. If the trainer dances then the client imitates that; if the trainer claps their hands then the client imitates that; if the trainer sings a tune then the client imitates that. In this way, a greater variety of outcomes for imitating occur so that imitation is more likely to maintain.

Example. Young, Krantz, McClannahan and Poulson (1994) trained four children with autism to imitate a variety of responses within four categories of responses: vocal, vocal-with toys, toy-play, and pantomime. A vocal imitation might be to imitate the trainer saying, "happy girl" or "blow bubble." A vocal with toys might be to hold a toy lizard by the tail and hop it across the table, saying "Boing" each time it hits the table. Toy-play might be dropping two letters into a mail slot, opening the box door and removing the letters. Pantomime were body movements, such as putting the thumbs into the armpits and flapping elbows up and down (Young et al., 1994).

When the children were trained on some of these they were given probe examples from either the same response group or from another response group. What was found was that the children would imitate the new ones from the same response group, but not those from another response group. So the generalized imitation still only worked within a certain type (topographical) of response group and not across to others.

Problems. Problems occur with imitation from having to assure that imitation will occur at all, and from the client learning to imitate unwanted behaviors—especially from generalized imitation training.

Simple Verbal Instructions and Prompting

Probably the most common way of training a new behavior is by some form of verbal instruction (more complex versions are in Chapter 6). This ranges from giving lectures to reading books like this one to teaching children how to do maths. Each of these involves saying or writing some words and a person hearing or reading those words and "doing what it says." This might not be so obvious in the case of lectures, but the lecturer is saying the words out the front so that the students can repeat them at a future point, not so that they do what they are taught about. What students are supposed to do with all those words is usually assumed to be known by the students. The more complex examples will be dealt with in the next two chapters.

The advantage of verbal instructions is that, once they are working, they can be very effective, can change a lot of behavior, and can "specify" very complex behaviors which would take ages to train by other means. I can ask you to do the following, and you should be able to do it, so long as you follow them at all:

> Stand up on your feet right now and start bouncing up and down without your feet leaving the floor. Do this more and more until you feet are *just about* to leave the floor each time you bounce upwards. Now hold you hands out perpendicular and see how this dampens your bouncing. Now push you hands downwards like you are swimming and feel how your bouncing goes up, even though the air movement is not pushing you upwards.

The point of giving this example is that to train the above through shaping or imitation would take a very long time. Verbal instructions do it quickly, *if the instructions are properly followed and the social conditions are right.* Getting instructions followed is perhaps the hardest part that needs most of the interventionist's attention.

Of course, saying that verbal instructions are a quick method is also a bit of a lie. People need to spend at least 10 to 12 years of their lives in schooling so that they can respond in certain ways upon hearing (or seeing) particular words. Once that is done, however, language use is quick and easy, but the process of learning all that is very lengthy.

Three problems arise straight away. First, just saying words does not make them happen–trying telling a stranger to stand on their head. Second, there are many events that we cannot really tell someone what to do, and I mentioned some of those in the section on shaping by successive approximations (driving a car, riding a bicycle, meditating). Finally, the fact that instructions are more likely to be followed if someone with power gives them means that the intervention might not work when that person goes away.

These points mean that it is crucial how the instructions are given and by whom. Once again, there are hidden social conditions necessary for instruction-following to work and these are a crucial part of the intervention. Like imitation, instruction-following itself might need to be taught first, or checks made that the person will follow the instructions. Again, just walk up to your boss and verbally instruct them, "Ok, now stand on your head!" You need to have a context for intervention in which the instructions will be followed. While this sounds silly, a large number of interventions have someone just instruct "Do not do this" or "Do this" and expect that people will then follow what was said. More on this in Chapter 5.

The second point means that the instructions need to be checked to make sure that they are possible to carry out and that they are both useful and appropriate. All these points are true also for "self-instructions." Just because I instruct myself to get up early out of bed does not mean that it will automatically happen.

I will have a lot more to say about verbal instructions through this book because they are the most common method of instruction. Most normal adults do all their learning through verbal instructions.

Problems. Verbal instructions rely upon the person following the instructions, and many social contexts can work against this happening–parents spend half their life telling adolescents what to do and they still do not do it. One of the most important lessons you can learn about interventions, although it seems either wrong or obvious, is that just telling someone to do something or how to do something does not make it happen. There are hidden social conditions necessary for those latter events to occur, as we saw in Chapter 1.

Graduated Prompts

A good technique for teaching quickly is with graduated prompts. This is just a mixture of three methods seen so far: verbal instructions, modeling and physical guidance. Once learned it can be done very smoothly and automatically–in fact, many people spontaneously use this without any training whatsoever. Graduated prompts start with verbal instructions and attempt to train the target behaviors that way. If that is not working, or perhaps not working on just one small component of the whole thing, then some very quick modeling is done followed immediately by getting the response under verbal control so instructions can again be used. If the modeling does not work then physical guidance is used, again, very briefly and quickly get the response under imitative control and then quickly under verbal instructional control. So you sort of go down the list if some part of your verbal instruction training does not work and then bring it quickly back up the list. As I mentioned, this can very naturally and very quickly:

> ok, try and move you arm up and down, up and down... [not working] That's good but see, it should look like this [modeling now], up and down, up and down... [still not working] here, I'll move you the right way, ok, keep that going now just like I'm doing... move your arm up and down like me, up and down... ok, so let's try that again, move your arm up and down, up and down...

Can you see in here the verbal instructions followed by modeling followed by physical guidance followed by modeling followed by proper verbal instructional control? The main idea of graduated prompts is to get verbal instructions working, so any modeling or physical guidance should be very brief, just until it is being done correctly. Otherwise, all the problems of those techniques can also be a problem here.

Problems. Graduated prompts can have all the same problems as verbal instructions, modeling and physical guidance, unless they are faded very quickly.

Role-playing and Simulations

A common way of teaching a new behavior, especially ones that are difficult to put into words (so you cannot use instructional control), is to role-play (Neef, Lensbower, Hockersmith, DePalma & Gray, 1990; Goldstein & Sorcher, 1974; Out & Lafreniere, 2001). Many organizational interventions that train behaviors have people act out what they are going to do in order to learn it. For example, in order to learn how to negotiate and mediate, which will be discussed in Chapter 7, I have classes play out some examples of mediations. One person plays the mediator, two others role-play people in a conflict situation, and a fourth person is there to watch and comment afterwards to the role-players about the whole performance. In fact, role-playing is actually identical to learning by being thrown in the deep end, like getting on a bicycle to learn how to ride, and is the same as rehearsing exam material at home before the exam to practice for the real thing, except that the content is verbal behavior.

In organizations, there are larger forms of role-playing that usually get called simulations instead. These usually extend over time and can be quite complex. There are now many similar role-play situations on computers, in which you are in charge of a city and have to make decisions to keep the city functioning. A simulation can become so realistic that it becomes the real thing, at least in fiction (Card, 1977).

Example 1. An interesting example of role-playing, and some beneficial side-effects, was presented by Fowler, Dougherty, Kirby and Kohler (1986). They had three boys who were disruptive in class and generally had negative interactions with others. They were assigned to pretend to be monitors during the lunch break, when they had to award points (or take one away) for good behavior by other children. When they did this, their own negative interactions immediately decreased and in two cases the positive interactions increased. There was a little increase again in negative behaviors when they were stopped as monitors, and these results did not generalize to other periods of the day. So the role reversal worked but without much transfer, although this could probably have been improved with further training for generalization (see below).

Example 2. Another example that shows a variety of simulations comes from Gawron, Dennison and Biferno (1996). They outline the large number of simulations used for testing flight equipment. These might be mockups of a flight deck, at which a person performs; mannequin models that are built to simulate the physical form of humans; full-sized mannequins to test restraint systems; and even electronic simulations of humans to test parameters of flight. There are also full-blown simulators, in which a person feels like they are in a real airplane, with digitized screens to show the scene outside the aircraft and full controls to operate. If well done, these provide a very realistic way of having someone train on the task without having the usual dire consequences from making mistakes. There are also car simulators, in which a person feels like they are driving a real car, and in which a screen shows the terrain through which they are driving, and from which children can run out or distractions can appear (http://www.practice.co.nz/learners/cddrives.html).

Problems. The obvious problem with simulations and role-plays is that they are not real, and the usefulness depends upon the correspondence to the real thing. This is a necessary evil, however, and no one who uses role-plays or simulations believes that the person will learn the exact skills they need for the real thing. With a good role-play or simulation, however, they will learn enough that they can adapt (be shaped) quickly when they enter the real situation, and it also means that they have not caused major damage while they were just practicing.

Strengthening Behaviors

A common situation is that a behavior or skill has already been learned by someone, or is easy, but the person does not perform it very often or appropriately. How can that activity be 'strengthened" to increase its frequency?

Positive Reinforcement

Positive reinforcement is a procedure defined precisely in research with animals but which, I have argued, is mostly meaningless for adult humans (Guerin, 2001a, b, 2004). This is because what is called 'reinforcement' with adult humans is complex, involved with a long history of social relationships, and depends upon a large number of social conditions for it to work. Saying "Good job!" to someone contingent upon them doing a specified action is not comparable to giving a rat a food pellet contingent upon pressing a bar. This is not to repudiate the animal research but to understand that human behavior by adulthood is already far more complex. Most of my friends, if I started saying "Good job!" to them would think me strange and it would have little effect except to get me excluded.

The properly defined 'reinforcement' procedure has many conditions almost never achieved with adult humans—they must be contingent, immediate, not sated, appropriate to individuals involved, and stronger than competing contingencies. It is not that adult humans do not have their behaviors shaped by reinforcers, it is just that there are too many of them for each observable behavior and they are part of a complex system.

Having said all that, saying "Good job!" to someone can be very effective but we do not really know exactly why. It might strengthen their following my instructions in the future rather than 'strengthening' the behavior they are doing, or it might strengthen our social relationships and therefore the generalized social reciprocities that arise (Guerin, 2004) so that it looks like their behavior is 'strengthened'. In any event, it is not a simple process occurring that makes the contingent behavior more likely in the future—as happens to the animals.

So you will find the best trainers praising their people they work with (Goldstein & Sorcher, 1974), and you should do so yourself, but just do not think of it as a reinforcement procedure—you will be disappointed. It is just a general way to keep them onside.

Negative Reinforcement, Escape and Avoidance

Negative reinforcement, escape and avoidance are intervention techniques that are common in everyday life but usually not carried out professionally for ethical reasons. They each have the same feature that something bad is presented unless the person does a certain action: "Do this and we won't do X to you". They might escape experiencing the bad event or be able to learn to avoid it. The key point to remember is that this is a technique that *strengthens an action* because the people are doing it more frequently to escape or avoid something bad.

These techniques are common in everyday life. Parents can lock children's toys away and instruct, "*You are not getting your toys back until you start cleaning the sink every night!*" In the military it forms the basis of torture techniques; I keep hurting you until you tell me what I want to know. Something bad happens until the behavior is strengthened—whether sink cleaning or spilling the beans.

In general, avoid these types of techniques since for adult humans they are going to have multiple and unpredictable effects. In the same way that general praise and 'reinforcement' might work by strengthening our social relationships and the related generalized social reciprocities rather than directly strengthening the behaviors being praised, the use of negative reinforcement (and punishment below) techniques can collaterally weaken our social relationships. So I might successfully use the technique to strengthen your behavior but you no longer want to be my friend. We just do not know these sorts of collateral effects well (see below).

Weakening Behaviors

The other goal of training basic behaviors, beyond training new skills and strengthening actions, is to weaken or stop someone doing something. How do you get a child to stop sucking their thumb? Once again I will urge you, as others will, to avoid these techniques and instead concentrate on increasing good behaviors while perhaps merely ignoring the bad (see *extinction* below).

One of the problems with weakening behaviors is that doing so does not teach any new behaviors to replace the old—the techniques just get rid of the old ones. What fills that gap could actually be worse than the one being weakened in fact! Second, the techniques rely on setting up aversive conditions, meaning that some contingent painful or bad event is usually used to weaken the behavior. Like negative reinforcement, there are ethical as well as practical problems with using aversive conditions. Some claim that there are no problems that cannot be dealt with by non-aversive techniques so there is no place for them anyway (Horner et al., 1990; Meyer & Evans, 1989). Finally, from a loose argument I have, it appears to me that any increase in a person's repertoire of actions is a good thing; while any decrease is a bad thing. This vaguely stems from believing that even the bad things we learn could be of use another day in another setting, and so long as no harm is being done, adding new behaviors is better than trying to get rid of behaviors. Do we really understand everything about thumb sucking that we can confidently say it must disappear? We can stop someone being aggressive and fighting, but the skills could be useful in times of war or if they needed a job in the military. I am not entirely convinced by this argument but it is worth pondering.

Having said all that, the techniques are widely used (if poorly) in real life. The government stops criminal activity by contingently locking people up, parents hit kids to stop them doing things, and people yell aversively at one another to stop the other doing or saying something. Procedures of weakening behaviors, and punishment procedures in particular, are all around us, although this does not mean they must always be or that they are the best way of doing things.

To this end, I will outline something about extinction procedures, the kindest form of all, and then greatly summarize the rest. Most of these techniques are only used by professional intervention agents under very controlled and unusual circumstances in any case. So avoid these techniques wherever possible and look for alternatives.

Example. Sajwaj, Libet and Agras (1974) squeezed aversive lemon juice down an infant's throat every time food was being brought up. The baby was dying from undernourishment since it vomited all its food, and every other technique had been tried (the baby could not talk of course so they could not reason with it!). They discussed the ethical issues first but then went ahead. The baby rapidly gained weight and was saved, although others would say that there might have been a non-aversive technique that was not tried.

Extinction

Extinction in this context means to remove the consequences that have been maintaining a behavior. In most cases of intervention, this means removing some support for the behavior that is be reduced or weakened. For example, some self-injurious behavior such as head-banging have been shown to be supported by inadvertent social reinforcement or escape. Typically, someone who begins head-banging gets very quick social attention and sympathy, and can get whatever they want if they stop. One way to reduce the unwanted behavior, then, is to remove these sources of support and extinguish the behavior.

Such procedures are often difficult to carry out in real life as interventions, and have many ethical questions involved. They are prevalent in normal life, however, as when you ignore someone, stop paying attention to someone, withdraw your support for someone, or stop being friends with someone (*"If you keep sucking your thumb I am not talking to you"*). Usually there are other avenues for the person whose behavior is being extinguished, so the strategy is not that successful anyway. There are numerous social strategies for secretly hiding things from others or stopping them from finding out (Chapter 4 of Guerin, 2004).

There are also side-effects of extinction. If not accompanied by some positive support for desired behaviors, extinction also reinforces total escape. I might stop paying attention to you when you are annoying me so as to weaken that behavior (perhaps not as a conscious strategy, though), and then find that you have just left and gone and made new friends who do not mind your "annoyances." Similarly, I have problems when withdrawl of attention (extinction) is used with young children, because giving attention serves multiple functions, not just specific to that behavior being weakened.

Some other side-effects of extinction have been shown repeatedly in research, although there are conditions for their production and they might not work for adult human complex cases. Starting extinction leads to a rapid "burst" of the behavior to be weakened, and also often leads to aggression. If someone is "bugging" me and so I ignore them, they will often immediately increase bugging me, since that has been reinforced in the past, and they might accompany this by some aggression (perhaps verbal, though).

Example. Lerman, Iwata and Wallace (1999) looked at archival data on 41 cases of extinction being used with persons with intellectual disabilities who showed self-injurious behavior. The self-injurious behavior was found to be maintained by escape from demands in 21 cases, access to social attention in 13 cases, access to objects in 4 cases, and automatic reinforcers in 3 cases. That is, in some cases the self-injurious behaviors led to the person being relieved of some demanding tasks, in others the person got attention when they were self-injurous, in other cases they got things they wanted when acting self-injuriously, and in the last case it was deemed that being self-injurious led to some change in their bodily states or the pain was replacing some worse event.

These 'reinforcers' were withheld during the extinction phases of intervention. They found that extinction bursts occurred in about 40% of the cases, more when only extinction was used, less when extinction was used in conjunction with other intervention techniques. Extinction-induced aggression was found in 22% of the cases, again, slightly less when a combination of intervention techniques were used.

These results for a real intervention show that such side-effects are common, even though they do not happen all the time. In this case, however, an extinction burst of self-injurious behavior can be very serious, even if it occurs only 40% of the time. The technique is an effective one, even with this side effect, and dealing with self-injurous behaviors is very difficult by any other techniques of intervention.

Variations on Extinction

There are some versions of extinction that differ slightly. You do not ignore the nasty behavior but change it gradually. With the DRL techniques (Differential Reinforcement for Low rates of responding) you strengthen lower and lower rates of the behavior rather than stop reinforcing it totally and immediately as extinction would (Tarbox & Hayes, 2003). This is perhaps less aversive, but it takes time and also focuses attention onto problem behavior rather than better alternatives. In DRO (Differential Reinforcement for Other behavior) or Omission training, any other behavior besides the nasty one is strengthened (Wallace & Robles, 2003). So if the child takes the thumb and sits on it this is strengthened, thereby leading to the weakening of thumb sucking. However, this again focuses on the problem behavior and in fact could strengthen problem behaviors, say if the child stopped thumb sucking but started fighting with siblings instead. In DRI (Differential Reinforcement for Incompatible behavior) the replacement is one that is incompatible with the behavior to be weakened, so if the child sat on the thumbs this is incompatible with thumb sucking and would be strengthened (Wallace & Robes, 2003). This procedure usually focuses on good behaviors as replacements but there is sometimes a problem with finding good incompatible behaviors.

Punishments

Punishment procedures are strictly speaking the presentation of something bad or the removal of something good when the behavior to be weakened occurs (Wacker, Harding, Berg, Cooper-Brown & Barretto, 2003). If you suck your thumb I either take away something you like or present you something you do not like. Pain is always effective except under gross torture conditions where it can eventually lose its effect, so the history of humans is one in which punishment procedures involving pain have been extremely common.

Unfortunately, punishment is usually not done well, because there are a number of conditions that need to be met for it to be effective and these almost never are met. For punishment to work properly it needs to be immediate, intense, consistent, and with no escape possible from the situation. This means that in real life the punisher needs to have enough control that the person cannot just escape the situation and learn instead not to see you again. Parents often find this when instead of a child taking their punishment they begin disliking the parents or start staying away from them. This is a side-effect of poor punishment procedures that makes it not worth using most times. Most punishment procedures in real life have hidden conditions that make them seem to work, but most of us learn to escape from the situation rather than stopping the behavior. For example, speeding fines can in principle make you stop speeding, but it can also strengthen being sneaky about speeding and watching more for police cars and police traps.

While this might convince you to use punishment procedures properly instead of in a messy way, real life usually makes it impossible for good punishment procedures and we end up with hybrids that probably make things worse. This is a good argument not to use them at all. It is better to use other positive techniques than do a poor job on punishment, which is almost always the case. For example, we almost never have control over another person that they cannot just escape us rather than front up again for their punishment procedure.

Apart from the common hitting and fighting found in real life, there are two methods that are sometimes used in professional interventions when ethically sound.

Response Cost. Response cost simply refers to procedures that take something nice away when the behaviors to be weakened occur. Common forms are speeding tickets and fines (taking our money away). Everything I have said can be found for these types of examples, that they teach people to be sneakier or to escape the situations in which they are likely to be caught. They are commonly used, however, and often come in the form of a verbally threatened response cost: "*You do that and I will get rid of all your posters!*"

Timeout. Timeout is a procedure that again is commonly used (Friman & Finney, 2003) but usually badly. It is supposed to be an extinction procedure that weakens bad behavior by removing a child from whatever is reinforcing the bad behavior, but in practice it is commonly used wrongly as a type of punishment ("You do X and I will lock you in your room"). So it is no longer removal of reinforcement but presentation of a punishment that is being used. Worse, it is also inadvertently used by adults to escape the situation of a badly behaved child ("Thank goodness, I can send him off to timeout again and get some peace for a few minutes!").

There are other side-effects, such as if the child is bored or stressed out and therefore acting badly, timeout will reinforce the bad behavior for next time since they get to leave! This needs to be explored before doing your intervention ("*Know your social contexts*") but is almost never done in practice. Timeout is also not instructive in the sense we saw above that it does not actually teach the child what good behavior to do instead. In schools, it also takes them away from their learning environment which is not a good thing.

So most of the opposition to timeout procedures, and it is illegal in some places in the world, come from the technique not actually being done properly. The problem is that, like punishment procedures, reality probably dictates that it will very rarely be done properly since it needs a lot of monitoring and there is usually no one available to do that. So unless the resources are there for it to be done properly, it should not be used! And you can always find an alternative that promotes good alternative and incompatible behaviors rather than getting rid of bad behaviors (Horner et al., 1990; Meyer & Evans, 1989).

Collateral Changes

I have mentioned a lot of side-effects, mostly unwanted, that occur when we change a behavior. This is part of a bigger picture that can actually be useful. For adult humans I have outlined how many part of our practices are mixed in together– learning to like bananas changes our social life as well our eating habits; learn to water-ski and you get invited out more.

While some of this can be seen as unwanted side-effects, the potential is there to utilize collateral effects for positive change. If someone has poor social skills and has no friends, rather than train them how to make friends, it would be good to work indirectly (so as not to focus on them having a "problem" behavior) and train them to dance, water-ski, or whatever else it takes to get asked out and eventually make friends. We do not know enough about this at the moment, although many savvy therapists and others probably do this surreptitiously or inadvertently already (Haley, 1973).

Previously I have mentioned six possible ways that such collateral effects (or multiple contingency effects) might occur, but we will not know much more until the social contexts for people's activities are better understood (Guerin, 1994). Such effects probably occur commonly in real life, and people seem to just "snap out of" problems, or spontaneously get better.

Example. An example of this was a study by Bay-Hinitz, Peterson and Quilitch (1994) in which they intervened and changed cooperation and competition by changing the toys with which children played (an environmental intervention as discussed at the start of this chapter). Throughout the study, these authors measured the percentage of cooperative behaviors shown by children during both a *Game Time* and a *Free Play* time. After doing this for a baseline of one or two weeks, the children were given toys during the *Game Time* that required either cooperation or else competition. The idea was that intervening to change the toys from cooperative to competitive toys would change the children's cooperativeness during *Game Time*.

The results showed that in most cases, when given the competitive games in *Game Time* the children showed less cooperation, but when given the cooperative toys in *Game Time* they showed more cooperation. More interestingly though for the discussion here, the children's play in *Free Play* time showed the same changes although neither the cooperative nor competitive games were available. So changing the environment with which the children could play changed their cooperative and competitive behaviors, and even occurred collaterally outside of that situation.

So the message is that collateral changes can be your intervention-friend if you know what is going on, and in this case led to a better outcome of more cooperative play even in a situation where the intervention toys were not present. In this case, the collateral effect was probably from the intervention affecting the children's more general relationships and not just their immediate play with cooperative or competitive toys. Does this remind you of the start of Chapter 1: "*interventions are adjustments in social contexts and relationships*"?

Chapter 4

More Complex Skills Training

Everything we do can be considered a skill, even how we talk (Guerin, 2004). For this chapter, however, we will concentrate on training manual skills, and ones that are mainly pertinent to education and work situations. We usually use the word "skill" for an action that can be done better or worse, and one for which practice can make better. Thus we talk about both skilled welding, that an experienced welder develops, and skilled decision making, again that long experience can improve.

It is a sad indictment of western civilization that in many cases, after people reach 30-40 years of age, they no longer learn new skills. While not completely true, children are explicitly trained on many skills—thinking, riding bikes, climbing, skating, etc. Adults tend not to do this unless their work requires it. Some adults are now learning computer skills, but few take up roller-blading or ice-skating. So training of skills is something restricted to certain groups in certain situations, and in western societies training usually costs money even though the skills are there and open to anyone who tries.

What I am getting at, that I hope you can see, is that skill training can be a political and economic issue in western societies at least (Darrah, 1995; Latham & Saari, 1982). It is stratified into certain groups of people and must be purchased. While purchasing is not strictly enforceable for skills—for example, I was able to teach myself hypnosis quite easily—the practice and use of those skills within society can also be highly political. I must do certain things and learn only through certain groups in order to *practice* hypnosis without being sued. There are even laws in most western countries about the use of hypnosis, for example.

These points are not trivial, and need to be kept in mind when thinking about interventions to train skills. Many training techniques have been packaged and copyrighted, even though they amount to no more than some methods from the last chapter and some from this chapter. Like breakfast cereal, you are mostly paying for the packaging.

Informal Teaching of Skills

Every culture has ways of teaching, and there are at least two important considerations we must learn from this to apply to interventions that include training skills. The first point is that if people have a particular way of learning then your own style (or the western style if you think that is a gold standard still) might not work for them, even though the person is bright and motivated.

Goodnow (1980) compared different ideas about training, mostly as applied to children. There were ideas of *telling*, *showing*, *doing*, and *watching*, and different groups placed different importance on these. She recounts when she was in Rome she thought that the children she worked with spent much of their time "just sitting," but eventually realized that the children were learning through careful watching rather than wasteful trial-and-error doing. Goodnow also pointed out how there were also very different social reactions to asking and answering question; some groups around the world see it as rude to ask a direct question, while others see it as picking on them if questions are asked of individuals rather than the whole group (Guerin, 2004, Chapter 5). Likewise, whether one should respond to an error and point it out is also a social question; some see direct feedback as very rude, even if accurate, and find more informal ways of doing this.

There is no implication here that one system is superior to the other. The main point is that if the system you are using is not fitted to the social and cultural history of your groups (Table 3) then they are liable to respond in inappropriate or incorrect ways but for the wrong reasons. Pálsson and Helgason (1999), for example, found that the boat skippers who did best in the marine school were not necessarily the ones who ended up best on the fishing boats. They suggested that such practical skills were best taught *in situ* and the school taught them some things but not the dexterity needed for fishing skills.

Harris (1984) also reported varies styles of informal training that occurred in an Australian aboriginal group. The training was started at birth, was continuous through life although informal, and had a strong social element to it. Certain training was under the control of certain social groups within the larger group of the tribes.

Both these accounts, and there are many more you will find if you begin looking, are good to read because they give you very different perspectives from the usual education-is-the-only-way-to-learn approach that most western training promulgates (Beresford & Partington, 2003; Durrenberger, 1997; Harris, 1990). Most western talk about interventions assumes that education in the western sense—telling people, lecturing them and "imparting knowledge"—is the only way to go. But slick training packages are not the only way to learn, and there are many things they do not teach you.

My second point is that while non-western cultural learning styles might not be the most cost-effective in western terms, and do not fit bureaucratic models and time schedules very well, they more often than not have a second function of helping maintain the whole culture (Guerin, 2004). Teaching things in informal settings and through longer and more informal methods of intervention, are not just about teaching what is in front of you but also about teaching the children and adults the whole culture and way of life. Ruining those ways of learning by imposing a foreign—but perhaps formally more effective—method of skill training can ruin other aspects of the culture, and the learning of particular skills might not be considered that important by the recipients. Both these points must be remembered when training in particular groups, especially when they are not imbued in western ways. The methods reported by Harris (1984; and Prince & Geissler, 2001) were not only teaching certain skills but concurrently or collaterally teaching social skills, hierarchical skills, and survival skills. So using 'culturally appropriate' methods of learning is not just to help the 'student' learn what we want to teach them better, but also to teach them other important lessons of life.

So what will be given below is very much a western perspective in which specific skills are being taught in the most effective (cost and time) way between strangers and in the shortest possible time with no waste, and the procedures are not aimed at teaching anything in addition of a social or moral nature. If you are working with indigenous or traditional groups they might be skeptical of such methods because they feel a lot is missing. As part of your skills training you might then wish to work with them on the other social components in other ways (Chapter 6). The strength of their conviction comes from the western method being totally focused on training a specific skill and nothing else whereas 'traditional' teachings incorporate many more lessons within training a single skill.

The astute reader will also see that this goes directly back to Table 3 in Chapter 1 (yet again!). Close communities have very different properties of social relationships and this is usually taught alongside any more formal knowledge in traditional teaching methods. Western teaching is only half the story for these people and this is again because western social relationships are commonly with strangers and so we want to be taught through a learning package or school but without any social or moral obligation to the teacher if they have been paid for what they do. We are not expected to become life-long buddies with every person who teaches us, and we are not expected to look after our teachers when they are old and need caring. Likewise, just because you bought my book and maybe even read it, I am not expected to have you over to eat dinner with me.

The problem with this discussion is that we do not know enough about informal ways of learning in this sense for me to say much more. Most accounts leave out the full context of what is really being taught alongside the up-front material that seems to be covered. I hope we can get more researchers working on this to present a better summary in the future of how these "traditional learning methods" really worked and what else was taught.

Task Analysis

The first typical steps in training skills (western style) is to break the actions down into smaller skill units, train those skills separately, and then train the person to put those units into one skilful performance. The first steps are well known, and books exist to help you break down skills into smaller skills, and to make those skills something concrete and observable, so you can actually know whether they are occurring or not (Binder, 1996; Cooper, Heron, & Heward, 1987; Frederiksen, 1982; Gilbert, 1978; Hawkins, Mathews & Hamdan, 1999; Johnson & Layng, 1992; Komaki, 1998; Komaki, Collins & Temlock, 1987; Lofland, 1971; Mager & Pipe, 1984; O'Brien, Dickinson, & Rosnow, 1982; Ross, 1982; Sulzer-Azaroff & Mayer, 1977; Taylor, 1998; Taylor, O'Driscoll, & Binning, 1998; Vargas, 1972; Wexley, 1984).

***Intervention Analysis 6.* Typical Steps in Training Complex Skills (in the Western Manner)**

Break the actions down into smaller skill units (task analysis)

Describe and list those smaller skills

Train those simpler skills separately

Train the person to put those units into one combined performance

Let us look at an example. Suppose you had to teach first-time fathers how to give a baby a bath. What would be the steps? Put water in the bath, put the baby in, take the baby out?

Dachman, Alessi, Vrazo, Fuqua and Kerr (1986) developed a training intervention to do just that. The point here is that they spent a long time just developing the unit steps that needed to be trained. They first identified the major skills needed for looking after an infant by interviewing experts (pediatricians, early childhood workers, and parents) and by reading a large amount of source material. From this they found six critical skills: holding, feeding, burping, bathing, diapering, and temperature measurement. They then video-recorded early childhood workers doing each of these skills and then watched the videos and wrote down all the steps. This was done by independent observers who then conferred when they disagreed. They then had 60 (official) experts and 30 parents (unofficial experts?) to rate whether each of the steps was important or not.

A long procedure but comprehensive. For example, the task analysis of bathing the baby came to 12 steps, many of which had sub-steps to be learned. For example, Step 6, shampooing, had another 5 steps involved in it: place the baby gently on a dry towel and wrap; use the football hold over the tub; first wet, then place some shampoo on his or her head and gently massage in a circular motion using the flat pads of your fingers; squeeze clear water from the wash cloth onto his or her scalp, rinsing away all suds; pat dry. The total number of steps was 28! Just to wash a baby. Of course, teaching each of these steps does not take a long time since many are very, very simple.

Just to give you the idea of this intervention, let me quickly outline the training procedures for these first-time fathers. What I would like you to notice and learn is how the training is based on everything from the last chapter, despite having a unique problem and unique set of skills to teach.

The main idea was first outlined to the fathers verbally, and questions answered. The fathers then had one week to read a manual containing all the steps with descriptions, to go through review questions and a 20-item quiz, after which any further questions were answered. So far, everything has been verbal knowledge, using reading and exam techniques. The fathers were then given a baby doll (simulation of the real thing) and observed how they performed with no more training than this. (This was done as a control baseline for the experimental method rather than anything to do with the intervention)

The final parts of the training were simply observation of the trainer modeling the behaviors required followed by the father's role-playing with the trainer giving immediate feedback on their performance. Feedback in this sense would have been a mixture of praise to keep them going and verbal instructions to change wrong behaviors. Each father received either two or three of these sessions.

The first message, then, is that breaking down actions into components skills is an effective method for training, and indeed necessary for most complex skills. The second message is that the training of those component skills is nothing more than the techniques we have already learned: praise, shaping, verbal prompting, physical guidance, modeling, role-playing, and simulation. The only tricks are to be systematic and thorough, and have a way of checking whether it is working.

Problems. There are some problems with task analysis that should be pointed out. First, doing the intervention this way can take time and effort. Even though it might be effective, the costs involved might not warrant doing the whole procedure. For example, most fathers do not learn to bath a baby this way, they do it by jumping in the deep end—so to speak. Their wife or their parents might give them verbal prompts or model for them but there is none of the systematic application of those methods. And of course, this lack of system shows in the results, mistakes are made, it can take longer for a good performance to emerge if all the time is added up, and steps can be left out so baby is left a bit dirty sometimes and perhaps will get a rash. But like my discussion of informal training above, going through this messy and cost-ineffective procedures as a couple might have other important learning experiences involved. Moreover, those going through informal skill training will have seen thousands of babies washed by the time it is their turn. In fact, training is probably not necessary for anyone but western Dads!

A second problem concerns some complex skills, for which the "putting it all together at the end" phase is not easy. Piano playing, for example, is not a matter of learning to hit every key and then just "putting it together." The integration of the component skills is the major part and can best be considered as a skill in itself. Most conglomerates of skills flow nicely into one another so when re-combining them they flow easily together (like washing a baby). The first few baths given by the trained fathers were probably punctuated by pauses and little delays, but after some practice they probably could combine all the steps fluently. But the intervention person must be wary of this and carefully observe, or even train explicitly, the final integration. We will look at bit more at this question when discussing "fluency" below.

Evaluation and Assessment

The next topic to consider is the evaluation of skill training (Childs, 1996; Komaki, 1998). While this might seem better placed at the end of the chapter, training is useless without knowing whether it worked, unless your goal is to make a training package purely to make money. But of course, if it continually does not work, then you are unlikely to sell it in the future, so it is even in your best interests to find out what components are not working.

Evaluation of training is not simple, and mistakes have been made in the past. Many are due to poor research designs, although I cannot cover those here. Any book or University-level course of research design will teach you these. For example, if you measure performance, then do your training, and then measure again, and find that the scores were better afterwards than before, you cannot conclude that your intervention was successful. There are at least 10 ways that the results could have occurred even if your intervention was not at all effective (e. g., Campbell & Stanley, 1963).

There are no agreed upon principles or approaches here, so I will go through two good approaches that raise different issues for you to consider.

Example 1. Childs (1996) lists four broad types of training evaluation: the reactions of the learner and the trainer, demonstrations that learning has taken place, generalization to learning on the job, and operational outcomes and consequences of the learning (for example, increased sales for businesses). The first and last of these are called social validation in the applied behavior analysis literature (e. g., Quinn, Sherman, Sheldon, Quinn, & Harchik, 1992; Wolf, 1978). Evaluations can also occur in the development of a training package (formative evaluation), in the regular use of the training (summative evaluation), and in the relationship to the broader outcomes and how the training fits in with organizational goals and changes (operational evaluation). Each of these three needs continuous assessment and re-designing (Childs, 1996; Kaufmann, Majone, & Ostrom, 1986).

The actual details of evaluation depend heavily upon the task and the training, so I do not want to go into details here. It should be noted by the reader, however, that evaluation should accompany all your interventions to make sure they work, and that this does not mean that you or even the client just get a good feeling that it has been successful. A decent research design is needed. All too often, criteria for evaluations are either just handed down as acceptable or else are politically motivated (Komaki, 1998).

Example 2. Komaki (1998) presented another approach to targeting behaviors for intervention and the criteria used to assess the effects. She proposed five criteria for selecting good criteria, which she called SURF & C:

Are the target behaviors	Sampled rather than decided?
Are the targets behaviors	Under the control of the clients?
Do independent observers get	Reliable agreement?
Are the assessments done	Frequently?
Are the target behaviors	Critical for the performance?

Komaki (1998) then follows this scheme up with a long example based on research done with Marine Corps who dealt with preventive maintenance of equipment such as jeeps, howitzers and trucks. As she points out, preventive maintenance is an interesting job to evaluate because it is difficult to see and has no outcomes (if everything maintains ok). Probably because of this lack of immediate and obvious outcomes, most workers are not motivated to carry it out. I will not go through all Komaki's example, but it is well worth reading for the detail and the many uses of training techniques that figure throughout the present book (also Komaki & Collins, 1982).

Generalization/Transfer and Maintenance

One of the most common problems in all the different writings on training is that of transfer or generalization, in which I will include generalization over time or maintenance (Rusch & Keller, 2003). A generalization problem is said to occur when training is successful but the behaviors do not then happen in different settings, particularly when they do not happen in the setting for which they were designed. So I teach children I see in my office to brush their teeth (using the 15 smaller component behaviors we saw above perhaps) and they do it successfully, but when they go home they stop brushing their teeth: the behavior I taught has not *generalized* or *transferred* to other settings or situations.

Once again, there are no agreed upon answers about how to improve generalization or transfer, although the proposed methods are all very similar. I will outline a few approaches, taking the examples from very different areas to give you a range of ideas about how you might improve generalization of your training procedures.

Example 1. Goldstein and Sorcher (1974) suggest four techniques to improve "transfer of learning" from the training situation to the real thing. First, they suggest teaching *general principles* that mediate their performance so trainees can use the learning on new tasks and in new settings. This does not mean learning abstract principles but more like learning the big picture, so they have a fuller understanding of what they are doing than just, "Do A then B," "If C happens then do D." Second, *response availability* means that the behaviors are strong, well-rehearsed and fluent (see next section of this chapter). Having *identical elements* means making the training situation closely resemble the actual situation in which the trainees will work. This supports the use of on-the-job training or vestibular training (see later in this chapter). Finally, having *performance feedback and reinforcement* on the real job is also important. This is really saying that motivation to perform at all is part of getting a successful performance after training has stopped. The motivation to do well at training might be very different at the real setting, so this needs to be checked and something put into place.

Example 2. In a classic paper from behavior analysis, Stokes and Baer (1977; also Chandler, Lubeck & Fowler, 1992; Kirby & Bickel, 1988; Stokes & Osnes, 1988, 1989) suggested seven methods of training for generalization, to replace the most common method that they called "Train and hope" (simply assuming that what you train will work under other conditions). The second method, and the first useful one, is to put into training several situations gradually coming closer to common ones. So train the activity and if it does not generalize to a new setting, say, then train in that setting. This is kept going until "spontaneous" generalization occurs.

Intervention Analysis 7. **Ways of Generalizing Trained Skills beyond the Training Setting** (Adapted from Stokes & Baer, 1977)

Train and just hope it works (the typical strategy but not recommended!)

Praise any generalizations that do happen to occur spontaneously and train more examples closer to final situations

Look for behaviors that are normally in the relevant setting

Train many diverse exemplars not repeat the same ones

Avoid salient and predictable features in the training situation

Use situations likely to be found in the real setting

Strengthen verbal self-reports of behavior that can mediate in the real setting

Train generalization itself as well

A third method for increasing generalization is the use of *natural contingencies*. This means finding out what works to keep behaviors maintained in the normal setting and try and train that into the program. For example, if you train children to do maths problems for sweets, this almost never occurs in the real maths situation in classrooms, so the behavior is unlikely to transfer. Training maths problems through using teacher praise would be more promising. Notice that this method requires that you spend time studying what actually happens in the real setting. I mentioned in Chapter 1 that this is always a good idea in any case—generalization or not.

A fourth generalization technique is to train many examples of the behaviors required. The behavior might be taught on many different machines, for example, or with many different people. This related to the next method of *train loosely* allows that there should be no stimuli that have strict control over the behavior. For example, if all the training is done by one trainer then that trainer and their praise and style probably will gain a lot of control over the required behaviors. Unless that person is present in the real setting, the behavior might not occur. So rather than training in a tight, experimental fashion, training should be loose in the range of manners and settings in which it is done.

Related to this is the method of using *indiscriminable contingencies*, meaning that the sources of control should not be so obvious and absolute that they gain full control of the behavior as we saw for the previous method. Keeping the parameters of training unpredictable can help in this regard, as can intermittent reinforcement. *Program common stimuli* is close to the "identical elements" method of Goldstein and Sorcher (1974), while *mediate generalization* is similar to Goldstein and Sorcher's "general principles." The generalization is mediated to the new situation by language (principles) or generalities learned during training. If all else fails, their last method is to train generalization itself as a skill, as a few people have done.

Overall, Stokes and Baer (1977) suggest looking for behaviors that are normally in the setting, train many diverse exemplars, avoid specific and repetitive stimuli in the training situation, use stimuli likely to be found in the real setting, strengthen verbal self-reports of behavior that can mediate in the real setting, and reinforce any generalizations that do happen to occur.

Example 3. In an organizational context, Wexley (1984) points out methods that can enhance transfer of training. He notes that the whole "organizational culture" is important, that if managers do now allow some freedom and variability and therefore risk, then new learning will not transfer. Some of this is what Goldstein and Sorcher (1974) called having performance feedback and reinforcement on the real job, and what Stokes and Baer (1977) called having the natural contingencies in place in the real setting present during training.

Example 4. Sulzer-Azaroff (1990) discusses some of the strategies to maintain a behavior over time, which I consider to be a generalization of training over time. The same ideas as presented so far are relevant here, once they are seen over a period of time. For example, the natural contingencies need to be maintained if the new behaviors are to be maintained. She also notes that self-instruction following and self-control skills can be useful to make the person somewhat apart from the system of contingencies in place (see Chapter 6). She also mentions fluency as important for maintenance, but that will be covered below.

Sulzer-Azaroff points out, however, that social systems are less likely to change than individuals, and so for longer term maintenance of behavior changes, the system often needs to be changed. Sometimes this can result in major organizational changes, and this needs to be thought through before training occurs or the whole training might be a waste of time. For example, you could have a great program to teach self-assertion to women, so they can stand up to their dominating husbands, but if the social system is not changed, this might just mean an escalation of pressure from the husband and eventual failure of transfer and disappointment all round. This does not mean you should give up but find other ways of doing the same, possibly trying to involve the husbands for example.

Likewise, many changes in health behaviors require a complete *lifestyle change* (see later in this chapter) to maintain any behavior changes. If someone learns to do regular exercise and eat vegetables and fruit each day then they will almost always need to change the way they shop, stock their fridge, and organize their time (to fit exercise classes in). There are many practical problems that need solving before maintenance works. I will say it again; these need to be thought through before training begins, as part of "*Know your social contexts*" (Chapter 1). Finally, Wexley (1984) suggested for organizational training, helpful clues can be obtained from the relapse prevention literature, and the many interventions proposed to help stop people from relapsing after they give up addictions (Brownell, Marlatt, Lichtenstein & Wilson, 1986; Irvin, Bowers, Dunn & Wang, 1999; Muehrer, 2000).

Fluency and Mastery Interventions

A common theme running through most training ideas and ideas about generalization and maintenance of training, is that the skills should be "overlearned" or "fluent." Some have taken this idea by itself and developed interventions to "mastery" or "fluency," claiming that there will be all sorts of problems with training that does not reach such criteria. The main problem we have in this area is the lack of published evidence; there is good evidence (Binder, 1996) but we need a lot more and a lot of the evidence is anecdotal. Different versions exist, variously named mastery learning, direct instruction, fluency training, precision teaching, and generative instruction. Much of this is used by an international maths and language teaching group for children called Kumon.

Strictly speaking, fluency means that not only can the trainee get 100% correct on the skill being learned but that they can do it in a certain time. It is one thing to learn all your times tables from 1 times 1 up to 12 times 12; it is another thing to be able to instantaneously give an answer to any one of these problems at random. Once you can do that, your skill is said to be fluent. Most people learn something until they do it once or twice correctly, and assume that is enough. Fluency or mastery assumes that you must overlearn or learn to work perfectly but in a shorter time period.

To give an example in more detail, teaching long division or mathematical equations requires the constant use of simple addition, multiplication, division and addition. If these have not been learned fluently, or to mastery level, then the learning of long division or equations will be futile. Direct instruction would first revise simple maths processes until they are fluent–100% accuracy *and* done in a short time. Only then would the more complex mathematics be trained. Intervention programs like these claim huge gains for the trainees (e. g., Johnson & Layng, 1992).

The proponents of fluency also claim that problems with training and transfer/ generalization involve the lack of fluency in basic component skills (Binder, 1996; Daly, Martens, Hamler, Dool & Eckert, 1999; Englemann & Carnine, 1982; Hempenstall, 1996; Johnson & Layng, 1992; Shipper & White, 1999; but see Lai & Biggs, 1994). The component skills might be learned to 100% (sometimes!) but not to fluency, but the problem is that they then have to be used on a regular basis in order for the composite skills to be learned. What this means, proponents claim, is that the complex, composite skills can be performed but they are never properly learned until their component skills are fluent. The intervention method is typically one of heavy overtraining of component skills so that learning the complex skills then take less time and give less trouble.

Example. To give an example from organization training, Shipper and White (1999) looked at training the frequency and mastery of managerial behaviors. Although they did not define mastery with the same precision as others mentioned in this section, their research shows how fluency can be applied in non-academic areas of skills. They measured both frequency and mastery of managerial behaviors, as well as effectiveness of outcomes. It was found that increasing the frequency without increasing the mastery sometimes led to less effective situations. For example, the managers might spend more time talking to employees but did not do anything useful when they did talk—increasing the frequency did not help without better mastery skills of what component behaviors they should be doing when they talked to staff.

Common Components of Skill Training

We have seen already that training skills relies primarily upon the techniques outlined in Chapter 3. There are, however, some specific adaptations of those techniques for the sorts of skill training situations we are dealing with here (Duncan & Lloyd, 1982; Holding, 1970b; Muchinsky, 1990; Welford, 1968; Wexley, 1984), in a similar way to there being specific adaptations to training animals (clickers, knowledge of flight distance, etc.). The other important aspect of this is the training situation, where the training takes place. That is usually broken down into in-the-job or off-the-job training.

Intervention Analysis 8. **Common Components of Skill Training**

Knowledge of results or feedback

Goal setting

Self-pacing and behavioral self-management

Practice

Aims and incentives

Knowledge of Results or Feedback

One of the most basic procedures in training is to give the person feedback or knowledge of their results. This is deceptively simple-sounding. For a start, the fact that the person needs feedback at all means that the task is not one of shaping, in which there is "automatic" feedback because the outcome would already be directly controlling the performance. Second, the use of feedback means that the "knowledge" of results is in a form not directly related to what is being done, in the way that falling off a bike is feedback in the same form as doing the task whereas a list of how many times you fell off would not be. What this point means is that the factors that control even attending to the feedback, doing something about the feedback, or seeking feedback, can be completely unrelated to the performance (Cone & Hayes, 1980). The obvious example is having people perform a task and then telling them the percentage they got correct–the feedback is not part of what the person is doing; nor do you perform the task while thinking about percentage correct. My point is that these considerations are true of all feedback and they need to be carefully considered in every use of feedback. Locke (1980), for example, suggested that informal competition is often an unreported factor that makes goal-setting and feedback effective in the first place. This analysis of feedback means we most often do not know what is really controlling the use of, attention to, or usefulness of feedback.

Having said this, there is good evidence that knowing something about how well you did is better than not knowing at all, although the task and the form of the feedback are obviously critical in whether this works (Fairbank & Prue, 1982; Holding, 1970b; Welford, 1968). Feedback is normally a necessary but not sufficient condition for learning skills. Most of the examples of feedback failing are due to either poor quality feedback or the feedback being too distant from the performance, distant in terms of either time or measurement. Being told at the end of the month what percentage correct you made will not help your next performance much by itself. Similarly, being told feedback about a group performance requires very special social conditions before it will affect the performance of individuals– it is not automatic (O'Leary-Kelly, 1998).

Example. Crowell, Anderson, Abel and Sergio (1988), for example, intervened to try and improve the client-friendly services of bank tellers. They did a very simple intervention for which the most part was just giving feedback to the tellers about how they were doing. It turned out that this alone was sufficient to improve the client services and make customers more happy with the service; just adding feedback (probably for the first time ever for these bank tellers) led to an improvement by itself.

Goal Setting

Goal setting is a procedure whereby the client or trainer sets specific goals and an effort is made to reach those goals within a certain period usually. This is used in industry a lot, as well as in sports training. An athlete might set a goal of swimming ten laps of the pool in a certain time by the end of the week, and trains towards this specific goal, rather than just training to "get better" by the end of the month.

Goal setting has been shown to be an effective method of training under some conditions, but those conditions again need to be thought through very carefully (Fellner & Sulzer-Azeroff, 1984; Kanfer, Ackerman, Murtha, Dugdale & Nelson, 1994). Like feedback, goal-setting is usually a verbal event; there is a verbally stated goal which is necessarily removed from or not part of the actual performance. The conditions that get a person to agree to a goal, even agreeing with themselves about a goal, are not necessarily going to be the same conditions that get them performing (see again the section in Chapter 1, "*Analyzing the Contexts is more important than Finding the Causes*"). I might agree verbally with a teacher to try and reach 50% on the next spelling test, but agreeing to a goal with a teacher is based on very different control than learning and performing my spelling. On the other hand, not having a goal at all, or having a very vague goal, might be worse.

Most of the disputes about goal-setting revolve around this point. Those who find goal-setting always useful forget or are not aware that they are using other methods to get the people to agree in the first place with those goals; those who do not find goal-setting working probably do not set the goals very realistically (Latham & Saari, 1982). Like feedback, goal-setting is not a simple procedure. New controls are added with goal-setting to the simple performance situation, and those new controls are usually social ones—what the coach will say if the goal is not met; who knows about the goals; even what people will say if they find out you cannot follow goals properly, that in itself can be punished in our society.

Example. A good example of this point, that is also a good example of scientific practice, concerns the different findings on the issue of whether or not it is better to let people be involved in setting goals or whether they should just be assigned ("reach this goal..."), and how that affects commitment to carry out the achievement of goals. Notice that this research question is the very point I have been stressing; what is it that keeps a person trying to reach a goal, as opposed to what happens when they reach that goal (or not)?

The two researchers, who had found opposite findings, met with another researcher as the mediator and looked for variables that might have affected their different results. They then designed four experiments to test between these (Latham, Erez & Locke, 1988). The report is worth reading in its entirety, but it turned out that one main factor was the manner in which the participants were given their goal: one of the researchers was more warm and friendly and *sold* the goal-setting idea to the participants; the other more or less just *told* them to achieve the goal. So the impetus to even try and achieve the goal would have been very different in these two cases, and an experiment supported this (Latham, Erez & Locke, 1988).

Self-pacing and Behavioral Self-Management

Self-management methods have the same constraint as goal-setting and feedback—there are forces (or contingencies) operating to keep the person self-managing other than the one that produces the actual performance. If that other source stops or does not generalize to other settings, then the self-management will fail. For example, I might work out a time-management procedure to increase my writing production and the contingencies making me follow this procedure might be comments from my wife that I am too haphazard. So the impetus for self-management is escaping my wife's comments or attempting to look good to her, and these have nothing to do with the writing itself and its consequences. If my wife changes her story or I completely impress her another way, the self-management procedure may stop whether or not it was helping my writing. The hope, of course, is that an increase in writing will be sufficient to keep the self-management going but this is in no way guaranteed (cf. "Train and hope" in *Intervention Analysis 7*). To help you realize that there is no magic "self" to keep "self-whatever" regimes going, consider how many people begin self-quitting programs, self-dieting plans, and self-managed exercise programs, and stop after a short while.

All the self-management programs need this extra social impetus to work, and for ones that usually work there is usually a hidden source somewhere. This might be just the opportunity to tell people how well you are doing, it might be avoidance of looking silly and haphazard, or it might be avoidance of looking weak when you stop half-way. The problem is so big that any self-whatever programs of training need to consider this questions carefully before starting.

If the self-whatever programs can be kept going, for whatever the forces in place, then the evidence is that they can be very effective, although we must watch out for the generalization problem, that the hidden background impetus might not generalize to other parts of the person's behavior (Andrasik & Heimberg, 1982). Even just making self-recordings of one's own behavior can produce changes that are quite pronounced (Andrasik, Heimberg & McNamara, 1981). For example, keeping a record of how many times I say "ok" in a lecture was an eye-opener for me; I found out that I was constantly saying it. But again, the impetus for doing the recording, and maintaining that recording, and even being surprised by the recording, did not come from any source that would change me–I still do it. Ok?

Example 1. A nice example of these points was shown by Kirby, Fowler and Baer (1991). They measured the baseline of maths performance of some children, and then gave them materials to record how many problems they did while encouraging them to complete more each time. This was effective and the number of maths problems completed increased, although not for recording alone, but for recording plus asking them to beat their best score. They noticed that the increases coincided with *more comments from peers*, so a second experiment manipulated when peers were allowed to make comments. They found that for the maths problems, there was an increased number of maths problems done when peers were commenting on them, although this same effect did not occur for alphabet problems.

Example 2. Another example of a full self-training program was conducted by Ninness, Fuerst, Rutherford, and Glenn (1991). They recorded that for 3 seriously disturbed adolescents, 90% of their misconduct occurred when the teacher was not in the room. This meant, of course, that teacher interventions might not work because they could not be implemented at the time they were most needed. So, after

a task analysis of the behaviors involved (see their Table 1), the adolescents were trained on social appropriate behaviors, first by using instruction, modeling, and role-playing—our standard but important techniques from the last chapter. They were then trained to carry out self-assessments, self-recording, and "self-reinforcement." After 5 weeks there were substantial improvements even when the teacher was out of the room, but generalization in another setting did not occur until they were trained to do the same self-management procedures in that new setting.

There are two points for discussion contained in the Ninness et al. (1991) paper that are instructive. The fact that generalization to another setting was poor is indicative that there was a source of contingencies, or impetus as I have been calling it, that was maintaining the self-management procedures separate from the outcome. This was probably something to do with the social situation of peer or teacher encouragement. Second, the "self-reinforcement" method is real but is a misnomer (see Chapter 5 for more). While you can give yourself reinforcers contingent upon certain behaviors, in line with what we saw in Chapter 1, this is again a complex situation. Something else is controlling your carrying out this procedure and not simply taking all the reinforcers anyway. Whatever is controlling that is playing an important role in the whole procedure, so it is not simply a case that you are only reinforcing yourself.

Practice

It seems obvious that practice is important to skilful performance but it is not clear what exactly is done through practice (Muchinsky, 1990; Rabbit & Banerji, 1989; Taylor, 1998; Welford, 1968). Saying that practice strengthens associations or reinforces habits merely makes a tautology. It could be though that practice might give the context, objects, and procedures better time to take control and shape the behavior, therefore improving performance. Practice might increase the density of reinforcement for correct performance and so increase performance. Practice might bring performance up to fluency or mastery standards by increasing speed while maintaining accuracy. Practice might also work to change incompatible collateral behaviors rather than have anything to do with the behavior itself. It is not clear what is going on except that "good" practice helps a fluent performance.

There is some evidence that distributed practice is better for perceptual-motor tasks whereas massed practice is better for verbal tasks (see Dempster, 1988; Kanfer, Ackerman, Murtha, Dugdale & Nelson, 1994). Distributed practice mans a little practice regularly, whereas massed practice, as you might guess, means doing a big lump of practice at one time. Studying through a semester, a little bit every week, is distributed practice; cramming for exams is massed practice. For example, common thought has it that doing one or two hours piano practice a day is better than doing 10 hours practice on one day a week, although it might never have been researched.

Practice is certainly task dependent, and if you are doing interventions you will need to give some thought to it. Nonverbal (perceptual-motor) tasks have different requirements from learning of verbal material, and rote learning capital cities of the world has different requirements to comprehending a novel and remembering the intricacies of the characters.

Aims and Incentives

From everything that has been said above about feedback, goal-setting, and self-management techniques, a lot more enters into the training situation than is obvious. It should come as no surprise, then, that aims and motivations to learn also enter into the equation (Muchinsky, 1990). We have already seen that attending to feedback, pursuing goals that have been set, and maintaining self-whatever procedures usually depend upon a whole range of motivations unrelated to the task at hand. Many times this makes no difference, and the person attends to the feedback, improves, and the improvement then maintains further attention to feedback. But in many other cases, remove that initial irrelevant motivation and the whole intervention fails. As an extreme example, you might sell the idea to someone to keep a diary of their eating, so as to design a dieting or healthy-eating program for them. Imagine now that the person overhears you making jokes about them to a friend; the self-diary is unlikely to maintain because it was your social consequences maintaining that part of the intervention, not the losing of weight.

Example 1. Darrah (1995) investigated a workplace training intervention in which classes were presented on Quality Assurance and Production. He found that the sessions were not just simple instruction classes, but were a mixture of many agendas by the people running the classes and the people taking the classes. There was no simple giving of information but discussions that involved work problems and political agendas.

Example 2. Durrenberger (1997) criticized what he called the "Education is the answer" method, that problems arise because someone does not know something or cannot do something and so we must educate them. He suggested that this encourages blaming the victim, that there is an ignorant person who needs educating so things can work properly. For his example, learning about the union and how it works and helps with grievances, he suggested taking part in real grievance handling situations. Basically, he is arguing that for his example, learning cannot easily be done through a lecture or presentation format, and must be done "hands on."

Example 3. Another example of the bigger motivational picture of training is that of Quinones (1995), who ran training sessions that were either labeled as "remedial" or "advanced" even though they were identical. Differences were found between participants run under these two "frames" for training, and the larger picture of "motivation to learn" was affected.

Methods of Training Skills

Most of these methods to be mentioned will not be new to the (astute) reader. But putting them in the following format, based on Muchinsky (1990) and Taylor (1998), is helpful for thinking about interventions and how they work.

Intervention Analysis 9. **Methods of Training Skills**
(based on Muchinsky, 1990 and Taylor, 1998)

Off-site training methods

    Lectures
    Audio-visual material
    Programmed instruction
    Computer-assisted instruction
    Conferences
    Simulation and role-playing
    Sensitivity training and outdoor wilderness training

On-site training methods

    On-the-job training
    Vestibule training
    Apprentice training
    Job rotation
    Job design
    Organizational development
    Process consultation
    Team building
    Critical incident analysis

Off-site Training Methods

Lectures have a place when the skills to be learned are heavily verbal or rule-governed. When you must learn the three things to do before beginning to weld, it is helpful to begin with a written list of instructions or someone talking to you (lecturing) about those instructions. This does not mean you are necessarily going to do them always after you leave the room, but if the three rules are not obvious from the welding situation itself, and rules are usually developed when things are not obvious from the situation alone, then lectures in this broad sense can help. Academic subjects clearly use them a lot, but most academic subjects require more skills than just learning of words. For this reason, most tertiary teaching incorporates other techniques below.

Audio-visual material can also help in two ways. First, like lectures, if the material is heavily verbal then seeing them written or hearing them being said can help. Second, an audio-visual presentation can act as a modeling situation, if the thing to be done is modeled on the screen. *Programmed instruction* is a method of writing verbal material that has been shown to be very effective for learning although intensive for preparation (Crosbie & Kelly, 1994). The material is read and immediately tested. There is repetition until 100% accuracy is achieved, and sometime fluency. More recently, *computer-assisted instruction* has become more popular, although in many ways the only differences to programmed instruction are that it is more "cool" to take part in, the programs are often worse than programmed instruction because they people writing the instructions are commonly trained to be programmers rather than trained to teach, and finally there is probably more distraction on computers to spend time fiddling with screen-savers than learning, but a good programme should not allow that to happen anyway (Andrewes, O'Connor, Mulder, McLennan, Derham, Weigall & Say, 1996; Muchinsky, 1990; Twamley, Jeste & Bellack, 2003; Wexley, 1984). The overall effects of computers for training are not clear (Brown, 2001).

Conferences are any form of discussion sessions done in conjunction with lectures or visual material. The advantage is that people being trained can discuss and clarify, and perhaps also get some practice or rehearsal while discussing what was said. The person doing the training can find out problems or areas for which the lectures or materials did not get learned.

Simulation and *role-playing* we have already come across in Chapter 3 (Wexley, 1984). They are useful in giving the person some experience that is not verbal, but for which they do not have the usual consequences if something goes wrong, and which they can repeat to improve their performance.

Sensitivity training and *outdoor wilderness training* are methods that have fads occasionally. The aim is to train generic skills of interpersonal communication and problem-solving, but not ones necessarily specific to task requirements (Eggleston, 2000). Sensitivity training groups go to a retreat and practice communication skills, trust, and other human relation skills. Sometimes these border on being trendy psychotherapies, but sometimes they teach useful interpersonal skills that are difficult to specify exactly and therefore get lost in task analyses otherwise. Wilderness training usually involves outdoor exercises in problem-solving and working as a team. Small groups might have a problem to solve, like setting up a camp and building a fire from scratch. They need to pool their talents and work together. More organizations are now providing these for staff, although I have not seen any good research on their effectiveness.

Clearly, the reader will be able to imagine problems with these sorts of methods; a wonderful group experience is had by all but when they return to work on Monday it is back to normal. This illustrates that work situations constrain what can be done in organizations. Businesses are there to make profits to survive, and a manager might not be able to be all buddy-buddy with someone who they have to tell what to do. So the pressure is also on the boss to be competitive in the wilderness so as not to lose face when back home in the office. But I hope the reader can also see some possible benefits from this; everyone working more peacefully together and finding out that the others in the office have some useful skills that they can depend upon in the future. There is so little good research on these that we do not really know how effective they can be. Even an office sports club or volleyball team might help to the same extent as these expensive corporate methods.

On-site Training Methods

On-the-job training usually consists of watching a more experienced worker do the task and then imitating while they talk a little about what you are doing (some verbal prompts). This is done on the spot with the same equipment as will be used in the real work. The main problem is that it can be rushed and not properly trained, leaving the person to make mistakes when they do it for real. It also uses equipment that should be used for making profits and can slow production down.

To overcome the slowing down of production problem, *vestibule training* sets up the same equipment nearby in a place where people can learn or just practice if they are unsure. Sometimes old machines are set up for new people to practice or learn on, so there is no wastage of machine time. Something like this happens with families who buy an old car for their children to learn to drive. This means that the family car is not taken out of service while a child is learning or after a child has an accident.

Apprentice training has been around for a long time, a procedure in which a new person works with an experienced person for a longer period learning many skills. This is particularly used in trades that have several main skills that are required for a competent worker. The apprentice might start learning the easier (or more boring) tasks by the same methods we have seen all along: modeling with imitation, verbal instructions, physical guidance, and even lectures in a broad sense. Eventually they would get to try the more complex tasks once they have show mastery of the easier ones. In some ways, doing a PhD in British countries, Australia and New Zealand is like this. A student works on a full-time research project with a supervisor or two, and learns about research as they go along. There is no course-work. The supervisors talk to the students about faulty designs they might propose, how to solve problems with the analysis, and how to write up the results, as well as teaching the student about the academic profession, about how to present at conferences, how to address a publication rejection, and how to write a research grant. In this way, a PhD is like an apprenticeship for academic life.

Job rotation is a common method that has a variety of functions. People are moved around a company or workplace and try out various jobs. Banks, for example, might have new people work as tellers and learn about that, and then have them move onto the desk that works with foreign currency exchanges. In this way, the person learns many of the tasks they will need wherever they might end up. It also gives them a better idea of what other groups do in the bank and the day-to-day problems those groups face. When they come later to send messages or plan for those groups, they will better understand the sorts of things that can and cannot be done there. If someone is sick, it also means that a variety of people can fill in temporarily.

Job design means changing the situation rather than the worker. Rather than train someone to do an extra task, you redesign the work situation and change the tasks that need doing. Job design has mostly been about enriching people's work, so they do not end up doing one little action over and over again until they get stressed or bored or both. In the early 1990s Australia went about restructuring work places with the idea of making them more interesting and more effective. There were many situations in which, for example, someone would need to put up a fence so they would dig the holes for the poles, but then someone else had to do the cementing, so they would call them in and perhaps a day later those people would come and cement in the poles. This was obviously inefficient. If the pole-diggers could also do the cementing a lot of time and money would be saved and the job would be more interesting for the workers. The problem, of course, was that from the workers (or unions) point of view, this led easily to making many workers redundant and getting rid of many workers. It as also the case that someone who could do a variety of tasks (like plumbers and electricians do) should be paid more but this was not likely to happen. So there was opposition and negotiations needed to be worked out.

On a bigger scale, *organizational development* redesigns entire organizations to make work more efficient and better for the workers (Dunphy, 1981; Hall, 1982; Schein, 1969). This can involve *process consultation* in which groups are interviewed or taken into conference and the problems and inefficiencies are aired. This is done throughout the organization and the consultants and management work on a plan to change things with the workers and unions. Jobs might be redesigned, new roles established for people, work descriptions changed, and layers of management removed. Once again, the problem can be that jobs are lost and therefore workers and unions often resist such moves.

Another organizational development intervention is *team building*. The idea is to develop teams that can work more independently and more effectively. Groups are worked with as a whole to brainstorm, problem-solve, and collaborate to make a more efficient work situation. Organizations can be *surveyed* to find out about problems, gripes, inefficiencies and innovations. This can be especially useful to find out what is happening with the lowest status workers. Such people might be reluctant to speak up to a process consultant hired by the boss, but they might show their attitudes towards their work and the company through a survey, if handled properly.

Another useful method is *critical incident analysis*, in which examples of events that were either good or bad are looked at closely. All the people concerned might be interviewed, and the different versions of what happened carefully compared. Notice that good examples should be used along with bad examples; always focusing on what went wrong is typical of organizations and for better interventions, both are useful sources of information. So in a recent study looking at clinical psychology with indigenous people, practicing psychologists were asked about a good example of their work and an example that they now could have done better. They are interviewed about these cases and learn from what happened in these "critical incidents".

Some Examples of Training Skills

In these examples, notice how the entire intervention is made up of things we have learned in this chapter and the last. Techniques are used in different ways but the problems and good features we have covered apply.

Example 1. Meyer and Raich (1983) trained sales representatives to improve sales and customer satisfaction using a "behavior modeling training program." They broke the sales down to units such as "approaching the customer" and "explaining features, advantages and benefits" (*tasks analysis*). They explained guidelines (*verbal prompts*) and followed this with a *video* of a *model* carrying out each of the procedures according to the guidelines. The participants then *role-played* the same situations while the trainers were *reinforcing* and *shaping* good performances. They found increased sales by these trained representatives compared to some control groups.

Example 2. Olson-Buchanan, Drasgow, Moberg, Mead, Keenan and Donovan (1998) developed a laser disc of conflict situations at work, to use as a training assessment. They first interviewed managers to find some real conflicts that had occurred (*task analysis* through *critical incidents*), and made 15 of these that were short enough unidentifiable. They then asked 110 experienced managers how they would handle these conflicts. The options were further tested and brought down to 4 options per conflict scenario. They checked that these fitted with a model being used to provide a spread of conflict situations. They wrote scenario scripts including follow-ons from the selection of any option. Finally, they hired actors to perform the scenario scripts (*modeling*) and filmed them from the manager's point of view, and converted this to a laser disc. This meant that they had a computer disc that would play conflict situations and stop at various points and ask for a choice of four options for how the watcher would respond, followed by the actors playing out the finish. The authors used this to compare to other assessments of conflict resolution skills, but clearly the computer disc can also be used for further training purposes.

Example 3. Simon and Werner (1996) measured how 160 novice computer users at a Naval Base learned to use computers under one of four conditions that had the same basic material. The *instructions* condition had a lecture plus discussion format in which the trainees were told general rules and given a slide presentation, followed by questions and discussion. The *exploration* condition put the trainees in front of a computer with a manual and told them to work through the manual. Questions were referred to the manual. The *behavioral modeling* condition gave a lecture format at the start but then the trainer demonstrated various actions on a projected computer screen and the trainees tried it for themselves on a computer. In a *control* condition participants were allowed to try other computer programs on the computers but not the one being taught. It was found that the behavior modeling condition worked best, although it must be remembered that this included aspects of the other two conditions.

Example 4. Komaki, Collins and Penn (1982) intervened to increase safety behaviors in a poultry processing plant. After making a *task analysis* of safety procedures ("when sharpening knives, use only the top 2/3 of steel"), there was a lengthy baseline of measurements followed by two conditions. In the first conditions, antecedents of the safety behaviors were presented, consisting of explaining safety rules with a slide presentation (*verbal prompts*), a prominent display set up with examples of the rules (*verbal/visual prompts*), a rule-of-the-week was regularly given, and there was a weekly safety meeting. Following this there was an intervention aimed at consequences to safety (or no-safety) actions. This consisted of a *feedback* graph of performance, photographs of safe actions, *encouragement* from the supervisor to do better, and weekly meetings reviewing the current performance. The antecedent conditions produced some decrease in unsafe actions, but most of the change occurred after the consequent conditions were implemented.

Training Decision Making, "Life" Skills and Changing Life Systems

Sometimes doing "Band-Aid" interventions is not enough. You can train a skill but the person is in a larger social system that will always revert them no matter how good the training. Send the person back home, or back into their neighborhood, and they will start over as they were previously. In such cases, difficult ethical and practical problems need to be discussed and addressed. The main ways to do this are to teach some generic decision making or life skills, or to actually have the person leave the situation. As we saw in the last chapter, these cases usually need wide involvement besides just the person and their intervention agent, and government agencies are usually involved. So treat these cases as very special in most instances, because of the drastic changes and commitments needed.

Training Problem-Solving and Decision-Making Skills

I have not written very much about training people to improve decision-making or problem-solving, but there are a number of training programs available (D'Zurilla & Goldfried, 1971; Janis, 1982; Kurfman, 1977; Luthans, 1982; Wheeler & Janis, 1980). All are very similar in that the goal is to identify the problem, explore or brainstorm as many options as possible, identify the consequences, both benefits and losses, to devise ways to implement the different solutions, and then to carry them out. Wheeler and Janis (1980), for example, define five steps:

> Accept the challenge (to make a decision)
> Search for alternatives
> Evaluate alternatives
> Become committed to decision or course of action
> Adhere to the decision or course of action

Most of the variation in training programs that occurs is in the details of how to do these steps. Sometimes there are problems with the person not being committed to a solution and so special steps must be taken for this (e. g., Hoyt & Janis, 1982). Other problems occur in getting the person to brainstorm the options, and outside help might be required for this. Usually there are problems in moving from talking about a decision or path of action and carrying that action out, so special consideration is needed for this in all the training programs. Finally, like any intervention, larger changes might be required before a preferred option can be implemented—what I call "lifestyle" changes below.

So how you train for problem-solving and decision-making will depend directly on the area of life involved and the person's situation, although training more generic problem-solving procedures and self-management of actions is probably worthwhile for all people. The training programs are very similar to negotiation and mediation procedures of intervention, which will be discussed in Chapter 7 (see *Intervention Analysis 15*). In those cases, however, the conflict is between two or more parties rather than between two or more conflicting courses of actions for the same person. A one-sided equivalent is the idea of "life-coaching" (McGoldrick & Carter, 2001).

Changing Life Systems

At a few places in this book I mention interventions in which to change someone, or even to change a group of people, we 'must' change a large part of how they conduct their life—change their lifestyle as some would say. For example, in Chapter 3 I mentioned that there could be drastic cases in which the persons are recommended to move and start life again somewhere else. I cautioned about not doing this flippantly, since the ethical considerations are so serious.

In other cases, the persons do not have to move but they must change a large portion of their life. For example, in intervening for obesity one must change dietary habits, exercise habits, how one spends the day, and possibly friends (cf. O'Halloran et al., 2001). The same discussion applies here—one must be very cautious about such widespread changes since we do not know much about the total effect of changes like these. If the person was to lose most of their current friends but not actually make new friends, then this could lead to problems. Such cases need to be monitored carefully.

Example. A good example of such a change is through the Alcoholics Anonymous (AA) program, which does not just work on alcohol consumption but works (in generally considered and nice ways) to change values, beliefs, health habits in general, a number of common practices, and require regular meetings (McCrady, 1994; Valverde & White-Mair, 1999; Wilson, Hayes & Byrd, 2000).

In other words, joining and maintaining an AA program is no light undertaking, but AA proponents make this clear beforehand so people join with realistic goals. The perceptive reader will also be thinking at this point about my discussion way back in Chapter 1: "*Analyzing the Contexts is more important than Finding the Causes*". A lot of the success of AA probably occurs at the start, from the conditions that are required to get the person to agree to participate fully in the first place (remember the bit about hypnosis really being caused by whatever gets the person up on the stage in the first place?). This is not a problem if it works, but we must remember this when considering the "causes" of AA's success and how we might adapt components of it for other arenas of life.

Training Life Skills

The other area for large-scale changes with individual lives is with the teaching of "life" skills. As we saw for "collateral changes" with very simple behaviors in the last chapter, the idea is to not focus on the "problem" behavior necessarily but to teach a range of other skills and see if the "problem" just disappears. For example, if a teenager is starting to use more and more drugs, then teach them some good social skills, some decision making skills, get them a job and friends, and maybe only tackle the "drug" issue peripherally or a little. If carefully monitored (so they do not just spend all their new salary on more expensive drugs!) then this can often solve the problem without focusing on the problem.

The most common life skills are the decision making ones discussed above, social skills and social competency, employment-related skills, academic skills to get an education, martial arts training if appropriate, and other skills that give a better sense of responsibility to the person and control over situations when things do not work out (Bierman, Greenberg and the Conduct Problems Prevention Research Group, 1996; Botvin, 1996; Danish, 1997; Dunn et al., 1999; Murphy, Pagano & Marlatt, 1986; Pierce & Schriebman, 1994; Pierce & Shields, 1998; Platt, 1995; Segrin, 2003; Weissberg, Barton & Shriver, 1997). There are many variations on these, but most are combinations of these often with a few more specific training programs added according to the population involved (such as drug and alcohol training, sexuality and safe sex programs, or anger management).

Example 1. Danish (1997) described a GOAL program for adolescents. They run a series of workshops that use techniques of role-playing, information presentation, praise, various fantasy verbal techniques from the next chapter, group discussion, and social support seeking. The focus for life skills is on finding positive life goals, focusing on the process of achieving those goals rather than the outcome, learning generic problem solving and decision making skills, learning to identity health promoting and health risking behaviors, learning how to get social support, and how to transfer (generalize) from these specifics to new situations (explicitly programmed generalization training).

As you should note, these are nothing new, but are a combination of techniques from the last two chapters. However, it does not matter that there is nothing new or mysterious here, the program seems to work well and is flexible to add new content and methods for specific groups.

Example 2. Botvin (1996) described the Life Skill Training program (LST) for substance abuse prevention. The methods should also be familiar from these last two chapters, and include lectures (didactic teaching), group discussions, demonstrations, and skills training. The skills include personal self-management skills such as decision making, analyzing and resisting media influences, self-control for anxiety and anger-frustration, and self-improvement. The students also learn social skills such as better communication, interactional skills and conversation, girl-boy relationship skills, and assertiveness. Finally, they get drug-related information and skills, such as consequences, knowledge, physiological effects, media and advertising pressure, and peer resistance training.

Chapter 5

Changing What People Say and Think

There are many problems that stem from the way people talk—not only talking to others about things and events and people, but also talking to yourself. For example, I might talk to myself or others about the existence of pink elephants in my house or how the CIA is tapping my phone and secretly wants to arrest me on suspicion of crimes I did not commit. I might also talk to others about my disbelief that exposure to the sun leads to skin cancer or talk about how immigrants should be sent home or talk about how there is no solution to my personal problems and that I might as well be dead. I might talk to others about my disbelief that exposure to the sun leads to skin cancer but talk to myself that it does. All these cases involve more than just "mere" talk, of course, but a large part of what is going on seems dependent upon the talk.

For these reasons, there is a long history of interventions that try to change the way people talk about themselves or about things. Propaganda campaigns try and change how opposing factions think about themselves and the opposition, psychotherapies try and change a person's "self-talk" and how they talk about people close to them, and negotiations attempt to get the other person talking about a compromise solution in a positive way. Television advertisements tell us that we should say nice things about this product, or that we tell ourselves not to drink and drive or that we should tell others about the dangers of smoking. While it is not the case that such interventions are necessarily effective, a lot of time and money goes into trying to change the way people talk and think about things.

The other reason words are important to interventions is that the majority of interventions utilize language in some way. In Chapter 3 we saw some ways to train without using language, that could be used with dogs, for example, but for typical training of even simple activities we use verbal instructions. While some of the examples from earlier chapters will be partly covered here again, the main reason for having a separate chapter is to put the total use of language into context.

How the Use of Language can be Effective in Doing Things

A bit needs to be said about the basis for language use that I assume here, although greater coverage is given elsewhere (Guerin, 2003a, 2004). I view language as just another way of acting or behaving, no different in principle to, say, waving your arms or digging with a spade in the garden. The important thing is to find the conditions under which such actions have an effect (and hence consequences). In the case of digging, the spade and your movements have an effect upon the soil; something is done—events occur, something grows.

In the case of language, despite a long history of misunderstanding, it can be rather simply put: language only has effects on other people (including yourself in special cases). When you speak, the only thing in the universe that can be affected is a listener or reader, not even the thing talked about. If I say "cat" then the cat is not affected, only someone listening. But just having a listener is not enough context to make something happen. The words will only have an effect if there is an appropriate history, that is, if the listeners also have learned the language—if they are trained in the same way that you are. This is the first point we must remember about interventions to change talking: that the consequences of talking will be effective in so far as people are changed by that talking, not in so far as the words correctly refer to something past, present or future.

Intervention Analysis 10. **Main Points about the Effectiveness of Words get Anything Done**

The consequences of talking will be effective in so far as people are changed by that talking and do something, not in so far as the words correctly refer to something past, present or future

Talking by itself cannot get things done, even to other people; resources consequences and context are needed to get the person to do something

Language does involve consequences but only consequences from listeners

People will say irrational or false things if the social consequences for doing so are effective

Talking to oneself is no different to the above and relies on (eventual) effects from others

---

The second relevant point about language use is that talking by itself cannot get things done, even to other people. If I were to walk up to you and say, "Please give me all your jewelry," not much would happen except that the police would be notified. If I were to point a gun at you, then things might be different. If I were to offer you four times the value of the jewelry on the spot in cash, then things might also be different although you might wonder about my "motives."

This is related to the next point about language use. Despite appearing to involve no consequences, language does indeed involve consequences, and if there is repeated use of language with no effects then people will not follow language. Language must have "power" behind it to work. We are taught this in stories like the boy who cried wolf. Repeating things over and over with no effect extinguishes the effects of language. If you walk up to a stranger and say, "Stand on your head, please," they will not do it unless there are consequences or something is exchanged for their standing on their head. More relevant to this book, if you just put a sign up next to a road that says, "Please slow down," people will not automatically obey those words without consequences. If a therapist tells you to stop smoking this will only work if there are certain consequences. Notice that most of these consequences are social. We will come back to this.

Our experience, however, tells us that often people do in fact seem to follow our words without any obvious consequences. So why do people so often seem to be affected by our words when we have no obvious guns pointing at them nor money to tempt them? The answer is that most of our social interactions with people are supported or maintained by *generalized exchanges* rather than immediate exchanges of items or events (Guerin 2004). Most of our interactions are with people we know and with whom we already have reciprocal obligations. If I help a friend with some work they do not immediately go and do some work for me in return but rather, they might cook me dinner, help me out at another time, or even get someone else to help me out on their behalf. That is, the maintaining consequences or exchanges usually occur at a different time, by a different person, with different behaviors involved, and in different situations. Rarely do we get things back immediately for helping people out.

Now, this scheme of things is the very basis for language working at all. If language use had to be reciprocated immediately then it just would not work. If I said to a friend, "Oh, look at that," and in order for them to look I had to pay them $1 on the spot, language would not accomplish very much. So language depends upon generalized exchange systems throughout a language community already working. If I am going to get you to say something after I speak then we need some exchanges, and generalized exchanges are going to work best (Guerin, 2004).

The final point about language use is that because being in groups with generalized consequence systems is so important, people will do or say things that keep them in that group, even if what they do or say seems irrational or false. It is not actually irrational, however, because successfully remaining in the group brings about more beneficial effects than acting "sensibly." So people will carry out all sorts of strange rituals that have the function of keeping them in a generalized exchange relationship. They will make jokes they do not "believe," they will say one thing and do another, they will talk about nonexistent "things" as if they were real, and they will criticize people who are not part of their group. All these forms of talk are important to them but their "truth" is not what gets them the exchanges; just doing or saying these things gets them the exchanges because it keeps them part of that exchanging social group. The effective of word to do things is not necessarily related to the "truth" of those words, just to the effects on listeners.

Putting these points together, these are the things I would like you to watch out for when considering whether or not to use language for interventions. Is it worth teaching someone to say something; will it change what they do? What else will be needed? Is it worth teaching verbal statements to someone as part of your intervention; will it change what they do? Where are the power and consequences to make words have an effect coming from? Who is supplying them? Is being a therapist or psychiatrist enough status and resource power to get people to do what you say, or only when you are around?

Once we draw out the social properties of talking and its effectiveness to do anything in this world, these are the points I want you to consider, even if not fully convinced immediately:

1. There are many influences that get people to talk other than what is being talked about or the truth of what is being talked about. People talk about fictitious urban legends just as happily as if they were true. In fact, having them untrue and fantastic makes them even more enjoyable in some contexts—but not in court, for example (Guerin, 2003a).

2. Words only affect people if there are consequences of those words and those consequences are unlikely to be related to what is actually being talked about. The consequences for telling a good urban legend probably have nothing to do with the urban legend itself but the context in which it is said—maintaining social relationships and having fun.

3. Close friends and family who are involved in many exchanges can usually get effects with their words without any obvious or specific consequences being needed. Close friends can typically say, "Hey, listen to this story I heard," and the others will listen. We would get a different response if we walked up to a stranger on the streets and said, "Hey, listen to this story I heard". This is not because of magic but because the reciprocal exchanges take place later or elsewhere in life.

4. Teaching someone to say words to follow might be completely unrelated to what influences them to do whatever it was. For example, being able to get someone to say that smoking is a health hazard might rely on consequences that have nothing to do with the health hazards of smoking; likewise, "knowing" that smoking is a health hazard does not mean a smoker will stop if the consequences for talking are different to the consequences for smoking (which they almost certainly are).

5. When someone seems to act irrationally or says things that seem false or irrational, look to see what that language use gets them socially. What would happen to their relationships if they did not say those things? And remember that the maintaining consequences of what they say might have nothing whatsoever to do with what they are saying. This will be especially important for delusions and obsessions which can be totally effective even if totally false.

These points make verbal interventions very difficult, but they are all properties of language that make language most useful (Guerin, 2004). For example, if language was maintained only by whether it was true or not we would not get far in life.

With these points in mind, I want to run briefly through some important areas of intervention for which words are either used by the intervention agent or else for which the intervention itself is to get someone to talk in a particular way. This could even include areas like brainwashing, in which the idea is to get people to talk *to themselves* in a certain way.

One final point, however, before we begin. A lot of what is called "cognitive" psychology, "cognitive" therapy or "cognitive" anthropology is really about the use of language in controlling our lives. If you examine the cognitive therapies closely you will find the only distinguishing feature is the use of language—challenging what the client says, teaching the client to say things, explaining things to the client and hoping the attribution will have an effect, and teaching the client to see/perceive/ categorize (which mean "talk about") things differently. This does not mean that these cognitive therapies are wrong, just because they are dressed up in a language of their own; in fact, they often have been shown to work very well. They will be incorporated here, however, without using their own jargon of a mind and a mental realm. The point they miss, I believe, is the powerful social basis that makes language work in the first place—even when telling yourself things. The framework of cognitive psychology avoids the real basis of language (social relationships) through the mental metaphors that are used. They make it as if the person spontaneously says things from nowhere without a context. So for the first time I will be reviewing cognitive techniques of intervention but putting them together with other interventions in a framework that makes more sense to me overall.

Types of Interventions Using Words

From the discussion so far, there are six main ways of intervening using words. We can (try to) use words to get people to do things, we can use words to get people to do things to others differently; we can use words to get people to say or think things; we can use words to get themselves to do things; we can change what people say about themselves; and we can use written rules and laws to change what people do (if the contexts and resource consequences are there).

Probably two of these methods were used first once people stopped just telling people what to do, telling people to say things and getting people to tell themselves what to do: the first represents psychoanalysis and most psychotherapies. Later came behavior therapies in which people were told what to do (behavioral homework) followed by getting people to say things to themselves in order to get them to change ("cognitive therapies" and "narrative therapies"). There has also always been a bunch of wacky and not so wacky interventions that get people to say all manner of weird things to themselves, supposedly to change them (mantras, prayers, self-esteem training). As indicated earlier, we do not have to think of a whole new mental or spiritual realm of the universe to encompass all these; we do not need to have cognitive processes separate from social behavior.

***Intervention Analysis 11.* Types of Interventions Using Words**

Using Words to Get People to Do Things

> Instruction following
> Giving advice and warnings
> Teaching "Facts" to Change What People Do
> Intervening With Written Laws, Policies and Rules

Getting People to Do Things to Others Using Words

> Communication training
> Assertiveness training
> Training managers, executives and trainers
> Persuasiveness training

Getting People to Say or Believe Words

> Teaching "Facts" to Change What People Say
> Teaching People the "Facts" are Wrong
> Helping Recall: Facilitating Verbal Control/ Cognitive Interviews
> Interrogation and Questioning
> Changing Attitudes and Beliefs

Getting People to Get Themselves to Do Things Using Words

> Self-planning, self-control and self-management techniques

Intervening to Change Peoples' Words about Themselves (Self-Talk)

> Self-esteem training, identity training, image management, feedback

Using Words to Get People to Do Things

The first idea here is a simple and ubiquitous one: tell people what they should do so as to intervene and change for the better. An even more common form of this intervention is to give people information and assume that they will act appropriately on that basis. So in the first case we *tell* someone that our best advice is to stop smoking and assume they will change and do what we say; in the second case we *tell* someone everything about the bad health and social consequences of smoking and then assume that they will then stop smoking.

Unfortunately, things do work out so simply as that. We do have a lot of what we ask followed casually and unthinkingly by close family and friends ("*Pass me the bread, would you dear?*") but beyond that, things get worse. It is amazing how many intervention agents are piqued when their super information message is understood but no one does what they are supposed to do afterwards. This is exactly why I put the use of language in interventions into the framework I use, so as to make absolutely clear that any effects from using language rely on a whole set of social contexts and consequences and they do not happen automatically. The evidence is actually that when people do follow information messages or advice given it is not automatic anyway, people usually run it past friends and family first to get reactions.

So this problem is going to re-occur through most of the following, that just telling someone good advice or the accurate bad consequences of what they are doing will not necessarily change what they do.

Direct Verbal Instructions: Presenting Advice and Warnings

Our first category of direct verbal instructions was given as an example in Chapter 3—the use of verbal prompts in simple training situations. We saw then, as I have urged now, that it relies heavily upon the relationship between the trainer and the trainee. Most interventions with strangers (Table 3 in Chapter 1) have a period of "rapport building" which really means heavy social influence is used to get the person into a relationship context where they will follow at least simple instructions. I have also urged (Chapter 1, "*Analyzing the Contexts is more important than Finding the Causes*") that there is far more to this than is usually realized—a large part of the actual intervention is contained in doing the "rapport building", just like hypnosis.

Whether the advice, instructions or warnings are followed therefore depends not only on the correctness of the words but also on the trust in the speaker, the probable consequences of doing what is suggested, the social consequences of not doing what the speaker tells you to do, and who else is involved. Since we usually judge these accurately in life, by giving the right level of request to the right person, many of these simple interventions might actually work. Advising someone to cut back a little bit on the drinking might succeed relatively easily (maybe it would not maintain though without further contact), but advising someone to leave their spouse and start a new life in another city is going to require a lot more to have the listener follow your instructions!

Example 1. Russell, Dzewaltowski and Ryan (1999) conducted a simple intervention to try and get more people to use the stairs at the university library, rather than using the elevator. In the control or baseline phase their sign read "Elevator" whereas in the intervention condition the sign read, "Elevator for physically challenged and staff use only, others use stairs please." There was some evidence for increased stair use during the intervention period, although this was mainly for younger males, and it occurred only between Monday and Thursday and not on Friday (which was interesting!). Clearly, putting up signs is not any sort of panacea to change behaviors. Kerr, Eves and Carroll (2001) found that placing bright messages on the risers of the stairs increased usage more than posters.

Example 2. Babor (1994) reviewed studies that tried simply to dissuade or advise a heavy drinker to stop or reduce their alcohol consumption. Advice was given through reasons or exhortation, not through coercion or bribery. The results showed that dissuasion worked with those heavy drinkers who had not had a long-term addiction yet. In a study Babor reviewed by the World Health Organization, for example, it was found that five minutes of advice was just as effective as a behavioral self-control training manual. How to give the advice was more ambiguous because of the many social contexts and people involved. Babor (1994) pointed out nicely, however, that many more complicated "talk" therapies could be working because of the advice giving, motivational cuing, and generalized social contingencies (compliance/conformity, Heiby & Frank, 2003) to do what an authority says (cf. "motivational interviewing", Borsari & Carey, 2000; Levensky, 2003; Miller & Rollnick, 1991).

Example 3. A lot of the research on warning signs and labels has been done in the context of safety messages (see the special issue of *Public Policy & Marketing*, 1998, number 1). Two quick examples will be given here. First, Cecil, Evans and Stanley (1996) asked adolescents to rate the health warning labels on cigarette packs. Overall, the smokers reported less belief in the validity of the warnings than did non-smokers. This might have been because they could not really say they believe them if they wanted to appear consistent, or because they "actually" believe them less. In either case, the message is that warning labels might only have a public influence on those who are already converted. Second, Hankin, Sloan and Sokol (1998) found only a medium size effect of warnings on alcoholic beverages for pregnant women. They also suggested that warnings are not enough to make a real change. What we do not know is whether these sorts of labels have any long term impact which has not been measured properly. It could still be that not having any labels at all might be worse or that the long term placement of labels eventually has an effect, perhaps in conjunction with other influences though.

Indirect Verbal Instructions: Teaching "Facts" in Educative Interventions to Change What People Do

We have already seen in Chapter 4 that teaching verbal knowledge is a widespread method of intervention, and incorporates education, lectures, computer-assisted teaching, pep-talks, and a lot of consultation. From what has been said above about the control of our actions by what we verbally "know," more needs to be done for interventions than just teaching people about things. Most people who still smoke verbally "know" the risks but other things obviously keep them smoking. Despite this, teaching verbal knowledge will remain part of most interventions because, if nothing else, it is easy to implement and difficult to prove that it is completely ineffective. It should be improved, however, by trying to incorporate more than just "book learning."

There are some situations, however, where little else can be done than teach verbal knowledge. Ethics or practicalities might preclude other interventions. For example, we cannot go around and teach everyone face-to-face about the risks of smoking, and show them through medical sampling what their own lungs look like, since this is very time-intensive. So teaching verbal knowledge through the mass media might be the only practical way. We also cannot just burst into peoples' homes and teach them a new way of parenting their children by demonstrating on their own kids; that would be unethical unless the people asked for it or the police or welfare services had legal rights to intervene. But broadcasting on TV verbal messages about better parenting is not unethical although we might never know whether it was effective or not.

Finally, there are many situations in which the material to be taught is purely verbal anyway, and lectures and the like are probably as good as any means for interventions. Teaching someone to ride a bike through written materials is not very useful but to teach the names of all the capital cities of the world, a verbal intervention is necessary. Teaching philosophy and abstract concepts is also a good realm for lectures and teaching through talk.

Active Watching of Videos. Some of these points can be seen in the study by Cugliari, Sobel and Miller (1999) that used videos and written information, or written information alone, to change the behavior of people in hospital. The area the authors were interested in was that of appointing a health care proxy—someone who could legally make decisions should the person fall unconscious or something. The United States federal law now requires patients to be informed about their rights of proxy. Cugliari, Sobel and Miller (1999) had a sample of hospital patients who received written information and another sample who received both written information and watched a video presentation about the issues involved, including discussions of case-studies.

What they found was quite typical of this area, although it goes against common "wisdom." The patients reported that the video presentation was clear and useful, more so than just the written information. So far, no surprises. However, when the authors looked at how many people actually signed on health care proxies afterwards there was no difference between the two groups. So the video was interesting and clear but did not affect the viewer's behavior afterwards any more or less than just written information. Before writing off videos, though, remember that we do not know the long-term effects of the videos; some researchers believe that there might be longer term effects that studies such as the present one do not pick up. A year later, and out of hospital, the people who had viewed the videos might remember better about health care proxies and also do something about it.

Passive Watching of Videos. O'Connor and Innes (1990) wanted to find out whether playing videos of educational health materials to parents in the waiting room of a large children's hospital would have any effect—where it would only be passive watching. Their argument was that most educational materials are viewed by parents who do not need the material, because they probably already know it. By placing the videos in a large hospital they could get a wider range of people viewing the material. They placed the waiting room chairs so that they video was right in front, but did not draw attention in any way to the video. On the screen, 1.5 hours of programmed material about children's health was played 24 hours a day, but only on certain days. They developed a measure of knowledge about children's health to test the effects of watching the video, or at least having it present in a hospital waiting room.

Parents with children in the waiting room were interviewed about their knowledge of children's health either one week or two months after they had been there. Two groups were interviewed—some who were present when the video was playing and some who were present at times when there was no video playing. The authors found no difference between knowledge one week or two months later, for either group. However, those who were present when the video was playing had higher scores on the children's health knowledge test than those who were not. This was true whether the test was given one week or two months later. So there were some effects, at least on this simple intervention, for a passive video playing educational material. Similar results were found by Mathews, Ellison, Guttmacher, Reisch and Goldstein (1999).

Written Materials. When left to their own devices to come up with an intervention, many people think about using leaflets of information that can be distributed. These seem like a good idea.

Newell, Girgis and Sanson-Fisher (1995) gave written materials about better health to people, either by mail or from a general practitioner at the end of a consultation. They later interviewed all the people they could locate and who agreed, two weeks after they got the material. For those who got the material through the mail, 77% remembered getting it, 75% said they kept it, and 67% reported reading it. For those who got the material through their GP, 91% remembered getting it, 93% said they kept it, but only 56% reported reading it. So those who got it from the GP remembered getting it and all, but the final reading of the material was a little higher for the mailed material, regardless of whether or not it was kept. So in terms of real intervention and utilization, the mailed material was more fruitful in the end. The authors also point out that given not everyone attends a GP, the mail methods would get to many more people in any case and would be read by as many or more people.

Becoña and Vázquez (2001) sent self-help guides through the mail to smokers, and half also received personalized feedback. They found that both groups were better than controls up to six months after the intervention, and that getting personalized feedback helped more than just receiving the mail self-help guides.

Castle, Skinner and Hampson (1999) gave half their sample of young women a pamphlet about the effects of sun on skin cancer. The leaflet increased knowledge scores but did not change reported health beliefs about sunbathing. Strangely, while no control participants changed whether they were active or nonactive about sun protection measures, after reading the leaflet eight of the 57 experimental participants went from reporting an action stage to a nonaction stage. It was suggested that some experimental participants who were active about sun tanning protection beforehand might have realized either that they were not taking effective measures anyway and so reduced their effort to protect themselves, or discovered that they were not as much at risk as they had thought and so reduced. While these interpretations are without evidence yet, it should not be assumed that more knowledge means that people will be more active in doing something about it. In this case it seems that the knowledge led some already active participants to become less so.

Segan, Borland and Hill (1999) developed similar materials that were given to tourists going to high sun-risk locations. There was some evidence that those who received the brochure spent less peak-hour time in the sun, but there were few other effects. The authors suggest that the materials might be useful as priming material but that they need to be followed up at the tourist location with further interventions.

In an unpublished study (see Cuco & Pierce, 1977, p. 104) educative material about family planning was sent to physicians in Colombia. The material was either sent in the mail or else there was a visit to the physician's office followed by a mailing. They reported that the visit plus mailing was more effective than the mailing alone, although it cost more.

The problem with leaflets and pamphlets then is not just one of people not reading, not understanding or not remembering the information. There can also be much confusion in producing such materials, and there are inconsistencies in the information and sometimes scant idea of who produced a leaflet making people disregard the information (Dixon-Woods, 2000). An example was given above also of the converted being affected by written labels but not the target audience (Cecil, Evans and Stanley, 1996). It is also the case that most people have developed large story repertoires of challenging what is said about their doing things they do not want to do (Guerin, 2004). We can get a sun-safe leaflet but simply report to others that it was propaganda for the sun-screen makers and throw it in the bin.

Intervening With Written Laws, Policies and Rules

In Chapter 2 it was mentioned that one of the best ways to change the actions of people to improve life is to change the laws of a nation. If, for example, tobacco could be made totally illegal then the use of tobacco would drop dramatically (of course, black markets would crop up and lead to other problems). The problem, as you can see by this last example, is that changing laws is very difficult because so many people and considerations need to be addressed. Such a law change would be fought very strongly by the very rich tobacco industry giants.

Most of the details of changing verbal rules and laws will be addressed in Chapter 6, on community interventions, since laws are rarely made to just change the behavior of a few, select individuals (see Guerin & Elmi, 2004, for an exception to this).

Getting People to Do Things to Others Using Words

Another situation of words in interventions is training people so they can get others to do things better. There are some shonky uses of this, such as teaching salespersons to sell more broken widgets, but in many cases people are not good at getting what they want from others so some training is needed for their own benefit. This is probably more so in western societies where stranger interactions are prevalent (Table 3 in Chapter 1). In close communities everyone has grown up together and knows what to do and what obligations people have to reciprocate.

This category is unexplored, and the examples I will give can probably be integrated better by future research, and other areas of intervention I have not put here linked in. (Translation: I am making this up as I go along.) There is also a long tradition of research in management which is specific to work situations (almost solely in western bureaucracies) but which has some interesting things to say about interventions (but less evidence). A little bit about two areas that are relevant.

Example 1. Communication Training. There are a large number of interventions across all disciplines that train people to communicate better (Marshall, 2000; Oliver & Margolin, 2003; Segrin, 2003; Vine, 2004). Communication is an abstract word, but the useful focus for us are cases in which communication training means being better able to get people to do things. I am tying to explain what our work group has to do, or what procedures we must do, or why the company is doing a particular action, and good communication skills means being able to present things in an accurate way that the listeners understand and hopefully are persuaded by. Training someone in communication skills means they should be able to do things to others better—whether that is giving information, getting actions, getting motivation, etc.

The many communication training packages are mixtures of all the techniques in Chapters 3, 4, and 5, especially including exercises, role plays or simulations (Withers & Lewis, 2003). There is also a specialist literature about training people to get things done with people from other "cultures" (Hooker, 2003; Landis, Bennett & Bennett, 2004).

Finally, most, but not all (Thomas, 2004, is a start), of these training interventions are directed at western-style social relationships consisting primarily of strangers in work places and stranger communities (Table 3). Many of the methods taught as better communication would not work in close communities that have their own ways of doing things. Wearing a slick suit and speaking precise and sleazy English would not go down well in communities in which family ties and obligations better get things than any way of persuading someone with words. We have yet to see good interventions trialed for these groups.

Example 2. Assertiveness Training. A related area is assertiveness training, in which timid or oppressed people are taught how to stand up to others better and get their own way more and get others to do ting more (Duckworth, 2003; Segrin, 2003). While not meant to be teaching bossiness, this is a useful skill for many in western societies needing to get others to do things for them.

Withers and Lewis (2003) for example, have an exercise called "Say it, Shout it, Skip it" in which people learn to "understand the differences among assertive, aggressive, and nonaggressive communication. Explains why assertive communication is most effective." (p. 116). The caveat I hope the astute reader is expecting now, is that there are different social systems that will require different approaches, so "most effective" really means in western societies with western properties (Table 3). I am sure their book was really only intended for those areas of the world, but the intervention agent needs to be cautious.

Getting People to Say or Believe things Using Words

The third big category of using words for interventions is intervening to get people to say or believe things. This is the goal of many suspicious groups and governments, to get people to believe they are the best leaders or governing parties, and also the goal of brainwashing, to get people to believe something they presently do not. From these examples it should be clear that ethics is vital to interventions that try and get people to say things a particular way. We need to be sure about what we are persuading them to believe.

Some of the interventions try and persuade people about things "well-known" to be risky or bad for your health. Campaigns tell you that smoking is bad, drink driving is bad, staying out of the sun is good, using sun block is good, and using heavy drugs is bad. These are either based on scientific evidence, what the majority think is correct, what the laws of the land dictate, or what the most popular religion or set of values says is correct. Examples of these respectively, might be smoking is bad for your health (scientific evidence), nudity should be kept private (what the majority think is correct), you cannot drive more than 50 kmph in the city (what the laws of the land dictate), and all people should be treated equally without discrimination (that the most popular religion or set of values says is correct). We can have public information campaigns to convince us of these things.

Such campaigns are obviously similar to advertising campaigns that try to make us say or believe something that will lead to good sales and profit for the company. Indeed, we will see in the next chapter that those trying to persuade people about important social issues or health behaviors turned in the 1980s to social marketing techniques to try and sell their messages better (but see Rothschild, 1979). The gap between the two is trickier than we like to imagine, and a message sold to the public by one government might be replaced when the next government comes into power. The social psychology literature on this topic in fact goes back to early research by Kurt Lewin and colleagues during World War II trying to get households (mothers that is!) to use more liver and offal in their meals so meat was not wasted as part of the war effort.

The point of this is to put the use of getting people to say or believe things into a proper perspective which is not straightforward, and to get you to think carefully about the ethics of what you are doing, even if you are writing a stop-smoking campaign message to present on the media to millions of people. Be careful about the messages you are trying to sell.

Teaching "Facts" in Educative Interventions to Change What People Say

In the last section I looked at ways to teach people "facts" to change what they do. This is usually part of any campaign to change what people say or believe. You mostly want people to say, believe or like different things so that they will do something different. We try to get people to say bad things about smoking, believe smoking is bad for your health, and think it to themselves in order to get them to change their own smoking or that of someone they know.

Most of the literature on this has been covered there, in the use of videos and leaflet to "sell" a message, usually to get someone to change what they do or say. For example, the study by O'Connor and Innes (1990) changed how much people waiting at a medical services knew (could say) about children's health. They directly wanted to change what people said and thought about children's health, and in this case I personally have no problem with such a goal.

A lot of the early models and theories of psychotherapy and psychoanalysis also tried to intervene to get clients to think about their problems in certain ways—in agreement with the therapists' own theories usually. After this was found suspect, most therapies became 'non-directive' and tried to get people to come up with their own chosen values and solutions, whether or not the therapist agreed. For example, if a client brought up that they might be gay the therapist should accept that or get the persons themselves to start thinking about it, but the therapist should not try and persuade the client that being gay is wrong and they should change their beliefs and attitudes towards homosexuality. How much this was the case, and how much secret directing occurred, is unclear. It is also likely that people went to certain therapists who they thought agreed with many of their own value and beliefs in the first place.

So while the cases for intervention by changing what people say, believe, or value are difficult, and need careful thought about what we are selling, we also have to bear in mind is that persuasion and selling thoughts and ideas is very common in life (Dillard & Pfau, 2002; Simons, 2001; Woodward & Denton, 1996). Somewhere in the middle of selling "Stop smoking", "Do not be racist", "Democracy is best for everyone", and "Buy my burgers" we all find a line in which useful intervention becomes marketing and brainwashing. It is best to remember that the line is never clear.

The final point is about the difference between learning to say something and actually believing it. I see these on a continuum and "truly believing" something has a lot of other behavior wrapped around it. Most importantly, I believe, what we label as true or strong beliefs are statements we act committed to across a wide range of audiences and people (Guerin, 2004). We say them across a wide range of contexts and take the consequences for that. In essence, calling something a belief, opinion, vagary or attitude is in itself a social strategy for doing things to listeners. Calling something a belief means the audience knows they are going to have to mount a strong challenge if they want to criticize you, meaning that they are likely to go along with it (mission successful for that strategy!). Calling something instead as "a sort of thought I sometimes have heard people say" leads to very different effects/ reactions from listeners. They are more likely to challenge what you say but you have *hedged* (Guerin, 2003a) and so the consequences for being wrong are much less.

Helping Recall: Facilitating Verbal Control/ Cognitive Interviews

There are many situations in which people have trouble recalling verbal "facts" and there are interventions that can help with this. This section concerns remembering when the person is trying to remember, whereas the following section is about interrogation—when the person is trying not to say anything but an interrogator is trying to get them to talk. Both literatures have a similar problem, getting the person to "remember" without adding extra fictitious facts. In the present case these are called false details and in interrogation they are called false confessions. With enough pressure people will say false "facts" even if these facts incriminate them (cf. Garven, Wood & Malpass, 2000).

Most of the work on cooperative remembering interventions has been in the context of witnesses in legal cases; can someone remember more about an event they saw than they can recall at first. I will not include the "Improve Your Memory in 10 days" types of intervention, although they all rely on the same principles but just dressed up a little to sell books and seminars and to make money. Key issues have been how to get children to recall without distortion, and how repeated recall affects the "facts" remembered. There are no firm answers at present but some recent key research will be presented briefly.

The basic idea in all these interventions is to reconstruct the context that surrounded the original event–this is the same for hypnotic techniques, the cognitive interview, and behavior analysis principles (Mantwill, Köhnken & Aschermann, 1995; McCauley & Fisher, 1995; Sheehan & Tilden, 1983; Skinner, 1968, 1983). In some manner or another, the context of the event needs to be reconstructed without introducing prompted information or strengthening verbal guesses.

One method that seems successful is called the *cognitive interview* (Mantwill, Köhnken & Aschermann, 1995; McCauley & Fisher, 1995). There are four basic strategies in the original intervention. First, the person is guided to reconstruct the context of the event they saw, forming images and re-sensing all the emotions, feelings and thoughts they had at the time. Second, the person is encouraged to say anything they recall without editing it first, so without worrying whether the listener will criticize or otherwise punish them for any aspects or inconsistencies in their report. They are encouraged to say what seem to be insignificant details or incomplete aspects. Third, they are asked to put some temporal order into the events, and start recalling from different times. For example, they might be asked to remember not from the beginning but from halfway through; "Let's start from the part when you saw X do Y. What happened next...?" Fourth, they are asked to say what they saw while taking different vantage points, as if they were another person watching what they saw from a different angle. The most recent version of the cognitive interview also works on the social context of the interview itself, and enhances rapport, interview sequencing, and the use of gestures.

Results of such a procedure show between 25% and 30% more details recalled than standard interviews or police interviews, and without increasing false details. Studies have now been done outside the research environment of the originators, and found similar results. This is perhaps not surprising, given that a combination of some fairly standard and well-known techniques are used, but the absence of false details is encouraging.

Example 1. As an example of the sort of research done, Mantwill, Köhnken and Aschermann (1995) showed a video of a blood donation event to 30 experienced blood donors and 30 non-donors, and they were all later questioned about what they had seen. Half were given the cognitive interview and half a standard structured interview. It was found that the cognitive interview led to more details being recalled than a standard structured interview. However, more incorrect details were also recalled. These two effects were not different for experienced donors and non-donors, although experienced donors tended to add details not at all in the original video, presumably coming from their own experiences. These authors tend to downplay the increase in incorrect details found with the cognitive interview, although I consider this quite important to remember. In real life there is probably no way for even police to tell which are correct or incorrect details, as could be done from the video. This would render such results highly open to criticism in a legal setting. If the intervention is just to recall as much as possible, however, then the cognitive interview clearly does that despite producing some extraneous details along the way.

Example 2. McCauley and Fisher (1995) looked at the repeated use of recall on children. They played a game of Simon Says and were interviewed within 3 hours using the cognitive interview or a standard interview. They were then interviewed again 2 weeks later. It was found that the repeated use of the cognitive interview led to more details being recalled, but once again, more incorrect details were also recalled. Like the previous research, these authors point out that the accuracy rate (proportion of facts that were accurate) was higher for the cognitive interview than the standard interview, to try and play down the increase in incorrect facts. Once again, I urge caution, however, since we cannot usually determine which are which in real life and in a legal case this could be a devastating criticism and the whole interview thrown out of court.

There is a lot of debate at present on children as witnesses, and the role of suggestibility in children's recall. A recent review points out that the real question is not whether suggestion can bias children's recall, but whether it does so *more* than with adults, who also show such effects (Ceci & Bruck, 1993). As we will see with interrogation below, questioning and talking always depends upon the social context and the social relations between the speaker and listener; the problem is that such social relations are very different with children and therefore require other ways to get recall without bias. Ceci and Bruck (1993) conclude that although recall gets better with age, and there is some evidence that preschoolers are more suggestible than older children, there are good examples of very young children resisting leading questions and threats from attorneys. The issue is not clear and obviously depends closely on the social context surrounding the events.

Interrogation and Questioning

Another situation involves a person not wanting to tell or remember information and an "interrogator" who is trying to get them to reveal something. Most often equated with police and military interrogation, there are many other circumstances where this situation arises. I will not go into specific methods here but draw out the overall pattern involved (Leo, 1996; Kassin & McNall, 1991; McMahon, 1995; Underwager & Wakefield, 1992).

In essence, the reliance on getting people to say things as a social process is fully revealed here—there is essentially a "game" (in the sense of game theory) of negative consequences for telling and negative consequences for refusing to tell (Guerin, 2004; Leo, 1996). Through a social relationship developed between person and interrogator, these consequences or removal of resources are balanced, shaped and distorted until telling becomes preferable. The problem is that at some point, if the consequences in general become too great, the person can falsely agree with information or break down completely. At that point the information becomes unreliable. In some cases the social relationship is not all that is involved and painful consequences are added to the mix through punishment or torture techniques. In many cases, though, the social relationship is developed to just facilitate cooperation rather than the stereotype of a nasty competition between the two.

From this analysis of the intervention, it is clear why the two main strategies are to either downplay the importance of telling or to exaggerate the seriousness of not telling (Kassin & McNall, 1991). Another technique understandable through this brief analysis is to have one interrogator build a friendly social relationship ("Look, I'm trying to help you, tell him what he wants to know") and the other an unfriendly relationship ("Look, I'm quite prepared to sit her all night without you eating if you do not talk").

Finally, many of the negotiation and mediation techniques from Chapter 7 are involved, except that the consequences or resources negotiated are very serious.

Teaching People the "Facts" are Wrong

There are a couple of interesting intervention situations in which rather than trying to get people to say or believe something, we try and get them to stop saying or believing something. These two are not quite the reverse of each other.

Intervening With Rumors and Gossip. Rumors and gossip are present in all groups of people, and can cause a lot of harm as well as good fun (Allport & Lepkin, 1945; Deodhar, Yemul & Banerjee, 1998; Herr, Kardes & Kim, 1991; Rosnow & Georgourdi, 1985; Singh, 1990; Tishkov, 1995). While there is a lot written and researched about the factors that might influence rumors, little has been written and even less researched about preventing or stopping damaging or malicious rumors. As usual, then, I will make some suggestions and guidelines along the way, but readers are encouraged to experiment—we do not really know what works here. A slightly different social context might change what is effective in stopping rumors.

The only real attempt to systematize interventions to prevent of stop rumors is that of Difonzo, Bordia and Rosnow (1994), based in organizational rumors and gossip. They based it around their own way of thinking about rumors, but their interventions are not tied to that framework. They suggest three phases in the production of rumors, each of which might need different interventions, and then they suggest a number of ways of neutralizing rumors once they are out there. Their main concern was with organizational rumors that can affect a company's reputation or business, but the principles would be worth trying in other arenas also.

The first suggested prong of intervening against rumors is to reduce their generation in the first place. On the basis of their model of rumor, they suggest explaining unexplained events before rumors can even start. For example, if a Prime Minister or President suddenly announces their resignation from office, without explanation, rumors are bound to begin. Explanations should be given to try and prevent these rumors starting. Difonzo, Bordia and Rosnow's (1994) model also suggests that anxious or uncertain events trigger rumors, so interventions to reduce anxiety could help here. All they suggest, however, is that the people in charge attempt to have a "relaxed demeanor" and look calm, although people are now probably wise to that one! Finally, an explicit role for rumor anticipation can be used as a pre-emptive intervention. For major decisions made or policy changes, have someone in the know check them out for possible rumors. Notice that all these interventions so far require pre-thought about rumors, and such vigilance takes effort and planning.

The second prong of intervention is to reduce the belief (credulity) people have in a rumor. They suggest holding a workshop in which rumors and their properties are explained, although they mention that if there is distrust already then this will be viewed with suspicion and taken as a propaganda meeting. Establishing trust is important and anti-rumor statements can then be made and act to reduce people's belief in any rumors. But, like stopping rumors in the first place, this requires pre-planning and honesty, which in rumors situations might be difficult to muster.

The third attack on rumors is to try and reduce their dissemination once they are formed. This requires being on a grapevine to pick up the rumors early, before they go too far. The authors suggest having a trusted aid who can report rumors to the management, but in reality I would guess that such a person would soon get removed from the grape-vine by others, if they knew the person was reporting to the boss! Difonzo, Bordia and Rosnow (1994) suggest that reporting can be nameless and not traceable to any individuals, but this seems unlikely in practice and over a long period. In many circumstances it might also be considered unethical or illegal.

The next question becomes one of what to do once there are rumors out there: a rumor spreads that the company is going to close down two main offices and make the staff redundant. What do you then do to neutralize the rumor? They suggest several options. As mentioned earlier, these will probably change in different situations, so your strategy is to learn them all and test them as you intervene.

The first intervention for neutralizing rumors is to ignore those that are "impotent." This is unlikely to occur much, however, and signals that there might be something to the rumor. Second, you can confirm the truth parts of the rumor. The authors cite an example in which the management quickly sent out information about what was actually happening to the workers. They strongly recommend that some comment be made about the rumor, because saying nothing implies that the rumor is true and the strangeness of not commenting itself can spark new rumors. They recommend that if no comment is to be made then a comment should be made about the reasons for this!

If the rumor must be refuted then Difonzo, Bordia and Rosnow (1994) suggest that denials are dangerous; they are suspicious. They suggest instead to base denials on truth, make sure there is consistency in what is said by different people, select an appropriate spokesperson, make them easy to understand, do not repeat the rumor, and if possible to again present the refutation in a "town hall" style meeting where dialogue is possible.

Responding to Normal and Destructive Criticism. Feedback is a normal part of life, and indeed people seek out comparison information from others as a normal routine of life from early childhood. Two cases will be briefly mentioned, learning how to respond to "normal" criticism, and responding to destructive criticism.

1. Training Criticism Acceptance as a Social Skill. Some studies have intervened to train accepting criticism as a social skill, for people who cannot take it. As always, this is done by breaking it down into component skills and training them individually (Hazel, Schumaker, Sherman, & Sheldon-Wildgen, 1981; Quinn, Sherman, Sheldon, Quinn & Harchik, 1992). The component behaviors trained were these, adapted from the last-named authors, and trained according to Chapters 3 and 4 if this book:

Nonverbal Components
    face the other person during conversation
    no movement away from person giving feedback
    keep eye-contact with the other person
    keep a neutral facial expression
    keep a straight posture
Specific Verbal Components
    paraphrases to check their understanding of what was said
    apologies
    asks for suggestions
    accepts the feedback
General Verbal Components
    maintain a normal voice tone
    no angry statements
    do not interrupt when other person is talking

These, then, are component behaviors that could be used to train up listening to feedback skills in people who lack such social skills. They have been used, for example, to train people with intellectual disabilities, who might otherwise be taken advantage of by unscrupulous characters. One must doubt the generality of these components, however, for other people and other times beyond western samples. The best idea would be to learn these ones and then adapt them based on testing to the populations you are working with.

Example. Quinn, Sherman, Sheldon, Quinn and Harchik (1992) made video-tapes of actors performing such component behaviors either well or poorly in a realistic setting and asked judges to rate how well they handled the situation, how pleasant was the interaction, how acceptable was their behavior, how much they would like to respond to such a person, and how likely they would respond in this way to the person. In all cases they found the most positive ratings on these questions for the videos with all components performed well, the lowest ratings on videos with all the components performed poorly, and middling ratings when only some of the components were performed poorly.

2. Responding to Destructive Criticism. In some cases, criticisms are destructive and need not be accepted. Such criticism might include sarcasm, or be "biting" or harsh. Baron (1990) argues that this can happen in organizations in which feedback is regularly given by managers. Managers often report skipping feedback that is negative because giving such feedback is aversive to them but eventually they get annoyed and the feedback might be given more destructively than planned. Parents and teachers, also, sometimes put off negative feedback so as not to ruin their relationship with the person, but eventually give it when it becomes too much, thereby unleashing more destructive feedback than planned.

Baron (1988) found that destructive criticism can have widespread effects, beyond what happens when negative feedback is presented in a constructive manner. People who have been criticized destructively change many of their behaviors, and in ways that have poor outcomes for themselves. In the light of what was said earlier in this chapter about language use, this is not surprising. Our relationships involve multiple generalized exchanges, most of which are difficult to observe under normal circumstances. When something like destructive criticism occurs, however, many seemingly unrelated changes can take place as a direct result.

Example. Baron (1990) looked at four ways that the effects of destructive criticism might be repaired. If someone has given destructive criticisms, what should they do to counter the effects they might have had? Baron had participants in a laboratory task prepare an advertising campaign for a shampoo. A second participant, who was really working for the experimenter, then evaluated their work and either gave them constructive or destructive criticisms. An example of the latter as this: "I don't think you could be original if you tried. Dull stuff!"

After going through the criticisms, participants took part in one of four interventions to counter the negative effects of the criticism. In the *incompatible response* intervention the participants were asked to rate cartoons that were considered funny by similar others. In the *external attribution* intervention participants were given some reasons why the evaluator had been harsh, reasons other than things to do with the participant. In the *apology* intervention the experimenter passed on that the evaluator felt sorry for the harshness of their criticism and apologized. Finally, in the *catharsis* intervention they were later able to rate the performance of the evaluator on some rating scales, so they could express their irritation towards the person. There were also two control conditions, people who received no intervention after receiving either constructive or destructive criticisms.

A number of measures were taken, including reports of anger, happiness and fairness, reported methods for handling future conflicts, and task performance. Overall, the apology and the external attributions interventions worked best, and the catharsis intervention worked least well. In fact, the catharsis intervention led to greater anger and worse task performance than the other interventions, putting doubt on interventions that promote catharsis as a method (cf, Guerin, 2001b, d).

Finally, a second study asked real managers in real organizations to rate the four methods for countering destructive criticism. The results matched those of the first study; that external attribution and apologies were the best interventions.

This is only one research report on this area of verbal interventions. Notice that both the behaviors measured and the interventions were verbal: offering recompense was not considered as an option for an intervention. A lot more needs to be done before we can be certain about what interventions work in different situations and with non-westerners or other groups. The point of this for the present chapter is to sensitize you to such interventions–that they occur and that some research has been done on them.

Intervening to Change Peoples' Self-Talk

Psychotherapies have always involved a lot of talk, even after "behavioral homework" became popular (Rosenfarb, 1992). Perhaps implicitly, it was assumed either that talking could cause people to change what they were doing or else that the major problems of life were "talking" ones. This perhaps seems naive now, but it seemed to work in the hey-day of psychotherapies–just talking it through was enough. However, things tend to be talked through ad nauseam these days and the problems are still there, meaning that resources and outcomes need to be always monitored carefully in such interventions and not rely on some magical power of talking about things to cause any changes (Chapter 7). While behavior therapies provide a corrective to these practices, they are perhaps weakest when dealing with the problems that do seem to be most closely related to talking. This is probably why cognitive-behavioral therapies have been popular, because they at least acknowledge that self-talking is the source of many problems. As mentioned at the start of this chapter, I think the "cognitive" metaphor avoids dealing with the social basis of self-talk, but ignoring self-talk altogether is probably worse.

Another arena in which self-talk interventions have taken off is in sports and sports psychology (Bloom, Durand-Bush & Salmela, 1997; Janelle, 1999; Munroe, Giacobbi, Hall & Weinberg, 2000; Thelwell & Greenlees, 2001; Theodorakis, Weinberg, Natsis, Douma & Kazakas, 2000; Van Raalte, Cornelius, Hatten & Brewer, 2000). There are many examples now of the same "cognitive" techniques being used by coaches and sports science researchers. Coaches give pep-talks to help the players relax or concentrate, and they also use imagery and guided talk to help the players focus on winning. Such techniques are even used for training cognitive therapists in the first place (Ronen & Rosenbaum, 1998).

I will not go through in detail the idea that "self-talk" is socially controlled. Elsewhere I have given the finer details of how this probably works (Guerin, 2001c) and there is a long history of such views (Bentley, 1935, 1954/1910; Berger & Luckmann, 1967; Cooley, 1909; Guerin, 1994; Josephs & Valsiner, 1998; Holquist, 1990; Kantor, 1969; Langford, 1978; Lohdi & Greer, 1989; Marx, 1961; Mead,

1922, 1924/1925, 1934; Michael, 1997; Miller et al., 1990; Rose, 1996, 1999; Sampson, 1993; Searle, 1995; Skinner, 1957; Wallis, 1925).

The basic idea for the reader to grasp is that even if saying things to yourself changes what you do and does not look social, the act of saying of those things itself depends crucially on other people. Notice just above I wrote that "Coaches give pep-talks to help the players relax". Notice that the coach is organizing, supporting, providing and strengthening the self-talk of the players. There are arguments about the finer details, such as whether self-talk can maintain itself if it leads to benefits, but I want to leave those out here. For you as an intervention agent the key thing is to look for the social control of any act of talking, whether to yourself or someone else. People cannot keep self-talking unless there are social consequences.

One reason why looking for the social control of all these acts of talking is important is that they are mostly hidden (Guerin, 2001c, d) and get overlooked. As pointed out elsewhere, most of our social behavior works best if the social control is hidden (Guerin, 2001c). Other people influence our self-talks in a generalized way ("significant others", Cooley, 1909; Guerin, 2001c; Mead, 1924/1925, 1934).

Another reason for analyzing the social control of self-behaviors is that social control means that biases from others can creep into our thinking. In fact, the biases from others are always there; the proportion of influence can change or multiple audiences can interfere with doing anything. Elsewhere I have suggested that the "cognitive" biases from cognitive psychologists actually have a social basis when you analyze how they are set up in the first place and look at the discursive analysis of what is going on, the same maneuver as we saw in Chapter 1 *"Analyzing the Contexts is more important than Finding the Causes"* (Guerin, 2001d, 2004).

To give an example of this from interventions, paradoxical interventions mean that if a client is ruminating on an unwanted thought, such as "My life ruinous", then the therapist urges them to say to themselves as much as possible "My life ruinous, my life ruinous, my life ruinous" until it "becomes meaningless" and reduces in frequency. If a client is depressed then they might get them to say over and over, "Let me be really depressed, let me be really depressed, let me be really depressed". But the shrewd reader will have noticed the same issue we encountered in that famous section of Chapter 1 mentioned above. The real control going on here—the real intervention—comes with the therapist getting the client to say what they say in the first place. A lot of urging and cajoling goes on before the self-talk even happens, and more to keep it maintained long enough. This is the real control going on, and the point here, once again, is that we have a generalized and disguised social control operating, not an autonomous, agentive, or private decision by the client.

Finally, this means that different groups of people can have their very way of thinking shaped by the different ways that groups organize themselves. When considering the methods given below we must remember that most have been investigated and published using people from western-organized societies, with the social properties shown in Table 3 from Chapter 1. When communities are organized differently this can mean that the people think in different ways (talk to themselves in different ways): they can emphasize different aspects of the words;

they can value social relationship thinking over logical thinking; they can think non-logically in the sense of more loose associations or creative leaps between self-talks; they can "think" in paragraphs as it were rather than single words or sentences; or they could talk to themselves using the main discursive strategies of language use (Guerin, 2003a, 2004) in very different ways to what "we" might think. There are many potential possibilities but we know very little about this because these self-talk phenomena have been researched with non-social models in mind. Hopefully more is to come as the social and resource basis of self-talk gets researched more, and recent discursive approaches open up the social strategic nature of language use.

The upshot of this is that whether or not you believe all these arguments about the social basis for self-talk, watch carefully what is happening in your interventions with self-talk and its audiences, especially multiple audiences with conflicting pressures (Guerin, 2001d). Also then watch for people from differently organized communities than your own, for how their self-talk proceeds and the outcomes because they might be very different to your own.

To help this out, I will briefly give two examples of approaching "cognitive" interventions from a social, conversational approach. This is similar to discursive and narrative forms but the language use is drawn much more closely back to material interactions and resources (Guerin, 2003a, 2004).

Example 1. A lot of the recent "cognitive therapy" push is about biases or errors in "cognitive processing" and how they can lead to the symptoms of mental illness. For example, Gottlib and Krasnoperova (1998) go through a number of cognitive biases that can be "suggested" to underlie symptoms of depression. Usually these are attentional biases, memory biases, and thought biases. So depressed clients are said to attend and remember more negative stimuli than positive, so they are always focusing on the negative outcomes likely in life (also Lange, Richard, Gest, de Vries & Lodder, 1998).

I have argued, along with many others, that these phenomena are about talk and conversation and therefore are rehearsal for action in future interactions with others (Guerin, 2001c, d). They are about having and rehearsing the conversational resources to engage strategically, in these cases in a depressed manner (for whatever reason), with people during social interaction. What is being rehearsed ("in your head") does not matter until such times as you talk to someone when it can have consequences. Like traumatic thoughts, they are not a problem until you have to talk to them about someone (Guerin, 2001b). So for these sorts of reason and observations, I would still look for the social basis to biases memories and attentional patterns; I argue they are shaped by others and are directed towards future strategic interactions with others. Similar rethinking would go into other approaches (e. g., Teasdale, Taylor, Cooper, Hayhurst & Paykel, 1995) but I will not go through more in detail.

Attending more to negative "stimuli" and remembering more negative "stimuli" are part of a bigger pattern concerned with being able to talk in strategic (in this case negative) ways with others. Why the person is strategically adding negatives to conversation must be part of your wider analysis (Guerin, 2004), but one possibility (to give you the flavor) is that conversationalists who talk negatively can either *lose* their audiences if the negative emphasis is inappropriate or not done in a fun way (and hence support their socal avoidance or social escape), or interestingly *gain* an audience when the negatives are focused in an attention-getting way. There are many situations in which negative conversations are most favored, such as the strategic use of complaining and controversy to *enhance* relationships (Alemán, 2001; Alicke et al., 1992; Baumeister, Bratslavsky, Finkenauer & Vohs, 2001; Drew and Holt, 1988; Hutchby, 1992; Schiffrin, 1984; Staske, 1999).

The upshot of this is that social relationships with the person's typical audiences needs careful analysis and intervention in terms of these attentional and remembering rehearsals. That is where things are happening rather than in the attention or remembering itself, so I am not arguing that the cognitive therapy models are wrong or the therapies do not work. I am arguing that the metaphor they are using is mis-directed and we need to focus on the social and conversational uses of this material in the person's strategic social life. Negative talk can be useful and strategically adapted to either gain or lose audiences and social relationships, as can grumpy behavior.

Example 2. Another example will be based on a useful model of anorexia nervosa by Garner and Bemis (1982). They also used a metaphor of biased or distorted cognitive processing which supposedly "leads" people to a number of systematic distortions. In this case it might be easier to see the conversational links since conversational and discursive analysts have shown the very same conversational patterns in "normal" strategic social uses of language (summarized in Guerin, 2003a, 2004). These are part of our usual ways of influencing people in everyday social life but the anorexics likely use them for strategic purposes others do not.

For example, Garner and Bemis (1982) list six "distortions" in their Table 1: selective abstraction, overgeneralization, magnification, dichotomous thinking, personalization, and superstitious thinking. Completely functional uses of these in "normal" conversation can be found in many other analyses (summarized in Guerin, 2004). For example, talking in more abstract ways (selective abstraction, overgeneralization) has clear social properties that affect listeners—more easily hedged if challenged, sound more definitive because wide-ranging, etc.

Magnification is the use of *extremes* in conversational and discursive analyses, and using extreme language ("I've gained, like 20 pounds!"), affects listeners in a pattern of ways again because of their social (not cognitive) properties (as two examples: if you make extreme statements you can later hedge when challenged but still end up ahead of the other person: "Okay, not 20 pounds but at least 15!"; and extremes can gain people's attention.).

Dichotomous thinking is common in the strategic use of categories for conversation, and has social properties of sounding definitive (and hence not worth challenging), being easily hedged afterwards, and sounding factual. Known under different names such as bipolar categories (Guerin, 2004), it serves many functions in conversation and everyday social strategy (Lévi-Strauss, 1949, 1966; Tajfel & Wilkes, 1963).

Finally, talking in terms of personalization or self-reference has a huge variety of social properties that can affect listener in strategic ways (Antaki, Condor & Levine, 1996). In particular, most self-references are also abstract and have those social properties we saw above as well, and self-references are very difficult for listeners to monitor for truth, since they use a metaphor of an inner person that/who cannot be seen. I have argued, in fact, that the lack of monitorability of self-reference statements has led to increases in monitoring the consistency between different versions of self-references to check on what is being said, since the self-reference cannot be observed (Guerin, 2004, p. 212, Analysis 30).

Once again, my point here is not that the six distortions do not occur and are not useful for interventions—quite the opposite! Rather, my point is that the metaphor of cognitive distortions is not the right one and takes attention away from the dynamic and strategic social bases of talking and self-talking, and leads interventions away from social analyses of the everyday social life of the people involved. Talking in "distorted" ways comes from conversational shaping in socially strategic ways, not from a passive effect of a cognitive information processing architecture.

How People "Normally" Self-Talk to Intervene

Before looking at the methods for changing self-talk, I want to direct the reader in the direction of studies that probe how people "normally" use their self-talk when in problems situations. The main point to take from this is that the methods are identical on the whole. The flashy methods of sport coaches and cognitive behavior therapists have all been used forever, and they are only different now because they are being researched more closely on the effectiveness and the details of what exactly is working. If you read the originals of the two examples below, also notice how similar are the methods reported in each.

Example 1. Weisenberg et al. (1993) gave questionnaires to Israeli children who had been through traumas of SCUD missile attacks during the Persian Gulf conflict. As part of this they asked about coping strategies used during the missile attacks without ever having been taught what they might do. Several of these were self-talk coping strategies, such as thinking of things not connected to the situation, making fun of the situation, wishing for a miracle, wishing that the missiles would fall elsewhere, praying, thinking of pleasant things that had happened to them, and acting as if everything was usual. Several of these verbal actions were shown to be (negatively) related to post-traumatic stress afterwards, that is, engaging in these verbal actions was associated with less PTSD.

Example 2. In an interesting paper by de Silva (1985), the methods used by cognitive behavior therapists for stopping unwanted intrusive thoughts were compared to methods promulgated by early Buddhists, and a lot of similarities pointed out. The methods were used by monks when meditating, supposedly with an empty mind. If they had unwanted thoughts there were five main techniques to stop the thoughts:

Switch to an opposite or incompatible thought
Ponder on the harmful consequences
Ignore and distract
Reflect on removal of causes
Control with forceful effort

Each of these is the same as some cognitive methods of intervention.

Methods Used to Change Self-Talk

Intervention Analysis 12 lists the range of "cognitive" or "self-talk" methods used in behavior therapy and elsewhere. Many have not been fully evaluated but rely upon self-reports that they worked. This is not just poor research but a result of the effects of such techniques being very difficult to evaluate. My arguments above that there are hidden social controls actually determining any "cognitive" or "self-talk" methods makes evaluation even harder.

With just a little bit of thought I have patterned these into three groups, although better research and more bits of thought would see a different version. The main methods, however, are very similar across a wide range of interventions by professionals, lay persons, and non-westerners, as we saw earlier. I will probably not do these methods any justice, but the aim here is to alert intervention agents to these techniques, or at least that they are known by others, and let the reader find out more as suits. Because of the way they are controlled, as suggested earlier, they are very likely to be context-specific and to make them work in other cultural, social, historical or economic situations you will need to change a lot of how they are reported done in the literature—especially in the relationship with the intervention agent.

Getting People to Get Themselves to Do Things Using Words

The first category I will use for self-talk is for the intervention agent to get the person to use self-talk to do things for themselves. This is usually part of everyday life, that in childhood we learn to "self-regulate" our own behaviors (at least in western societies we are meant to) and to plan for ourselves what we will do in the short-term and the long-term. Things can go wrong and people not learn this properly, and there are situations in which we must self-regulate our behavior that we are not used to or trained for in everyday life.

"Self-motivation". There are methods in which a trainer teaches someone to say things to themselves in order to motivate them to do something in the first place (Treasure, Katzman, Schmidt, Troop, Todd & de Silva, 1999). This might be unpleasant things or very difficult things. In cases of sport coaches the athlete is trained to make self-statements that get them to try really, really hard. This can involve other categories below, such as focusing (attentional training) on a very specific goal for finishing the race or competition (self-goal-setting).

Intervention Analysis 12. **Verbal/Cognitive Methods for Self-talk Interventions**

Getting People to Get Themselves to Do Things Using Words

Increase Verbal/Social Regulation
increase verbal sense of control
slogans, self-instruction following and self-statement modification
self-goal-setting
verbal commitments and contracts
self-help manuals and bibliotherapy
self-regulation and planning
diary writing and self-narratives for instruction following
self-motivational enhancement
mental rehearsal
self-negotiation or self-mediation
problem-solving exercises
mindfulness training and attentional manipulations

Intervening to Change People's Words about Themselves

Feedback
feedback or reality checking
guided self-dialogue
changing thoughts or thought stopping, especially "automatic"
        thoughts
guided discovery
self-monitoring
self- questioning
identifying patterns of negative thoughts
habituation of "negative" thoughts
mindfulness training
rational emotive therapy methods
talk aloud procedures (think-aloud)

Changing Social/Self Knowledge
imaginal exposure and imagery modification
providing explanations and reasons for social conversation
enhancing self-identity
making positive-self-statements
acceptance
anticipated consequences
reframing or (disputational) cognitive restructuring
pleasant activity training
paradox, metaphors and deliteralization
symptom prescription
break up current audiences
self-help manuals and bibliotherapy

Self-regulation. A great number of methods take the techniques from Chapter 4 ("*Common Components of Skill Training*") and make the people themselves do these, such as getting feedback, goal-setting, self-monitoring, behavioral self-management, practice and rehearsal, and setting up aims and incentives (Heidt & Marx, 2003; Kelley, 2003; Rehm & Adams, 2003; Rokke, Tomhave & Jocie, 2000; Skinner, 1983). Other are taught to keep diaries of what they have to do and follow that, others are taught time-management techniques that they have to learn to run themselves by telling themselves things regularly. Another intervention taught adults with brain injuries to self-administer written prompts (O'Reilly, Green & Braunling-McMorrow, 1990). Methods also can focus on "normal" instruction following and train the person to follow self-instructions in a similar looking way (Grote, Rosales & Baer, 1996; Grote, Rosales, Morrison, Royer & Baer, 1996; Henk & Helfeldt, 1987). Another similar version has been called self-statement modification (Duch, Hirt & Schroeder, 1989), used mainly to intervene with children for impulsivity or hyperactivity, disruptive or aggressive behaviors, delinquency and phobias or social anxiety. Other interventions, perhaps not always with western therapists, is to give the person slogans to repeat (Valverde & White-Mair, 1999; Wilkinson & Kitzinger, 2000).

Training attention and distraction. "Mental rehearsal" is common and makes the person say things to themselves over and over, which might partly be an attentional method but also a self-regulation method. Other attentional methods can train people to train themselves to watch and monitor what is going on, a method used in an interesting way for individuals with schizophrenia (Twamley, Jeste & Bellack, 2003).

Self-negotiation or self-mediation. We will look at interventions of negotiation and mediation in Chapter 7, but I want to point out here that once you get used to the idea that "self" events are really "hidden social" events, then many of these methods begin to look like a form of self-negotiation or self-mediation. Many of the same steps can be used but the person starts negotiating or mediating between patterns of what they do that are different because of different audiences or social controls over them (*Intervention Analysis 15*).

Self-help manuals and bibliotherapy. There is a long tradition of interventions that give people some books to read with no further contact by a helper, counselor or therapist (Rosen, 2003). Alternatively, people can buy "self-help" books in bookshops; indeed, they are usually some of the best sellers. While many therapists scoff at such books, the research suggests that, at least for some problems, bibliotherapy can be just as effective a contact with a therapist.

Marrs (1995), for example, reviewed all studies comparing therapist intervention with bibliotherapy. He found that overall there was no difference between the two on outcomes. Looking more at the details, bibliotherapy seemed to work better for assertion training, anxiety and sexual problems, whereas therapist contact worked better for weight loss, impulse control, and studying. Some therapist contact was also suggested for individuals with panic attacks by Febbraro et al. (1999).

In other studies, Jamison and Scogin (1995) found that bibliotherapy was superior in outcome to a waiting list control group for adult depression. They also reported less dysfunctional attitudes and less automatic negative thoughts after the treatment for those with bibliotherapy. Mimeault and Morin (1999) compared bibliotherapy alone, bibliotherapy with weekly phone contact with a clinician, and a waiting list control group, for insomniacs. Both treatment groups improved more than the control but the added phone contact seemed to make no extra difference. Jason et al. (1995) found little effect for smoking cessation for self-help manuals alone; contact with a social support group was needed in addition to have an effect.

Example 1. Taylor and O'Reilly (1997) trained participants with mild intellectual disabilities to carry out standard skills in shopping, such as lifting a basket, looking at the shopping list, going to the correct checkout, etc. To do this the participants went through four procedures for each step talking our loud but then later talking to themselves: statement of the problem ("I must get a basket"); statement of the response ("I will get a basket now"); report on the response ("I have got a basket"); and self-acknowledgement ("Well done!"). Participants could do their own versions of the statements.

They found that this was done successfully and participants could shop correctly from a list, presumably while using self-statements to "guide" what they were doing. To test this was actually happening, Taylor and O'Reilly (1997) tried "blocking" the self-instructions by training them to repeat numbers out loud that the instructors said. The assumption was that they could not self-instruct during this, and sure enough, performance was poor under these conditions.

Example 2. From a political point of view, Rimke (2000) argued that self-help books are acting as a pretend panacea for problems that have societal or structural causes. Like other cognitive instructional techniques (Wilkinson & Kitzinger, 2000), they allow blame to be placed on the person for not changing their own behavior, and failure becomes implicit or explicit victim-blaming. Thus it can be argued that the use of self-help books "is intrinsically linked to governmental management of populations, and so to less individual autonomy rather than more" (Rimke, 2000, p. 61).

Wilkinson and Kitzinger (2000), meanwhile, were working with women with breast cancer and looking at the language use. They found that there was a talk from doctors and others that the women must "think positive" and this will help cure them. As mentioned above, this lands the blame on the women for failure, since they obviously were not thinking positively enough! But it is also instructive that the women were given authority and explanations by medical staff as well as other women, for why they should say positive things to themselves and think positively in general. Many women actually developed methods of challenging this local "wisdom' (Kitzinger, 2000).

Intervening to Change Peoples' Words about Themselves (Self-Talk)

Interventions can also change what things people say about themselves even if these are not linked (at least directly) to instruction following. My hokey category system puts these into two broad methods, using words to get reality checks or feedback (not always positive), and learning to talk about yourself in a new way (usually a more positive way, unless it is a paradoxical intervention or Provocative Therapy).

What we will find about these interventions is that they are really about finding stories or statements about yourself that are acceptable, consistent or defensible to other people—your main audiences—rather than about acceptability to an "inner self". These stories need to fulfill all the criteria of strategic uses of stories and explanations that we tell others (Guerin, 2003a, 2004).

My view is that the main "work" done in re-addressing stories and statements about yourself (identities) is taken up with reality checking what your main audiences will accept, especially if those audiences have different expectations. The only real difference to stories aimed strategically for consumption by others is that "self" stories allow much greater hedging (Guerin, 2003a, 2004) since no one can really check or monitor the truth about what is said. What follows from this, however, is that consistency in telling stories becomes the substitute for observable monitoring of what someone says. So again, a lot of the "work" done when forming identities will be about checking the consistency and defensibility of stories across different audiences. It is no use waking up one day and revealing to family and friends that your true identity you have just "discovered" through consulting your inner child is as an ancestor of a Greek King who ruled seven kingdoms. You will need a lot of maneuvering to deal with the challenges and changes in how people treat you if you go through with this, although in some cases ("mental illness") that could provide a strategic way to move on from an untenable situation and escape or avoid a worse situation—so even that example is not totally silly.

Getting Better Feedback or Reality Checks through Words

There are methods used to get people to say out loud what they are telling themselves at present—and receive the consequences for this (*Intervention Analysis 12*). They can be called "talk aloud" procedures or "think" aloud procedures (Davison & Best, 2003; Davison, Vogel & Coffman, 1997). This could lead to positive or negative outcomes, of course, so it needs to be done under some control. You should not just tell a client to go and ask everyone they know what they really think of them; this could lead to problems and the person must be trained first in accepting negative criticism (see earlier section of this chapter) as well as basking in positive feedback!

People can be taught to self-monitor what they do and how others react to them, can be guided through by words from the intervention agent to have a dialogue (with themselves!) about how they see themselves and have the listener (themselves) judge the reality of this (cf. Ronen & Rosenbaum, 1998). The hypnotherapist Milton Erickson even used to do this but not have the people say anything at all to him about what they were telling themselves about themselves or even whether they then judged it as reality or not (Haley, 1973). People can also be taught to attend (see last section) to patterns of negative thoughts, and monitor when they occur and the contexts for them. Finally, methods of teaching "mindfulness" get people to attend more to what they are thinking, felling and telling themselves, and this may require telling out loud or not (Dimidjian & Linehan, 2003). People can learn to self-question and even self-interrogate, in the same way as I suggested earlier that self-mediation and self-negotiation makes sense.

Example: Delusions. Chadwick, Lowe, Horne and Higson (1994) tried two interventions to stop delusions. Most of the delusions in the people treated were long-standing ones, and most were verbal. For example, the participant HJ had 20 years of schizophrenia with delusions that an unknown man was persecuting her and trying to kill her; she got her evidence from auditory hallucinations; and also believed (talked about) that her mind was being read.

The orientation of this book, as I tried to get across earlier, is that upon hearing such verbal delusions the question should not be, "What is making her think these things," nor "What stimuli could she be misinterpreting as evidence for her beliefs," but rather, *to ask about the effects that saying such things has had on the people around her.* However, easier said than done, because a 20 year history of these symptoms means that a lot of effects would have occurred over the years and the maintenance of her beliefs could have changed many times from what they were originally doing strategically. But getting the approach is more important for now than being able to carry it out. The importance of this approach will become clear in the following discussion.

The first intervention by the authors was a traditional cognitive therapy one, of trying to *test the reality of the beliefs,* by collaborating with the client to find ways of testing the beliefs. For example, the client HJ suggested that if she wore earmuffs and could still hear the voices then they must not be real voices. However, can you see the problem here? If she can live with the first beliefs then it would be easy for her to come up with a new belief to cover the situation if the test failed. It is unlikely that if the voices stopped that she would passively acquiesce and agree that he voices were imaginary—she has 20 years invested in this and could look like a fool if found trivially mistaken. She already says that people read her mind so it would be easy for those same people to *implant* the voices straight into her skull. There are plenty of science fiction books that show how this could work!

So from the perspective of this book, the problem is that the beliefs are based on social maintenance in the first place, so testing them against some "empirical" (presumably this means non-social) reality is unlikely to work unless the therapists also implicitly persuade her (social effects again) of new beliefs. Which is probably what happens; the person is verbally re-shaped to talk differnetly across audiences.

The second intervention that Chadwick, Lowe, Horne and Higson (1994) tried was to actually challenge the beliefs verbally, rather than try to empirically test them. They gave evidence against the beliefs, showed them to be internally inconsistent, got their clients' alternative explanations for what was going on, and gave alternatives. I hope it is clear by now that this really amounts to re-shaping the client's verbal behavior (cf. Alford, 1986; Guerin, 2004). They are providing strong social punishment for holding the delusions and are reinforcing alternative beliefs.

It is not about the client re-thinking their beliefs but about the re-shaping of them through social influence.

The results, as might be expected after this brief discussion, were that improvement with only the reality testing was weak. Only with one client did it seem to work, and then not for long. But as I suggested, the intervention is only as good as your test of empirical reality and is as weak as your client's ability to invent new explanations is good! And most are good at this. With the introduction of more direct challenging, the intervention was more effective, and follow-ups showed improvements over the next 6 months.

Changing Social/Self-Knowledge

There are a variety of methods that change what we say to ourselves about ourselves, and how we describe ourselves. As should be clear by now, how we describe ourselves is vitally important to life but not because of close matching to an inner self but because of the social effects this has on our audiences and communities and how they in turn treat us.

Some methods try to present directly a new way of representing, constructing or framing oneself, using imagery modification, mindfulness, dialectics, defusion, reframing, guided mastery, (disputational) cognitive restructuring, public conversations, positive attention, emotion regulation, re-attributional training, urge surfing, or hypnosis (Akillas & Efran, 1995; Bell, Boggs & Eyberg, 2003; Bolton, Howlett, Lago & Wright, 2004; Capafóns, Sosa & Viña, 1999; Dimidjian & Linehan, 2003; Dobson & Hamiltn, 2003; Ellis, 2003; Fruzzetti & Fruzzetti, 2003; Fruzzetti, Shenk, Mosco & Lowry, 2003; Haley, 1973; Hoffart, 1998; Kelly, 2000; Laird & Metalsky, 2003; Leermakers, Perri, Shigaki & Fuller, 1999; Lloyd, 2003; Luoma & Hayes, 2003; Martin, Moritz & Hall, 1999; Newman, 2003; Scott & Cervone, 2003; Selby & Bradley, 2003). People can be guided, for example, to image new pictures of themselves and tell themselves about these new images. We can get people to talk to themselves about their identity and anticipate consequences and reactions from others, and devise new identities (stories) for themselves.

Another method is to have people come up with and repeat positive statements about themselves or think about pleasant activities, although once again (from Chapter 1) getting the people to the point where they can and will do this is probably the major part of the intervention, not the actual saying of statements (Lange, Richard, Gest, de Vries & Lodder, 1998). Most of these methods also probably include the types of feedback and testing of new stories we saw in the last section. It is not just about learning to say to myself, "I am a great writer", but also about monitoring the reactions to this and the actual outcomes (when everyone hates my books!). These methods also have to involve the social properties of story making discussed in the last section (and Guerin, 2004).

Other versions of these methods have people make up fictitious stories or metaphors in which they are a character playing a role (Gordon, 1978; McCurry & Hayes, 1992; Ronen & Rosenbaum, 1998; Rosen, 1982). This again has all the properties we have seen: it is initiated by another person, it allows monitoring and feedback and gradual shaping to something acceptable to other audiences, and allows time to change and make new facets not in the original once doing that is safe. Hypnotherapists sometime use this but they do the job of telling the story and add changes that might reframe something for the person involved or show new possibilities to them they would not accept if just instructed to do so (Erickson, 1980a).

In my scheme, most of these techniques are likely to work by allowing time for the person to think through and rehearse explanations, reasons and defenses against challenges, and get ready for actual conversations with real people and real consequences. Coming up with these rehearsals is such a large part of language use and everyday life (Guerin, 2004) that much time is spent rehearsing what will be said (Guerin, 2001c). Part of it is also probably coming to terms with the reality from feedback and monitoring functions and coming to an *acceptance* that things cannot be as you might imagine or wish them to be, and so new stories, explanations, defenses, and framing must occur to deal strategically with these once they become part of your public behavior (Hayes, Jacobson, Follette & Dougher, 1994; Hayes & Pankey, 2003).

Finally, we saw self-help manuals and bibliotherapy in an earlier section discussed as methods for getting a person to get themselves to do something. They can also be a great source of re-making stories about oneself and finding new ideas or phrases that can be used.

Example: Stopping Obsessions and Thought Intrusions. There are a number of areas in which people have unwanted thoughts, obsessive thoughts, or repetitive thoughts that they say they would rather not have. The research strongly suggests that there is no difference in principle between clinical obsessions and everyday unwanted thoughts. That is, everyone has thoughts that they say they would rather not have and that they cannot "control."

This whole area is somewhat confused because of various metaphors for language and thinking. Thinking is usually considered under "volitional" control and so unwanted thoughts are considered "intrusive." In line with the approach to language given at the beginning of this chapter, however, we need to look more for our interventions through the social control of thinking, and in fact consider all "thoughts" as *social intrusions*. You do not know where any of your thoughts "come from" (how they are socially controlled) whether wanted or unwanted. Further, the content of those thoughts can have nothing to do with their timing or relevance if they are strategies to maintain relationships in particular ways rather than do something more direct (Guerin, 2004).

What we do know is that there are many "powerful" events that are used for social control through language (Guerin, 1997, 2004), and this includes rumors and urban legends, making a good story that holds a listener's attention (whether or not the content is truthful or a lie), scary stories and yucky things that people find aversive, talk about anxious events, and repetition. All these have been used for social control since the dawn of humans, and might have nothing to do with the "state" of a person talking about them. It is like telling a ghost story: it can allow me to control your attention (hopefully in a nice, friendly and useful way) whether or not I also "believe" the story.

So from a conversational view of "cognition" (Edwards, 1997; Guerin, 2004), when we find potent talk and the speaker unaware of why those thoughts are there (they cannot observe the generalized social contingencies of conversation), then that is a very good clue that the thoughts have been shaped socially through talk. This fits with Rachman's (1981) definition of intrusive thoughts: that they interrupt ongoing activity, are attributed to internal causes, and cannot easily be controlled by the thinker (also Clark & Purdon, 1995). Lack of control and intrusion are highly indicative of generalized social contingencies (Table 4 and Analysis 3 in Guerin, 2004), and such social contingencies have always been attributed to internal causes, albeit wrongly, because they cannot easily be observed (Guerin, 1994, 2004).

This way of viewing intrusive thoughts also fits other research. First, that there are positive intrusive thoughts as well as the negative ones studied as obsessions and anxieties (Edwards & Dickerson, 1987). Second, that obsession is related to feeling responsible for something and inflated feelings of responsibility (Wilson & Chambless, 1999). This is highly indicative of social contingencies, the talk being not unlike that of rumors and urban legends. Such talk is highly attention-getting, and this includes both getting one's own attention, and rehearsing for future conversation to others (cf. Mace & Lalli, 1991; Manne, 1999). Most worries, anxieties and intrusive thoughts are not such a problem until you have to talk about them to another person, or potentially talk about them (Guerin, 2001b, d).

Interventions for intrusive thoughts vary, but there are five major ones (cf. de Silva, 1985; Ladouceur et al., 2000; Weisenberg et al., 1993). *Exposure or Satiation Training* have people think (socially controlled by the therapist, notice) about their obsessional thoughts for a long period while kept relaxed (cf. Parkinson & Rachman, 1980; Foa, Streketee, Grayson, Turner & Latimer, 1984). The idea is similar to systematic desensitization, prolong the experience so as to desensitize it (Head & Gross, 2003). *Thought-Stopping* trains the person to stop the thoughts with a command as soon as they begin (cf. Foa et al., 1984). This is often difficult, however, if the obsessive thoughts are fast and unheralded (Robertson, Wendiggensen & Kaplan, 1983). *Distraction* gets the person to think or do something else, while *Thought Switching* has them think of something unrelated or very different. Finally, *Paradoxical Intentions* can be used, in which a person exaggerates the obsessional or intrusive thoughts and makes them even scarier or more responsibility-inducing. [This is related to *symptom prescription* in which the person is led (persuaded) to carry out their symptoms to excess (Akillas & Efran, 1995; Erickson, 1980b).]

Notice that in all case there is a social re-shaping of the verbal behavior occurring, with the intervention agent changing the nature of the listener for the obsessional or intrusive thoughts, or providing a new type of audience (McAndrew, 1989; cf. Emmelkamp & de Lange, 1983). The intervention agent provides a new source of social shaping of talk, but it must be more powerful than the original audiences if the treatment is to maintain or not switch to other thoughts.

Interventions That Use Combinations of These Methods

We saw earlier some of the methods being done "naturally" by people in tricky situations. I want to finish off by looking at a few areas where the methods discussed here are currently used in interventions. The main point of this will, in fact, just be to show you that there is nothing mysterious about these interventions—they are widely used whether people know it or not. They are also used in conjunction with methods from Chapters 3 and 4. [They are dressed up usually in magic jargon but they are not magic—because (1) it is the hidden nature of the social control that gives them this flavor, Guerin 2001c, 2004, and (2) because of the way people are brought to this point, as in my hypnotist example from Chapter 1.]

There are some good guides to the conglomerations of methods that make up other schools of therapy or training (Hawton, Salkovskis, Kirk & Clark, 1989; Hayes, Follette & Linehan, 2004; Hayes, Strosahl & Wilson, 1999; Hayes & Wilson, 1994; Nelson-Jones, 2002; O'Donohue, Fisher & Hayes, 2003) and that are not just recipe books. As mentioned elsewhere, recipe books are not much use here because contexts and situations vary so much from person to person, from group to group, that the recipes have to be hugely modified, and in fact re-written. A better strategy is to learn what these techniques are about and when they are useful and adapt them or radically alter them when dealing with people in a very different context. The annotated examples of Milton Erickson provide marvelous cases of all these techniques even if they were never labeled the way they are now back in his day.

Example 1. Elliott, Miltenberger, Kaster-Bundgaard & Lumley (1996) surveyed behavior therapists and asked them, amongst other interesting things, what treatment procedures they used and how often they would use them. The procedures most used by practitioners with clients were, from highest percentage to lowest: cognitive behavior therapy, relaxation procedures, modeling and behavior skills training, cognitive restructuring, behavioral contracting, self-management, problem solving therapy, operant procedures to strengthen behavior, couples therapy, thought stopping, operant procedures for decreasing behavior, systematic desensitization, therapeutic relationship enhancement, family therapy, exposure and response prevention, in vivo desensitization, rational emotive therapy, stress inoculation, group therapy, habit reversal, token economy, biofeedback, flooding, hypnosis, covert conditioning, facilitated communication, EMDR, and aversion therapy.

Most of these come from Chapter 3, 4 and 5, and should be familiar. Some in the list are already conglomerates of many methods, such as family therapy. But the list should give you the idea that these techniques are widely used, and that they are not special and we have covered them somewhere already in this book.

Example 2. Freeston and Ladouceur (1997) interviewed clients with Obsessive-Compulsive Disorder about the strategies they used to control intrusive thoughts and obsessional thoughts. For intrusive thoughts, they reported, from the highest to lowest percentage reporting: physical action, thought stopping, try to convince (self?) that it is unimportant, thought replacement, talk about the thoughts, do nothing, analyze, a religious strategy plan an action, evaluate thought as unimportant, relax or meditate, visualize the thought, act out the thought mentally, verbally check, use overt action to control activation, or think about it. Once again, similar techniques are used and most relate to the self-talk methods we have discussed.

Example 3. Gould, Damarjian and Medberry (1999) looked at the types of "mental skills" training used in youth sports by coaches and others, and at how the coaches taught them. These skills are the ones we have covered in the second half of this chapter, on self-talk, especially the self-regulation ones. Methods to teach them included these that we have already covered: consultants, using videos, parent education, building relationships with the clients, role modeling, shaping behavior, reflection and self-awareness (self-talk mixtures probably), analogies, concentration drills, simulations, imagery, goal setting, enhancing motivation, thought stopping, team activities, discussions, and relaxation.

Example 4. Another example from sports psychology is that of Meyers, Whelan and Murphy (1996) who reviewed cognitive behavioral methods used to enhance athletic performance. They found four main components that were important, each relating to parts we have discussed: goal setting, imagery and mental rehearsal, arousal management, and cognitive self-regulation. You should be able to link three of these easily to sections of this chapter, but one, arousal management, is a bit more obscure. It refers to methods of getting a athlete alert and attentive enough to concentrate on their sport, but not too worked up that they start making mistakes. This is a mixture then of attentional training, self-motivational methods, and self-regulation methods, as I have called them above.

Example 5. Hoberman, Clarke and Saunders (1996) reviewed interventions for adolescent depression. They present a variety of models that have been used, all of which are combinations of this chapter with parts of Chapters 3 and 4 added in. Nothing you could not handle this far into the book! To give you the flavor of these and the confidence that nothing mysterious is being added that you could not do, here are a few models. One cognitive-behavioral model (meaning Chapters 3 and 4 are used with some of the language techniques added from this chapter) consisted of group therapy that focused on: (1) recognizing feelings in oneself and others (no doubt monitoring and construction of self-stories involved); (2) assertiveness (from this chapter); (3) conversational skills; (4) giving and receiving positive feedback (because groups often only give negative feedback!); (5) giving and receiving negative feedback; (6) social problem solving (some skills from Chapter 7 and decision making skills from this chapter); and (7) negotiation to resolve social conflicts (also from Chapter 7). These topics were introduced to the group (more like lectures), examples given by group members, and role plays made which were videotaped. There was also practice for homework between sessions.

Another model of adolescent depression intervention (CWDA) had the following outline: (1) reviewing group rule and the rationale for what is going to happen, giving a skills focus or framework; (2) relaxation training; (3) identifying pleasant activities and giving feedback on the frequency of these, learning to monitor these and set goals for them and make a contract to carry out the goals; (4) "cognitive" (self-talk) sessions to challenge negative and "irrational" thoughts and teach self-questioning and challenge, and to act as their own audience and counter argue these negative thoughts; (5) social skills training focusing on conversational skills in particular, planning and self-regulation of social activities, and strategies for making friends; (6) basic negotiation, communication, problem solving and conflict resolution skills (next chapter); and (7) anticipating problems and developing a life plan with personal goal setting, and planning for a depression relapse.

I hope by now the components of these are familiar to you, and the similarities between these last two programs noted.

Finally, having read all this and seen all the common intervention procedures, be clear that this does not make you capable of using these methods—either practically or ethically. You still require actual learning, practice and experience of the methods under strict guidance and supervision. It also needs to be part of your wider learning so you can put the methods properly into their context in any case. You cannot just apply them to any old problem without analyzing the context first, and expect them to work. The earlier parts of the book still apply!

Chapter 6

Changing Communities and Societies

Over the last few decades there has been an increase in the number of reported community interventions, and the number of interventions which have collaboration between the intervention agents and members of communities. There has probably always been many community interventions, but they are being taken on more in the mainstream now and more reports are being published. Indigenous and other minority communities have also made more headway recently in demanding collaborative interventions rather than imposed interventions.

One foundation point of community interventions is that both changing and maintaining most practices depends on a large group of people rather than just the intervention. If we were to teach a single youth not to take drugs or to drink less alcohol that would be fine, but others of their peers, schoolmates and community members could easily undo all that training. The idea is that we need to tackle changing whole communities to support individuals within that community to make and maintain changes. There are also other problems that arise because of communities and these need to be addressed at a community or societal level.

The first immediate issue is the constituency of the "community" (cf. MacQueen, McLellan, Metzger, Kegeles, Strauss, Scotti, Blanchard & Trotter, 2001). If we think back to the famous Table 3 of Chapter 1, for western societies a community might primarily be a group of strangers who are accidentally or through stratification residing in similar places (neighborhoods or suburbs). For close communities, on the other hand, we might be talking about a group of people who are related, know each other well, have many interactions with each other every day, and inter-marry. These different types of community are likely to collaborate very differently and interventions will therefore be very different.

Three words of caution, though. First, most publications are about western societies so most reported "community interventions" will be about the first version of community. But this is starting to change and hopefully will continue. Second, most published interventions with close communities, on the other hand, are based around ethnicity or indigeniety as their defining feature, or sometimes religion, but this can certainly be broadened in the future. Third, different disciplines have concentrated on different forms of community on the whole but this is changing. Most early *anthropological* community interventions were based on close communities that made up all of a society instead of being a minority within a dominant "stranger" society. This is changing, and much more is done by anthropologists on close communities living within a dominant or colonizing society. Most *sociological* interventions with close communities were originally with groups within a western society but which were associated with a class, an economic stratification, or a rural/

Intervention Analysis 13. **Two Broad Types of Community Intervention**

(Based loosely on Table 3)

1. A community of "strangers" who each have a few close family and friends and networks of acquaintances but probably not locally

> Usually in western societies
> Usually one or two resource problems bringing them together as a community
> Might need work bringing the people together as a community
> Getting accepted in the community not such a problem usually but
> > leadership might be an issue in the community
> Commitment might be an issue
> Could be tied into a religious or thematic association ("mushroom club")

2. A community of closely related and inter-connected people, with strong family and community ties

> Could be a group within a western society or the whole society
> Unusually have problems with other groups, especially dominant groups
> Might take work getting accepted or finding a place or role
> Might want intervention agent to do peripheral and not central tasks
> Usually leadership is in place but this could raise other issues
> People usually committed to the community and want ownership

---

urban niche. Most *psychological* studies with communities were with western communities with western social relationships except for some "cross-cultural" (cross-national, in reality) comparisons which did not really take this difference into account and which treated any differences found as essential to the communities, their ethnicity, their race, or their indigeniety.

Basic Methods and Skills Needed for Community and Societal Interventions

The methods of community intervention are many and varied but the different "approaches" have a lot of overlap. While I might separate different approaches below, that is mainly historical and is done so that you can find these interventions in the literature. What they actually do in practice is amazingly similar. The 'action' part of 'action research', for example, is really no different to what applied anthropologists do except in how the background context is observed and assessed: Action researchers usually make some participant observations before intervening whereas applied anthropologists tend to take longer spending time with the people involved or even living with them for extended periods. These are only very rough differences, however, and the overlap is tremendous.

Intervention Analysis 14. **Methods and Skills Needed for Community Interventions**

Experience with diverse communities
Learning and understanding other ways of organizing communities
Experience with many diverse communities so nothing much shocks
Talking and interpreting languages and broken languages

Ability to use community research methods to help
Participant observation methods
Interviews
Running small groups or focus groups
Surveys and rapid assessments of needs or impact

Working as a team
Able to work in teams
Able to drop out or have a back seat as necessary

Getting communities on-side and organizable
Participation with communities
Facilitating community development
Building collaborations and trust
Giving technical, counseling and legal assistance

Facilitating learning in communities
Running public meetings and small groups including self-help groups
Simple presentations of complex information
Public education
Media and social marketing strategies
Being able to use all the other training methods in this book

Building ties between organizations and communities
Social networking with communities, government and non-government
Skills in negotiation, advising, persuading

Handling people, bureaucracies and opponents
Arguing as an advocate
Cultural brokering
Working with bureaucracies
Talking to government and business leaders and workers

Making things happen, getting some action
Marshalling resources, community funding and networks to do these
Causing things to be done through others
Gathering and summarizing research and literature for policy development
Formulating policy and seeing it through
Accessing the media where necessary

Most community interventions also use very similar skills and these are listed in *Intervention Analysis 14* (Alinsky, 1971; Gwynne, 2003; Nolan, 2003; Schensul, 1974; Segal, Gerdes & Steiner, 2003). For each of the approaches I will discuss later, you can find an emphasis on one or two of the methods or skills listed, but the others are usually there implicit anyway. I would favor getting rid of the traditional divisions used below, and focus on the skills and contexts needed for community interventions—regardless of the academic disciplines that happen to be historically implicated. Most of the differences are historical now.

A common feature of all these methods and skills is that they can only be learned in a very limited way via words—from lectures, discussion, or even from this book. They really need to be experienced and learned by trying them out. Setting up and running a focus group discussion between two or three different ethnic communities on the topic of fighting between their children at school can only be learned through words in a very limited way. The community equivalent of "on-site training" (from Chapter 4) is really needed. You need to watch someone who has done this before, then start working with them (or run like a "vestibule" focus group by using members of the communities well-known to you already), and then do an apprenticeship by running groups with the expert present. While you could learn it by jumping in the deep end and just doing it, one must be careful ethically of not making things worse for the communities this way or hurting anyone.

Experience with diverse communities. A key skill used in community interventions is to have, and use, experience with diverse communities, whether they are diverse on ethnicity, religion, location, isolation, etc. Having this sensitizes you to think of things before others do, and to anticipate what you can do to make things work better. It also means that you are not shocked at things you see and find, unless the communities' leaders will be pleased to see that you are shocked, of course, as they sometimes are. Having these experiences also means you will either learn other languages or you will learn to talk to people with different languages and education levels and be understood and understand them.

Ability to use community research methods to help. You need to be familiar with the community research methods, since you will either be using them as part of what you do or else the communities will ask you to help them with research that they can then use. Participant observation and ethnographic methods are especially important in community interventions, but you should also be fluent in interviews, running small group discussions or focus groups, and carrying our surveys and rapid assessment procedures (see below).

Working as a team. Most community interventions are as part of a team, and hardly ever will you venture into something alone. You need to be able to work well in a team and facilitate that team, but for community work you also need to be able to take the back seat or drop out altogether since this is appropriate for many communities. Some people find this difficult to do because they started the intervention and they think they should be allowed to finish it. You must be wary of ending up "owning" community interventions as your own.

Getting communities on-side and organizable. You have to be able to participate in communities as they allow you, and facilitate developments, again, as they allow you to do. Doing this gives the community more trust in you, but you will already need their trust before they will let you participate. Many people also give extra voluntary help (mostly because they like the people, not for the mercenary reason of getting the community to like them), such as legal and technical assistance, advocacy, counseling and advice giving, and generally helping with day to day living. Advocacy is an underplayed skill in many areas that could be better developed and better understood (Ernst, Grant, Streissguth & Sampson, 1999; Grant, Ernst & Streissguth, 1999; Hess, 1993; Mahmood, 1996; Sullivan & Bybee, 1999; Trinch, 2001).

Facilitating learning in communities. Most community interventions require you (and the team or community members) to give information or teach others in the community, in order for changes to occur. This usually happens through all the methods we have seen in Chapters 3, 4, and 5. Presentations need to be simple and clear, but not present a distorted view of the community and its relationships. This likely requires public education through running small groups, social marketing or face to face talking, depending upon the size of the community. At some point, you will probably also have to run a public meeting of the community or the "opposition" so you will need those skills as well (not always useful though, McComas, 2003). The other useful teaching you can do is to examine your role in the intervention and in the community and begin training leaders amongst the community members to take over from you—plan for leadership succession from the community itself.

Building ties between organizations and communities. Many of the problems for communities are about accessing or gaining resources from other organizations and from government. You should be able to network easily, with both government and non-government organizations, and this will include skills from Chapters 5 and 7 on persuasion, clear communication, and negotiation of resource allocation.

Handling people, bureaucracies and opponents. As well as building ties between organizations, you need to be able to handle people well, and be able to reason about and defend the community. This sometimes means being a cultural broker and working between organizations and the community, although it is easy to become the expert and start speaking on behalf of the community when you have no authority to do so. With some groups, especially diverse ethnic groups, bureaucrats often welcome a cultural broker not from the community for the wrong reasons, and prefer to speak with them rather than the community members. This needs to be watched, since it is flattering and good for your career but not good for the community. Again, if you are not from the community, plan a succession so someone from the community can replace you as the cultural broker.

Making things happen, getting some action. Finally, an important part of most community interventions is to get things actually happening. Sometimes this means working with the community to gain resources they need and the networks to maintain these resources. Sometimes people need to be mobilized to get things to happen, and managerial skills are useful here if the community does not want that role themselves. On the ground action is good but you also need to be prepared to work with policy analysts and work with literatures and discussions to formulate policy changes needed to make things happen. The hardest part about policy is following it through to make sure it causes things to happen in a good way. But it is an effective way to make things happen.

In all, there is quite a bit to do and quite a few skills needed for community interventions. This makes sense because in such interventions you are mobilizing a lot of different people and changes, and many things need to be done. But importantly, you should not be doing it alone in any case, and building up a good team, especially from the community itself, is the way to go.

Probably the most important consideration that cannot be stressed enough is to involve the community in the intervention from the very start. More and more research examples show failed interventions not from lack of consultation with the community but from lack of participation. Every different researcher and intervention agent has their own set of participation rules and procedures, but they are all very similar to the points made above (Austin, 2003; Barnes, 2000; Baum, Sanderson & Jolley, 1997; Belloni, 2001; Carr & Halvorsen, 2001; Costa, Kottak, & Prado, 1997; Davis & Whittington, 1998; Dunne, 2000; Fisher & Ball, 2003; Freitas, 1998; Herbert-Cheshire, 2000; Johnson, Lando, Schmid, & Solberg, 1997; Kowalsky, Verhoef, Thurston, & Rutherford, 1996; McComas, 203; Michaels, Mason & Solecki, 2001; Murray, 2000; Omidian & Lipson, 1996; Porter, 2002; Potvin, Cargo, McComber, Delormier, & Macaulay, 2003; Rowley, K. G., Daniel, M., Skinner, Skinner, White & O'Dea, 2000; Roussos & Fawcett, 2000; Russos, Fawcett, Francisco, Berkley, & Lopez, 1997; Snell-Johns, Imm, Wandersman & Claypoole, 2003; Yasumaro, Silva, Andrighetti, Macoris, Mazine & Winch, 1998).

Example. To give an example of combining all these skills, McGovern, Gerbeerich, Kochevar, Nachreiner and Wingert (1998) complied details of all the *community-based* violence prevention interventions in Minnesota, including child abuse, domestic violence, school violence, community violence and general violence. Their final sample was of 250 programs that met all their criteria and agreed to respond to some questions. Of interest here were the activities and services reported by these programs, that is, what sorts of things did they do—what interventions skills did they use?

Of all the 250 programs in the sample, these are the methods they used, with the percentage of programs using that method in brackets:

Public education (81.2%)
Health care, counseling, social service (74.4%)
Professional education (71.2%)
Advocacy (70.8%)

Policy making (51.2%)
Technical assistance (40.8%)
Legal assistance (37.6%)
Research (33.2%)
Mediation (29.2%)
Housing (28.8%)
Employment training (20.4%)
Other (15.6%)
(From McGovern et al., 1998, Table 3, p. 225)

By far the biggest was education or giving people facts, especially combining both public and professional education interventions. Also of interest is the high percentage using advocacy. This should give some clues as to the skills you require, and should acquire, to do community interventions.

Ethical and Practical Issues

It cannot be emphasized enough that working with communities can cause harm and hurt people, including yourself. Some of the relevant points have been made in the first two chapters, and these should be re-read. Most of the issues are discussed in all the literatures, whatever disciplinary background. These need to be taken seriously (Austin, 2003; Banks, 2001; Barnes, 2000; Costa, Kottak & Prado, 1997; Dunne, 2000; Fisher & Ball, 2003; Kowalsky, Verhoef, Thurston & Rutherford, 1996; Mahmood, 1996; Merrell, 2000; Potvin, Cargo, McComber, Delormier & Macaulay, 2003; Smith, 1999; Snell-Johns, Imm, Wandersman & Claypoole, 2003).

The main point to take away is the tradeoff between you helping a community, mobilizing them, teaching them, facilitating developments and getting thanked as a hero, and the community being allowed to determine and cause its own destiny, progress or development. Indigenous and ethnic minority communities in particular, have had centuries of everything being done for them but not actually in a way they want and without consultation. Check this regularly with your communities, informants and outsiders. As mentioned above, it can be flattering and very lucrative for your career to initiate intervention after intervention for a community, but in the long run this is not useful for the bigger intervention of getting the community to take charge over their own lives. Watch this closely if you are doing this sort of work.

Community Interventions

As mentioned above, community interventions usually fall into different approaches, some based around disciplines and some around a method. A close examination shows that they overlap more than they differ and those that focus on one method actually have the other methods implicitly in there somewhere. I want to quickly go through these here, with some examples, so you can source them better in libraries and internet searches. One day I hope they will come together, and that is what I am working towards (Guerin, 2004, 2005a).

Applied Anthropology

Anthropologists have always been strong on community interventions, partly due to the intensive time they spend with their communities, and partly due to the circumstances of working with the communities they do (Akwabi-Ameyaw, 1990; Fetterman, 1993; Gwynne, 2003; Hackenberg, 1999, 2002; Nolan, 2003; Podolefsky , 1985; Podolefsky & Brown, 1994; Schensul, 1974; Spicer, 1997; Sponsel, 2001; Stull & Schensul, 1987). In terms of skills, their biggest asset is indeed the time they are trained to spend understanding a community and learning its languages. Traditionally, anthropologists have also been among the best-trained advocates and cultural brokers. They have traditionally also worked mostly with isolated communities who form the dominant group (at least they have imaged them that way, Wolf, 1982) but they now work with all types of communities.

As something of a contradiction to what I have just written, anthropologists are also skilled in *rapid appraisal assessments*. This comes partly from their history as employees of government agencies that needed to find out population characteristics or just numbers rapidly. Anthropologists therefore have a history of conducting censuses among non-western populations, and rapid appraisals of social conditions or needs of communities. These are not meant—nor were they ever meant—to replace careful ethnography, but they were often a route to funding anthropological research and they also were perfect vehicles for mapping out the various contexts of a community before commencing the ethnography. They also were a way into the community. Even now, working with a migrant or refugee population in an urban area usually commences with a census of how many people are there and a needs assessment of what services and provisions they have and what others they require.

Rapid Appraisal Assessments come in many flavors and are not exclusive to anthropologists (Morrow, 1999; Murray, Tapson, Turnbull, McCallum & Little, 1994; Preston, 1994; Schwartz, Molnar & Lovshin, 1988; Vanclay, 2002; van Willigen & Finan, 1991). The basic ideas are to meet the community, talk to either key informants of the community or hold community meeting and discussion groups, gather any archival or file information that might be available, and put this all together with recommendations. This is meant to take between one and four weeks.

Example 1. Topper (1987) worked in northern Arizona when land jointly run by Navajos and Hopi tribes was divided between them meaning that 10,000 Navajos had to relocate. It was noticed that the Indian Health Services at this time had a big increase in the numbers attending with complaints of stress from the relocation. An anthropologist was hired to gather data on the problems, to assess the impact on the mental health services, and to advise on ways to minimize impacts.

Topper saw the process in terms of three stages: discovery, intervention and evaluation. In the discovery stage he gathered all possible information about the effects of relocation, and included newspaper analysis as well as key informant interviews. This showed that there would be considerable impact of relocation, and also revealed that the people themselves were not well informed about what was going on.

These results led to three interventions. First, a monthly newsletter was instigated to provide information he had found and keep people up to date on what was happening. Group sessions were also held with the main parties to answer any questions more directly from what was known. This had unexpected results, for example, of greatly reducing the number of rumors going around. It also led to the anthropologist being seen as a clinical resource for referrals.

The second intervention researched the mental health clinics through questionnaires about those using the services. The evaluation stage found greater numbers using the clinics and very high levels of distress from those who were to be relocated compared to those not being relocated. Depression was 7.5 times greater, and was especially worse for those less "acculturated" and over forty years of age. This led in turn to rapid development of tribal provision of help (which had started being planned anyway) and saw three tribal social workers and three outreach aides employed.

The third intervention was unplanned and involved working with other agencies to provide them with information and help them maintain relationships with the parties involved. It also showed a surprising amount of interest from lawyers, courts and other bodies in the clinic results. Many of these groups were supposed to be helping the tribes so new programs were implemented to help with the relocation issues. This led to Topper's fourth intervention as an expert witness to provide information and testimony for hearings.

Example 2. Podolefsky (1985) provides a useful lesson for would-be community intervention agents. He and his team conducted field research in a district of San Francisco, using formal and informal interviews with key informants, note-taking in community meetings, and program participation. The setting was that a crime prevention intervention called SAFE–Safety Awareness for Everyone was being implemented, and Podolefsky studied how the implementation worked. The actual SAFE intervention was typical of the sort described elsewhere in this chapter: there were volunteer community groups formed into neighborhood safety councils by a paid neighborhood coordinator. The main ideas were to improve communication between communities and organizations, reduce opportunities for crime, and encourage neighborhood responsibility and public awareness of crime. Inside all of this there were five interventions: Home Alert that organized groups block by block; a similar Merchants Alert for businesses; Operation Identification to label property; a crime reporting program; and a series of workshops and seminars on crime prevention.

In all, Podolefsky found a very poor response from the communities, the "community response to the SAFE Program was cool from its inception" (p. 37) for several reasons. First, the community idea was that crime had a socioeconomic cause and any program needed to address this if it was going to work at all, whereas the program was phrased in terms of wicked criminals who were abnormal (cf. Litton & Potter, 1985). Second, there was a history of programs being implemented for opportunistic reasons, such as up and coming elections. Third, some were worried about forming into neighborhood groups when they either did not know or did not want to know their neighbors (Table 3 in Chapter 1), or their neighbors were already probably involved in crime so it was awkward to include them. Fourth, focusing on particular targets worried many of the minority groups since that could lead to racism and discrimination occurring. Fifth, there was concern over the perceived role of the FBI in the program—people could get on with the police however much they complained about them, but not the FBI. Finally, there were many other issues such as lack of consultation, prior selection of the neighborhood coordinators, and duplication of programs already on-going. These amounted to implying that the communities had no leadership already so some had to be built, and there were protests over the arrogance of this.

In all, this paper is worth reading before doing community interventions. While not an intervention itself, it does report on the (unsuccessful) community intervention that was clearly rejected by the community.

Social Network Interventions

We saw some social network interventions in Chapter 2, when considering who might be involved in interventions. Social networks are a strong part of most people's lives, especially if family networks are included (Guerin, 2004), and support from social networks is a major part of helping people and keeping their stress levels down (Guerin, 2004). For this reason, building interventions by changing or working with social networks is an important area to explore (Copello, Orford, Hodgson, Tober & Barrett, 2002; Evans & Moltzen, 2000; Fontaine, 1986; Hogan, Linden & Najarian, 2002; Levin, 1993; also compare Carlsson, 2000).

Unfortunately, a recent review found some overall evidence for social support interventions working, but there were so many studies with poor design features and using different methods that it was difficult to make firm conclusions (Hogan, Linden & Najarian, 2002). The most common ideas are getting support person for people, or training people in social skills likely to provide them with a social network of friends. For example, people could have a smoking cessation program and then either be part of a supportive social network or not, and the difference in maintenance of smoking cessation measured.

Example 1. Levin (1993) created social networks for economic development in rural areas of Norway. There were few networks between businesses and entrepreneurs so the goal was to forge them. This was done through "action research" (described more below). Within this, there were many smaller interventions that should be familiar by now for community interventions: setting up committees, informant interviews, conferences or public meetings with communities, task force formation, meetings and reporting, evaluation of results, leadership training programs for locals, networking between the public sector and private businesses, and writing up the findings and dissemination.

Example 2. Copello, Orford, Hodgson, Tober and Barrett (2002) dealt with people with serious drinking problems, and in line with what was said in Chapter 2, explicitly brought relevant people in the client's network into the therapy. Network members were eligible, for example, if they did not have a drinking problem themselves, if they were not much higher or lower in power than the client (they needed to be about the same level), and were over 16 years old. They also had to be ready to support the person, agree with the drinking goals set (moderation or abstinence), and could offer positive but firm support to continue with the program and work towards the goal rather than criticism. During sessions a number of topics are taught to the support persons, seemingly by talking but perhaps with some role-modeling as well.

Action Research

Action research has developed in a few areas, most notably education and organizational development (Action Research Reader, 1988; Dick, 1993; Dickson & Green, 2001; Foster, 1972; McTaggart, 1997; Morrison & Lilford, 2001; Oskamp, 1984; Selby & Bradley, 2003; Selener, 1997; Trout, Dokecki, Newbrough & O'Gorman, 2003). The ideas behind action research approaches are not just (1) that there needs to be action to change things during research—opposing the mythical distant, objective scientist image—but also an emphasis on (2) repeated cycles of evaluation, planning, brainstorming problem solutions, problem-solving, and intervention, and (3) on involving the community members themselves in all these processes. So there is quite an overlap of skills outlined above with other approaches.

At the least, the cycle is one of planning for intervention, action, and then evaluation or review, all the while getting participation from those concerned (Dick, 1993). It involves research in the sense of getting information from participants and elsewhere for planning and action, and then researching the outcomes ready to go on with another cycle of planning and more action. It is also often described as a spiral rather than a cycle since the evaluation/review means that each successive attempt at intervention is getting closer to what is desired or is getting more meaningful (if the reviews find that the original goals need changing).

Beyond this, most of the skills and positive features are common to other approaches (Morrison & Lilford, 2001). While not ethnographic, the constant participation by community members means that much is learned informally as well, the advantage anthropologists have always had. Its basic philosophy is also shared with a strange bedfellow, behavior analysis, which also has an emphasis on the idea that to really understand or analyze what is going on you need to try changing something and observe carefully what happens—just continually talking about concepts and ideas gets nowhere.

Example. Selby and Bradley (2003) had found that discourses around youth in small rural town usually portrayed them as either *a risk* or *at risk*. Rather than just recording discourses, the research worked towards changing something, or acting. Seeing that the youth's voices were not being heard, they caused a group of youth (self-selected) to form a theatre "production" with some experienced theatre people, which they then proceeded to display in public. This was the youth's Public Conversation. [I am writing "caused a group ... to form" because of the discussion in Chapter 1, "*Analyzing the Contexts is more important than Finding the Causes*" about hidden social influences from intervention agents in just setting up the context for interventions.]

After going back to the planning stages a few times, the town agreed to hire some youth coordinators, a move which had been voted out several times in the past. There was a lot more involved in this intervention, however, including public meetings at which the researchers spoke and eventually one of the youth spoke as well. But the basic guiding approach was an action research one: plan, do something, see what happens, plan more on the basis of what you now know, more action, etc.

Community Psychology

Community psychology started mid-last century from a mixture of community studies in community mental health and Kurt Lewin's (1947) research on social change interventions (Kelly, Snowden & Muñoz, 1977; Levine & Perkins, 1997; Prilleltensky & Nelson, 2000; Rappaport & Seidman, 2000; Reppucci, Woolard & Fried, 1999). From both these sources there has been an intervention emphasis on group discussions, self-help groups, and counseling as interventions, and a lot of emphasis on presenting information as the way of changing behavior (see Chapter 5; also Davison, Pennebaker & Dickerson, 2000; Levine, 1988). Along the way, the limits of using these methods alone have been acknowledged and many other skills added in, all of which are found in the other approaches (*Intervention Analysis 14*; also Rappaport & Seidman, 2000). A large part of community psychology has been taken up with theorizing rather than interventions, however (see Levine & Perkins, 1997).

At present, then, most community psychologists also emphasize "new" intervention techniques such as participation by the community in interventions, media promotion and social marketing campaigns, action research planning, and policy links. The roots of community psychology still show, however, and less emphasis is placed on spending a lot of time with participants than I would deem necessary, and less emphasis on advocacy and volunteer work than other approaches (getting your hands dirty). On the other hand, more is done by way of groups and therapy still than other approaches might attempt, except perhaps social work. Finally, one other difference, which is true of the first two examples below, is that psychologists are still more likely to attempt experimental and control conditions in community research, despite the problems it can cause. For example, in both examples below the control groups missed out on useful learning.

Example 1. Sullivan and Bybee (1998) aimed to reduce violence for women with abusive partners by training community advocates (going against what I wrote above about community psychology and advocacy!). They used 143 female graduate students in a community psychology program as the advocates and gave them extensive training in listening skills, empathy, mobilizing and accessing community resources, and information about dangerous situations and what life is like for women with abusive partners. They worked with women who had been in a women's shelter for 4-6 hours per week with close supervision.

As would be expected by social workers or other community workers, the advocacy typically involved housing, employment, legal assistance, transportation, education, child care, health care, financial and material resources, and social support. Very much like action research (inadvertently I think), there was an explicit cycle of assessment of needed advocacy (planning), implementation (action, and included brain storming ideas), evaluation, secondary implementation, and termination.

The results were encouraging and, compared to a control group getting no advocacy, the participants reported less physical violence over time, better quality of life, more social support, less depressive symptoms, and more access to resources. Things did get better for the control group of women, but at a slower rate than having an advocate helping.

Example 2. Cronan, Brooks, Kilpatrick, Bigatti and Tally (1999) gave 277 parents of low-income families who were on a Head Start program a special training program aimed at helping the parents to read with their children and encourage their children to read (cf. Huebner, 2000). The intervention consisted of 18 visits by a trained tutor who modeled how to read to the child and listen to the child reading, taught the child various concepts, and sang songs. They also left a children's book at the house to keep, along with other materials, and on the first visit they helped the child make a "Book Box".

In the short term the intervention was successful in getting parents to read to, and be read to by, their children and gains were made in the children's literacy. However, at a one-year follow-up most of the improvements were no better than controls. Ways of improving maintenance were therefore highlighted for future studies.

Example 3. In a study very reminiscent of the origins of community psychology, de la Ray and Parekh (1996) brought together a group of teenage mothers to discuss their problems and issues. The facilitators used intervention methods from Chapters 4 and 5 to help this, especially audio-visual aids and games. The main part, though, was the presentation of information and group discussions (very like Kurt Lewin). They also trained the mothers to be facilitators in their own right, in an effort to promote more groups to form. While not explicitly evaluated, it was clear that the teenage mothers benefited from the intervention.

Protest and Radical Solutions

If community and social change is not forthcoming then two old and tried methods of intervention are to be more radical and to protest. This can go from agitation, revolution and semi-violent actions (Greenpeace falls into a middle potions here sometimes) down to peaceful protests and non-violent activism (Oskamp, 1984).

Saul Alinsky (1971) was well-known in intervention circles for these types of campaigns, although he usually relied on peaceful solutions. Many of his campaigns though involved embarrassing or inconveniencing the opposition, some campaigns used conflict but allowed the opposition to exist, and only a few tried to bring down the opposition altogether.

More recently Michael Moore has been doing similar campaigns on all sorts of social issues (2002, 2003). For example, a politician who opposed gay rights vehemently was targeted (Moore & Glynn, 1998). A gay men's choir was sent to the politician's offices in Washington and outside they sung "What the world needs now is love, sweet love..." The police arrived and told them they were not allowed to sing on Capitol Hill. So they went to the politician's residence and sung in the street outside, but his wife came out and thanked them but said he was not at home. While not an intervention in the sense of measuring outcomes, many of Michael Moore's interventions/stunts have led to social changes. The most powerful ingredient probably, unlike Alinsky, is that Moore films the events and gets them broadcast. For example, one of his most powerful intervention/stunts was following up a bank that offered a free rifle with any new account, so Michael Moore went in with cameras and set up a new account and filmed being given the rifle as his reward. Seeing this happen on film is very different from reading about the story in written form.

If you are looking for peaceful but effective methods of community and social change, the best is still the three volume series by Gene Sharp (1973). Sharp outlines all the techniques systematically and gives copious examples from historical and recent events. In Volume Two, which outlines the methods of nonviolent action, he divides the material into: nonviolent protest and persuasion; social noncooperation, economic noncoooperation (subdivided into economic boycotts and strikes); political noncooperation; and nonviolent intervention. To give you the flavor, Table 5 lists some of his finer divisions for social noncooperation.

Example. I will take an example from "Social noncooperation" as shown in Table 5. Under "Suspension of social and sports events" Sharp outlines the case of the 1940-1945 occupation of Norway by Germany. The Norwegians refused to join in any sports activities with the Germans, who had seen this as a way of building networks with the occupied people. This was done from the ground up rather than being a directive from above, which could have got people in trouble. Everyone heard by word of mouth that they should not join in sports with the Germans.

For example, in 1940 some German officers tried to set up Norwegian-German football matches but the Norwegians did not show up so the games were abandoned. When Germans tried to join tennis clubs, tennis clubs set aside a few days for the Germans to play (so they did not get in trouble) but no Norwegians "happened" to turn up on those days. Some Denmark-Norwegian wrestling matches had been planned but when the Fascist party official turned up he found that all 64 Norwegian wrestlers had stayed home.

Social Work and Community Welfare

Social work and community welfare come very close at times to community psychology but tend to differ by having more hands-on experience with the communities, being better trained as advocates, dealing more with counseling

Table 5. Methods for Social Noncooperation

(from Sharp, 1973)

Ostracism of persons
Social boycott
Selective social boycott
Lysistratic nonaction (spouses refuse sexual relations)
Excommunication
Interdict

Noncooperation with social events, customs, and institutions
Suspension of social and sports activities
Boycott of social affairs
Student strike
Social disobedience
Withdrawal fro social institutions

Withdrawal from the social system
Stay-at-home
Total personnel non cooperation
'Flight' of workers
Sanctuary
Collective disappearance
Protest emigration (*hijrat*)

approaches than therapies that have a foundation in psychology, looking more at the cause of problems being in social systems and societal level processes rather than being something about the people, and dealing less with theory and ideas about issues and more with actively changing them. This is all "in general", though, and there is much overlap (Banks, 2001; Harrison, Thyer & Wodarski, 1996; Mattaini & Thyer, 1996; Munford & Nash, 1994; Pease & Fook, 1999; Segal, Gerdes & Steiner, 2003).

The focus has always been on western urban communities and the problems that occur, and the various *communities* that do not do well in such centers—the aged, the disabled, those going through the 'mental health' services, the young, the disrupted families, the 'working class', the poor or low income households, adoption and foster care, diversity, immigrants, etc. *Issues and problems* dealt with have included community conflict, drugs, gay rights, women's rights, health issues including AIDS, employment, welfare, etc. *Interventions* have usually been a mix of talking and counseling services with a strong dose of advocacy to get resources and services for those who need them most (Segal, Gerdes & Steiner, 2003). Whereas many psychologists would work with the middle-class who can afford to see them, social workers have traditionally worked with the 'needy' and helped on the ground with getting more basic resources and rights established. Conducting group counseling sessions and group discussions have always been key interventions for social workers, especially between persons in the same predicament who might be able to help each other and share their experiences with the group.

Social workers have also traditionally been employed by government departments or a civil service, so this has meant (1) having to get a conscience for what they are doing with respect to government policies, (2) dealing with conflicts between how they would like to help people and what they are allowed to do under government policies, (3) learning well how to establish networks between government and non-government organizations and mobilize help and resources through those networks, and (4) living with restrictions on how much time they can spend getting to know families and communities (their employers will not allow them to spend weeks mapping out an ethnography of a community!).

All this is 'in general', as mentioned, and many exceptions will be found. For the purposes of examining interventions, however, the flavor will have been given of good networking and interpersonal skills gained through social work education, good advocacy and resource mobilization skills, and good skills with respect to a variety of diverse community groups (but very different from what anthropologists experience, however). There are social work academics who research and produce theories and abstract generalizations about society and the causes of social problems, but the average social worker is more on-the-ground and has skills to reflect this. They tend to work with 'cases' that are very real.

Example 1. Comer, Meier and Galinsky (2004) conducted two studies using an approach known in their area as the Research Intervention Paradigm (remarkably like an action research cycle). The first of these interventions focused on a problem of people with Sickle Cell disease (SCD) who often have high rates of depression. To deal with this they used a "psychoeducational" intervention, which just means giving information, some methods from Chapters 4 and 5, and group discussions between people with the same problems (see Botsford & Rule, 2004, for a similar psychoeducational intervention). After piloting, the basic procedures of intervention were to get a group of SCD people together in groups, have two leaders/ facilitators present some material, give some self-management suggestions, do activities for countering negative thoughts (Chapter 5) and stress reduction, and have group discussions about how support can be given and ideas for overcoming problems. This was nothing new to what we have seen in this book so far, except for the group discussions between people in the same predicament.

Example 2. In a simple but effective intervention, Ingersoll-Dayton, Schroepfer, Pryce and Waarala (2003) tried to empower caregivers (mostly family and aides) of people with dementia in nursing homes to find ways of overcoming the frustrating and messy problems that often occur—problems such as wandering, physical aggression, and verbal aggression. These problems can often sour otherwise useful relationships that help the patients. The idea simply was over seven weeks for the researchers to interview family carers and aides to have them talk about the person's past, their positive qualities, what they had liked doing previously, and suggestions for overcoming the problems that were occurring. The researcher then put these together into a plan with ideas that could be implemented, and the plan was reviewed by all those involved as it was three weeks after when the plan had been implemented.

Many of these plans were successful, such as the client who was aggressive when being undressed at night. Another aide told about an old friend Tom whom the client always talked about, so when the staff undressed him they talked about Tom and encouraged him to do so and he stopped being aggressive. The intervention was simply a type of reiterative problem solving (like negotiation or action research) that involved those closest to the clients who knew their historical context much better rather than just the current presenting problems.

Societal, National and International Interventions

There is a limit to what can be done through communities, and so we come to interventions that aim to change a whole society or nation, or to target smaller populations within that. These are notoriously difficult to evaluate, for many reasons discussed below. It is not just the size of them that makes evaluation difficult, but also the long-term nature of the outcomes and the politics involved in setting up and running such programs. Nonetheless, good outcomes have sometimes been measured.

Changing Nations through Large-Scale Public Good Programs

Large-scale programs are usually the resolve of government departments under public pressure, or the United Nations in under-developed countries. Without needing law changes (see below), large programs of a sweeping nature are imposed and carried out by government employees or subcontractors. Occasionally these have been developed through large, philanthropic research or welfare funds. They are usually for health, education, youth development, special needs groups, or housing. Sometimes they are after the event, such as setting up large-scale needle-replacement programs after a health epidemic has already begun. Other times they are forward-looking early or primary prevention programs that are not fixing up an already existing problem but preventing one from occurring in the first place (Albee & Gullotta, 1997; Allen & Philliber, 2001; Cowan, 1997; Durlak, 1997; Durlak & Wells, 1998; Edwards, Brown, Hodgson, Kyle, Reed & Wallace, 1999; Fengqin, 1999; Haines & Case, 2005; Kagitcibasi, Sunar & Bekman, 2001; Melton & Barry, 1994; Pérez-Cuevas, Reyes, Pego, Tomé, Ceja, Flores & Gutiérrez, 1999; Schorr, 1991; Sogoric, Middelton, Lang, Ivankovic & Kern, 2005; Weissberg, Kumpfer & Seligman, 2003). Programs such as these have usually had fancy names applied to identify them: the New Deal, Head Start, and DARE.

It is often complained that these programs concentrate millions of dollars into projects but never work, although it is better to say that we usually do not know the full impact of such programs—would things have been better if there had been no program, and are there trickle-down effects that we do not even realize stem from the program? Moreover, the programs are almost always surrounded by political and economic pressures, so the discourses surrounding them—before, during and after—need to take this into account. Those working on such programs also need to keep this politics in mind, because it means that they will not have an independent reign to do what is best according to current evidence—there will be political pressures from government and/or donors as to what needs to be done and to whom. Evaluations also need to remember this before condemning programs.

The details of the large-scale interventions vary tremendously, and will not be summarized in any detail. Many examples are given in Seidman (1983) and Joffe and Albee (1981) of the older programs. Current efforts are similar but make much more use of the mass media and social marketing techniques (see below). This does not mean they are more effective, of course, and sometimes it seems that a mass media campaign satisfies the instigators because they sound like they are reaching lots of people whereas in fact they might have little effect.

Finally, while not large-scale programs in themselves, there are many useful reviews of social interventions that review across a large number of programs and over a long time span. These provide a very good glimpse of what works and does not work on a large-scale, although one must take the costs into account if the best evidence interventions are to be utilized on a large-scale (Aguirre–Molena & Gorman, 1996; Biglan & Taylor, 2000; Card, 1999; Gorman & Speer, 1996; McGovern, Gerberich, Kochevar, Nachreiner & Wingert, 1998; Orleans & Cummings, 1999; Shiffman, Mason & Henningfield, 1998; Smedley & Syme, 2001; Wurtele, 1995; Zigler & Muenchow, 1992). The journals just cited are worth perusing for similar reviews in other areas.

Example 1. Allen and Philliber (2001) looked at the Teen Outreach program to prevent teenage pregnancy and failure at school by analyzing data from 3,300 teenagers from multisites. This is a national program in the United States that mixes many elements from earlier chapters. It is school-based that puts volunteer students into service in their own communities. The volunteer work, however, is not totally extramural but is linked to the school curriculum involving group discussions on social issues. So there is changing of talk during discussions and experience in advocacy and basic helping through the volunteer work.

The evidence is that the Teen Outreach program works to reduce teenage pregnancies and dropout rates at school (Card, 1999). A common question, though, is whether the students volunteering for the program are actually the ones who need it most, as one can imagine those most likely to dropout or get pregnant would not volunteer. Allen and Philliber (2001), however, found a broad range of students participated and the high-risk group were represented in the program and in the good results.

Example 2. A very different intervention was to implement a flood warning system in Australia (Handmer, Keys & Elliott, 1999). The task was to build guidelines for best practice in flood warning systems across the whole nation, and across all the different groups involved. This involved not only cooperation and agreement between many diverse organizations, but also the recognition by those organizations that something was even needed.

The process itself was something like the iterative cycle we saw for action research, but with a lot of consultation and involvement by all groups with a stake in the outcomes, even if they did not realize they had a stake. Active responsibility was needed by those concerned for the system to work. The following were the main steps needed to get to the end point of intervention completion:

> National conference to learn from recent floods and establish flood
>   warnings as a priority
> National workshop called to start drawing up best practice guidelines
> Time spent understanding and clarifying the tasks
> An ad hoc group started informally to draft guidelines
> An iterative process among informal networks to get comments
> Draft read by non-specialists (who found it too difficult)
> Made more reader-friendly
> Draft now widely circulated for comments and changes
> Endorsed by some of the main parties
> Publication of the Guide
> Endorsement by main CEOs so the Guide becomes their policy
> Continuing effort to implement on the ground

It can be seen that this is a long and complex process, and national changes usually take this long because of political necessity. Another example is given later of an international effort that required even more time, delicate handling, and cooperation (Lumpe, 1999).

Example 3. Seitz, Rosenbaum and Apfel (1985) made a 10-year follow-up on families from an earlier intensive intervention. The program had been set up by Provence and colleagues for "impoverished" families, to work intensively with them so as to provide better development conditions for their children. The families were originally recruited around 1970, after fitting a variety of criteria, and a matched control group was also included.

For the families, the program started when the mothers were pregnant and went on for almost 3 years after the birth of that child. There were four main components: home visitations, pediatric care, day-care, and developmental examinations. *Home visitations* were by social workers, psychologists, and nurses, who developed close personal links and helped with a range of practical and advocacy issues, as well as sympathetic listening. The *pediatric care* was close and intensive and allowed for house calls and one-on-one discussions between parents and doctor with no time limit, provided regular check-ups on the children, and often involved training and advice. The *day-care* consisted of an average of 13.2 months of child care by a highly qualified staff, and also allowed for discussion with parents and training as necessary. Finally, the children were given regular *developmental tests* and this was coupled with parental discussions on observing the children's developmental stages and learning about child care.

The results were impressive, perhaps not surprising given the huge amount of time and concentration put into the program details. After 10 years the mothers were more likely to be self-supporting, had better education levels than the controls, and had smaller family sizes. The children had better attendance at school, and the boys used less special services. While the program was costly with so much direct input from professionals, the authors estimated that there was a saving of US$40,000 (in 1985) from welfare services that potentially would have been used without the program being in place.

Example 4. A now famous example of a national (USA and elsewhere) program that did not work is the DARE program (Drug Abuse Resistance Education). In 1993 it was estimated that 6 million students were exposed to DARE, at US$750 million. This is not the only program since in 1997 it was estimated that in the USA US$2.4 billion was spent on youth drug prevention programs. The problem is, DARE does not seem to work even after allowing up to ten years for trickle down effects to appear (Brown & Kreft, 1998; Clayton, Leukefeld, Harrington & Cattarello, 1996; Ennett et al., 1994; Hansen & McNeal, 1997; Lynam, Milich, Zimmerman, Novak, Logan, Martin, Leukefeld & Clayton, 1999).

A curious feature about DARE that makes it noteworthy here, is that teachers and those running the program (the police) stand by the program and claim all sorts of successes, so there is now some literature and research on why failing programs are seen by some as winners (Brown & Kreft, 1998). This is worth reading since the things that affect believing a program to be strong have often been true of failures when measured properly. For example, people watch fear and scare tactics on television regularly, such as horrific car smashes advertising "Do not drink and drive", and this powerfully affects them, leading them to claim that it "surely" must be effective in reducing drink driving. However, there are all manner of reasons why this might not be so. For example, these advertisements mainly affect those who are already converted to the message, fear tactics do not teach you what to do otherwise, and fear tactics are easily discounted by verbal strategies for those who wish to justify or not assume responsibility for their drink driving. This is not to say that fear tactics cannot work, just that they are not simple (Hill, Chapman & Donovan, 1998; Keller, 1999; Smith, 1997).

The DARE program varies slightly from one implementation to the next, but typically consists of about 17 sessions delivered by police officers, focusing on social skills needed to resist "peer pressure", information about drugs and their effects, self-esteem building, training on decision making skills, and thinking about alternatives to drug use. It is one of a group of "Just say no!" programs emphasizing zero tolerance. So it has talk interventions from Chapter 6, skills training from Chapter 5, and some life skills training also from Chapter 5.

One of the likely problems is the link between programs at school and the outside life, in which there is exposure to a wide range of peers. There is also great scope to verbally discount the type of training that is given in DARE, with simple verbal strategies allowing one to overcome whatever resistance was trained:

"No, I don't want to try that stuff."

"Oh, you've done one of those resistance courses, eh wimp! You are now standing up to me and you're going to miss out because of some namby pamby teaching fill-in class in high school. Ok, miss out then, but you're the loser here! So you want in?"

One study even found that resistance training lead to more assertiveness which could be used both to resist peer influence and to cause it as well (Donaldson, Graham, Piccinin & Hansen, 1995).

Example 5. Surratt and Inciardi (1996) describe attempts to instigate drug use and HIV risk prevention programs amongst street youth in Rio De Janeiro. It is estimated that there are 800,000 children living in poverty in Rio, and estimates of street youth (which vary by definition) range from 20,000 to 1 million. There are differences between children on the street who work informally and make a living and those who live on the street. Many work during the day on the streets but go to a home at night, whereas as others truly live on the streets at night. More importantly, while some work at legal or semi-legal trades, others work at selling drugs or at prostitution, and violence is a daily event.

Put into this frame, any interventions to prevent drug use and unsafe sexual practices are fraught with difficulty, and the best in this field have been working with close community involvement and participation, while collecting the contextual details (recommended in Chapter 1) so as not to stereotypes the street youth or jump to conclusions (see for example, Campos, Raffaelli, et al., 1994).

Intervention strategies for this broad program were divided by Surratt and Inciardi (1996) into four types: correctional, rehabilitative, outreach, and preventive (following Lusk, 1989). *Correctional* programs see the street youth as under the jurisdiction of justice departments, and so they are placed into institutions that become crowded and abusive, although they could be done better. *Rehabilitative* approaches view the children as victims of poverty and neglect, and so smaller programs for drug use and detoxification have been set up by churches and other groups, although they only reach a small proportion of the street youth. *Outreach* programs train lay workers in counseling, education, and advocacy to work with the street kids and try and teach them some basics of life they missed out on and to get them more self-reliant and planning. However, these outreach programs can be overly abstract and not deal with the harsh realities of everyday living and violence. Finally, the *preventive* models work to educate policy makers on why there are street children in the first place and what their policies could do, and also to provide education, work, or alternative activities for the children and help prevent family disruptions. One program is tackling an estimated 80,000 children in this way.

Media and Social Marketing Campaigns

The major change to interventions for nations and societies in recent times has been the widespread use of mass media and marketing techniques to promote interventions for social change. This is especially so for health promotions, but is used in many other areas. Indeed, it would be strange today to have a major health campaign that did not involve social marketing and the mass media (Andreasen, 1995; Donovan & Owen, 1994; Elliott, 1989; Winett, 1993; Wurtele, 1995). Such approaches are not new, but the media has become much more sophisticated now in terms of what it can do (Mendelsohn, 1973; Rothschild, 1979).

It is worth thinking about differences between marketing for private profit-making companies and social marketing for social problems. Rothschild (1979) outlined one way to do this, such as product and price differences (most social campaigns only cost taxes or time and you usually do not get any 'thing' out of it), involvement (people are often not involved directly in social issues or even feeling the effects of the problems), and segmentation (it is often politically unsound to target the social problem communities directly but mass media can then end up preaching to the converted, Keller, 1999; Black, Blue, Kosmoski & Coster, 2000).

Rothschild summarizes across six marketing dimensions: situation involvement, enduring involvement, benefits, costs, cost/benefit ratio, pre-existing demand, and segmentation. For example, keeping people to a speed limit has low involvement and little interest for most people, although key for people's beliefs, few personal or even societal benefits, costs in time and image, a poor cost/benefit ratio, virtually no pre-existing demand, but it does apply to all drivers. In private marketing terms, this would be a very hard product to sell. Rothschild concluded that there is likely to be a very low impact of any such social marketing, although he did not take into account the cost of police action when you speed. In one sense there is also no market competition in social campaigns (no one advertises on television to go fast), but indirectly car manufacturers and those who build good roads contribute to speeding almost like a competitive market.

There are probably as many "success factors" for marketing as there are marketing firms. Donovan and Owen (1994) point to these ones from their healthy look at the literature: differential advantages over the competition; customer satisfaction; exchange of trading something for something; perceived customer value; selectivity in market segments; understand the marketing environment; market research; and strategic planning. Each of these means different things for social issues, and Donovan and Owen (1994) usefully go through the example of using social marketing to get people to do more physical activity in these terms.

A final general point is that despite some successes (Winett, Leckliter, Chinn & Stahl, 1984), the real effects of media campaigns are unknown. It is difficult to evaluate such campaigns properly, so many just end up reporting how everyone felt affected and changed by the campaign, whereas I reported earlier for "fear" campaigns that: people might feel affected but not change their relevant behaviors; that only the converted or non-targeted population feel affected; that people might report being changed but not do so since there is an obvious expectation that something should have changed; and the large expense often means government sponsored campaigns just want to show that something has been done with an obvious big splash effect and they are not really concerned about what really has changed from the media campaign.

Example 1. Rimal and Flora (1998) evaluated the effects of a major social marketing campaign on adults' and children's healthy eating. An intervention targeting two cities (with two other cities as controls) had large mass media campaigns focused on diet, activity and smoking. There were leaflets, television advertisements, television programs, health columns in newspapers, booklets, media events, and radio messages.

The evaluation found evidence that the campaign had an effect on healthy diet when the two groups of cities were compared (also controlling for a number of variables), especially for children since the adults were more likely to return to their old diets after the campaign finished. There was some evidence also that the children influenced the parents and vice versa, although the results were not as conclusive as had been hoped. In all, a large-scale mass media campaign seemed effective to a reasonable degree when compared to cities with no such campaign.

Example 2. Booth, Bauman, Olderburg, Owen and Magnus (1992) looked at the effects of a large mass-media campaign targeting increases in physical activity. The component interventions were television advertisements, education of professions such as doctors through circulated papers, radio and newspaper announcements, events incorporating sporting stars and celebrities, stickers, posters, leaflets, shirts, and the dedication of two national soap operas to the issues (cf. Piotrow et al., 1990 and Rogers et al., 1999 in the family planning intervention literature).

The authors found that after the campaign, 75% of a sample survey could recall the campaign message, but there was no increase in knowledge about the benefits of physical activity which they put down to high pre-campaign levels. Those over 50 years old reported increased walking after the campaign and the number of walks. The 'least educated' group also increased walking which showed that the messages did not just have an influence on those who might understand them better.

Example 3. Ratcliffe, Cairns and Platt (1997) report on a mass-media anti-smoking campaign in Scotland. The component interventions were similar to the last one with the exception of a telephone line: television advertisements, outdoor posters (including billboards), and newspaper and radio announcements, an anti-smoking booklet giving advice on stopping; and a free telephone helpline *Smokeline* that people could call for advice, information and motivation.

Using a few methods to determine the success of this campaign (worth reading since evaluation is difficult as I have reiterated), there was probably about 9.88% of smokers still quitting 6 months afterwards as a result of the campaign (coming from a sample who were followed up). In terms of the total number of smokers involved, this then translates into something like 6,000 people who quit.

Of more interest, is that the authors then did a cost/benefit analysis in terms of the number of life-years saved and the cost of this. Once again, estimating this is tricky (and worth reading for that reason), but they estimated that the campaign, which cost about £1.5 million, led to a cost of between £300 and £650 per life-year saved. Other campaigns they note were for nicotine patches in the USA of between US$4500 and $11,000 per life-year saved, and between $1100 and $1200 for a Swedish "Quit and Win" mass media contest. So despite the large outlay of about £1.5 million, the effects were quite reasonable compared to other methods. Later trickle down effects might also add to this, whereas nicotine patches probably do not have trickle down effects.

Changing Laws and Government Policy

Almost every area of intervention we have covered has suggested that changing the laws and policies of a country will also help change people (Carlsson, 2000; Findlayson, 2001/2002; Hackenberg & Hackenberg, 1999; Hess, 1993; Levine & Perkins, 1997; Palmer, 2001/2002; Parker & Langley, 1993; Pentz, 2000; Thomas & Robertson, 1990; Van Meter & Van Horn, 1975). I have pointed out in a few places, however, that policy changes are not easy because of politicking, uncertain side-effects of any policy changes, the cost of implementation once policy or law is changed, and the many steps and cooperative changes needed to get a good implementation of change. These problems are well outlined in Hess (1993), who shows the problems anthropologists face when they wish to use their knowledge to influence politicians and their representatives (also MacCoun, 1993; Nadelmann, 1989).

Social policy and public policy require specialized training but most of the skills are included in this chapter and Chapter 5. For example, using advocacy and social networking becomes transformed more into lobbying or hiring professional lobbyists, and the contextual analysis becomes much more focused on the political context and what is likely to work or not. For example, in many cases politicians want to see that 70-80% of people want the social policy change before they will consider pushing for it. This is a tall order for problems that people mostly do not care about (see Rothschild, 1979 in the last section) but the politicians do not want to end up looking like fools when no one else supports a bill or amendment they introduce.

The advantage of policy and law changes of course is that something gets done to a lot of people usually—there are large interventions that come from policy and law changes. It also takes a big effort to remove that policy or law once accepted, although this can be a negative feature if you wish to change negative effects of previous policies.

Example 1. Pentz (2000) looked at the policy changes that have been (and could be) implemented to decrease youth drug use, and the roles of communities in these. First off, community groups can lobby for drug changes through action councils, task forces, partnerships and coalitions (e. g., Carlsson, 2000). This is more effective than individuals lobbying, especially for the costs involved. Community groups such as these can also help shape enforcement procedures of policies if they are not being implemented properly. For example, Jason, Billows, Schnopp-Wyatt and King (1996) showed community methods that could facilitate the implementation of laws not allowing the sale of cigarette to minors, since this was a law not being properly enforced.

Pentz points out two types of approaches that can be used. *Programmatic* policies work towards education administration of interventions, youth funds in general, dissemination of materials, and changing norms of community acceptability. Each of these has a role to play in reducing youth drug problems. *Regulatory* policies are more about enforcement but not only work to restrict access and availability of drugs, but can also be used to enforce the monitoring of such policies. This can be used to train those who sell cigarettes or alcohol, support these people if they enforce the laws, and to work with schools to get their cooperation.

Finally, as we have seen many times in this chapter, community facilitation of policy change can be greatly helped if the community is allowed to participate in decision making, and if the community has strong leadership to make this happen. This means that training for leadership is a skill that in the long term can also help with policy changes for communities.

Example 2. Girgis, Doran, Sanson-Fisher and Walsh (1995) took a nice twist on the cigarette sales to minors by calculating how much revenue the Australian government was making from taxes on cigarettes illegally sold to minors, and then comparing this to how much was being put into interventions to prevent it happening. They estimated that there were 200,000 under-age children smoking 11.5 million packets of cigarettes across Australia in 1990. This meant that the government earned about *AUS$60* for every child smoking while it put in only *11 cents* per smoking child for anti-smoking campaigns during the same period. So only *0.002 percent* of the government's revenue was being spent on discouraging children from smoking. Their real point of course was that a lot more could be done to stop this problem and the government is directly making a lot of money that could be used.

Example 3. Robertson (1999; Busch & Robertson, 1993) looked at the effectiveness of a law change in New Zealand (the Domestic Violence Act 1995) that brought in stricter regulations for cases of spouse abuse. Of interest here was the finding that the law specified that the men must undergo counseling and intervention programs to change their practices. It was found that this produced all sorts of loopholes and problems because the law was unclear about the details and so the men and intervention agents did their best under a poorly described situation. For example, it was thought that some men learned from the programs better ways to disguise or hide their abuse, rather than learning to stop it altogether. It was also realized that the men only had to complete a training course and there was no legal requirement that they do well at it, or pass it to a certain standard, so many men just coasted their way through the programs without really learning anything or changing what they did. Finally, a lot of the considerations from focusing on changing the men led to conditions that could put the women involved at greater risk. So, while there were positive benefits compared to not having the law change there at all, significant implementation problems were found.

Changing the World

To finish off I will give just one example of international interventions. These are mostly coordinated through the United Nations or other organizations that help developing countries. They are fraught with a lot of politics, in this case between nations, which can lead to many problems and things going wrong. This is not just true of social issue interventions but also military protection interventions and even aid (Anderson, 2000; Bakewell, 2000; Bellamy, 1997; Diprizio, 1999; Harpham, Burton & Blue, 2001; Herbinger, Crawshaw & Shaw, 1999; Hill, 2000; Omidian & Lipson, 1996; Shawcross, 2000; Weiss, 1999).

Example. There have been brave international attempts to intervene and either restrict or totally ban the use of both land mines and small-arms. Reading the details of these interventions one is impressed with the tenacity of NGOs in pushing for these changes, and the tenacity of the major world powers to resist because they are also the major producers and profiteers from these weapons (Brem & Rutherford, 2001; Goldblat, 1999; Lumpe, 1999). This is so despite the NGOs mostly residing within the same major powers that are resisting.

What I want to get across from these examples is that the intervention process is long and hard and that it mostly is about policy and policy statements. While such policy statements often seem vacuous or abstract, especially if given within a very general speech, they can actually cause things to happen or cause things to start being put in place so things can happen. In an Appendix, Lumpe (1999) shows the large number of speeches and reports needed to get the small arms and light weapons intervention underway. From a speech in April 1998 by the UN Secretary General Kofi Annan based around a UN report of proliferation of small arms, other resolutions, reports, planning briefs, and statements were made which gradually shaped up into two UN Resolutions on 'illicit arms' and 'small arms'. A similar story is seen for land mines (Goldblat, 1999) but with some interesting differences between the two proposals (Bram & Rutherford, 2001). If you want to save the world, it is possible, but be ready for barriers to appear from nowhere.

Chapter 7

Putting it All Together: Negotiation, Mediation, Conflict Resolution & Problem Solving

Two of the most common things that intervention persons will find themselves doing are negotiating with someone to change, and mediating between two persons. The people involved probably have all the skills they need, so there is no need to train new skills. Instead, typically in these cases there are problems of resource conflicts, whether material or social resources (Guerin, 2004), and some settlement or balancing needs to be made. Even psychotherapists do this, with the resource conflict being one between the client and their families or the client and their expectations (history) of resources (Nezu, Nezu & Lombardo, 2003). International mediators in war-torn countries do the same thing on a bigger scale, in trying to make peace between two sides in a conflict. Another intervention situation, hopefully not common, is negotiating with people who have taken hostages or negotiating with "terrorists." Finally, the other common use of negotiation is in setting up any intervention in the first place. No one except police usually has the power to just move in on someone and tell them what to do and how to change what they are doing. Most sorts of intervention requires negotiating with the people involved, their families, communities, the politicians and lawyers in charge, as well as the persons being changed.

The perspective worked from here is that resource scarcity or allocation is at the root of every conflict but the route from resources to everyday practices is not simple (Guerin, 2004). There could be social resources involved such as attention, reputation, status or trust, as well as material resources such as food and shelter (Guerin, 2004). The former are probably the most common, but also the trickiest to analyze and hence resolve. The difficulties in analyzing such resource problems lead people to attribute the cause to a "disposition" of the person or parties involved: "The Serbs are just intransigent" or "My client is being resistant." Better analyses go beyond such descriptive labels and look for the resource problems at stake, even for resolving "personal" problems and crises in psychotherapies. The problem is that such attributions are also useful strategies to influence the other side, so they tend to proliferate and be believed. For example, if one side of a negotiation claims that the other is just pig-headed and intransigent then it (sometimes) forces the other side to appear the opposite and so give concessions: that is, the dispositional attribution *functions* as a strategy in itself so it complicates your negotiations (Guerin, 2004, Chapter 5).

So the issue in this book is that you can teach people all the skills you care to (Chapters 3, 4, & 5) but at some point you usually need to get people to re-allocate resources between them, and you can be a negotiator in this or a mediator.

How People "Normally" Negotiate and Mediate

Everyday Negotiation around the World

Several researchers have looked at negotiation and mediation in communities around the world, and while they have not always measured whether these interventions worked or not, they are instructive to find methods that are useful (Darr, 1999; Gaetz, 1995; Lee, 2000; MacCallum, 1967; Smith, 1996; Zartman & Berman, 1982). They have studied the different types of social relationships listed in Table 3, what is more.

Example 1. McCall, Ngeva and Mbebe (1997), for example, studied a diverse township near Johannesburg in South Africa. The first question they asked was: who were in conflict? They found three clusters: "marital" relationships, including ex-spouses and parents; non-family primary relationships, including friends and neighbors; and secondary relationships, including landlords, contractor-builders, employers, and teachers.

They then asked about the disputes and found 88 of these, which they put into seven categories: *third-party issues*, such as child-rearing, gossip, family interfering, adultery, favoritism, and jealousy; *relationships issues*, including abusive language, lack of trust, bad behavior, over-demanding behavior, and selfishness; *economic issues*, such as credit, unemployment, breaking contracts, exploitation, and use of facilities; *criminal issues*, such as battery, stealing and trespassing; *time/orderliness issues*, including coming late, space, and untidiness; *organizational issues*, such as division of labor, unfair dismissals, truancy, uniforms, and competition; and *other issues*, such as political affiliation, traditions, witchcraft, sexual abuse, and infertility. McCall, Ngeva and Mbebe (1997) next looked at which relationships had which of these issues as problems. Just to give a few examples, neighbors had conflicts over children, untidiness, jealousy, gossip, space, noise, and trespassing. Landlords and tenants had conflicts over rent, authority, children, untidiness, and use of facilities.

McCall, Ngeva and Mbebe (1997) finally looked at who mediated or negotiated these conflicts. They report that the traditional Bantu culture requires that resolution be kept private, within the family or the relationship but there were 55 external forums mentioned. These were put into six categories, of which three will be given in full to show the idea. The others were civic forums, educational forums, and other organizational forums.

Legal forums: police, lawyers, commissioner's court, magistrate's court,
    bureaucratic forums, social workers, psychologists, inspectors, town
    council, Transvaal Provincial Authority, and the Department of
    Education and Training.

Economic forums: Union, training center, manager, bank manager, con
struction manager, shop owner, parent's employer.
Informal/Traditional forums: community elders, yard elderlies, respect
able person, neighbor, friends.

These points give the idea well that there are a range of bodies that can intervene
and mediate or negotiate in a wide variety of circumstances. For most problems,
there are people around who can intervene to help if the conflict cannot be kept
within the groups from which it originated. These can be linked to the type of
relationship (see Table 3 in Chapter 1), as McCall, Ngeva and Mbebe (1997) showed
in their Table 5. To give a few examples from their study, spouses usually relied for
mediation on the Alexandra Civic Organization, social workers, the Commissioner's
court or the police. Teachers and students usually relied on the school Principal, the
School Committee or the Student Representative Council. Friends were reported to
rely on other friends only.

Example 2. James Wall and his colleagues have conducted some impressive
research on common negotiation and mediation strategies used in different Asian
countries (cf. Ma, 1992). They conducted interviews in China, Korea, Malaysia and
Japan about peoples' recent mediations and their social context (Callister & Wall,
1997; Sohn & Wall, 1993; Wall & Callister, 1999; Wall, Stark & Standifer, 2001).
One should not generalize to the whole of these countries from just these data, but
I will give some of the flavor of what was found to help you think about the common
negotiation strategies used.

The highest-ranking strategy for both the Japanese and the Korean samples was
to meet the parties separately and discuss the issues. The highest-ranking strategy
for the Chinese was to educate the persons. The other highest-ranking strategies
across all three groups, with one exception, were to gather information, to argue for
concessions, to listen to the other party, to state the other's point of view, and to
apologize. The one exception was the use of criticism by the Chinese sample, a
strategy that was ranked only 19th and 12th for the Japanese and Korean samples
respectively but ranked third for the Chinese.

While limited in generality, these data should give you the idea of what most
mediations and negotiations are about: meeting the parties separately, finding out
the full stories of what happened, being able to state both points of view and then
discussing the problems, arguing with one or both sides about the issues and trying
to get the sides to concede, and then getting a resolution. The last step takes many
forms, and this is indicative of Wall and colleagues' results, which found many
strategies for concluding a negotiation, but none of which was used all the time—
forgive, call for empathy, relax, threat, drink and eat together.

These are the sorts of steps that all negotiation and mediation go through. There
is a problem with resources, and you must sort out the stories about those resources
and what the problems are while getting both sides to see the other's viewpoint so
they make concessions and find a resolution. These steps form the basis of almost

all negotiations (Wall, 1985) and mediations (Wall & Lynn, 1993) and are worth spelling out in *Intervention Analysis 15*, since we will find the same forms through family mediation, international peace-brokering, and negotiating with terrorists:

Intervention Analysis 15: **Basic Interventions for Negotiation and Mediation**

Find out the full stories of what happened; get any other evidence

Meet the parties separately if appropriate

Be able to state both points of view to them

Discuss the problems of resource allocation and inequities

Find novel solutions and problem-solve

Argue and discuss with one or both sides about the solutions

Try to get the sides to concede to make a resolution

Get a resolution that will commit them to the future

Children's Negotiation

Cunningham and colleagues presented an interesting report of teaching students to use conflict resolution techniques for use in the playgrounds of their schools (Cunningham, Cunningham, Tran, Young, Zacharias & Martorelli, 1998). The aim was to measure aggression in the playgrounds and see whether teaching some students to mediate in conflicts could reduce it.

The researchers got volunteers (with parental permission) who were taken through a 15-hour training program on mediation. The training program used techniques already covered in the earlier chapters of this book: learning the concepts of mediation, modeling the steps of resolving conflict, and role-playing conflict resolutions to rehearse their skills. The results showed success: "Mediation produced an abrupt and sustained reduction in direct observations of physically aggressive playground behavior. Follow-up observations suggest that these effects were evident in the following year" (Cunningham et al., 1998, p. 658). Simple training and implementation produced good reductions in aggression in children's play.

How to Negotiate and Mediate Best

In looking at a few general outlines of how negotiations and mediation take place, or should take place, we must remember that the real issues are always over resources—whether material or social resources. That is, the question is one of power. Often it seems to outsiders that the question being negotiated is about arguments and logic—if only one side would see the rationality of accepting some obviously sound logic and agree to concessions then everything would be alright. What is being negotiated usually, however, are complex resources that are interlinked and nothing is as simple as it seems (cf. De Dreu, Giebels & Van de Vliert, 1998; Tjosvold, 1998).

As an example, one of the main obstacles to easy negotiations is the idea of "face-saving," making sure that one side does not come away looking silly or weak if they give in or concede. While this appears on the surface to be unrelated to negotiation over resources, and may seem a pure vanity for that side of the dispute, we must remember that face or reputation is what keeps larger communities and their resources together (Guerin, 2004) and if one side demands a solution that keeps their face, they are not being trivial. All future relations between that side and any other group, not just the one being negotiated with at present, depend crucially on saving-face in the present. It is not just a matter of self-image or vanity. If I look weak coming out of the present negotiation then all other groups with whom I deal will have an advantage in future negotiations with me. To protect future bargaining and resource allocations I need to save face now.

These sorts of issues, about reputation, trust, bluff and impression management, all make groups and people act as if "irrational" or appear to be blind, crazy or stupid (Guerin, 2004, Chapter 3). But looking at the problem as one of managing all future resource negotiations, acting in these ways is really quite rational-in-the-long-term. And mediators especially need to be very aware of this. This is why negotiations are often lengthy and repetitive, there is a need to argue and gain concessions while maintaining a decent future position for each of the sides. Such social issues are not trivial in comparison to making great logical arguments and devastating criticisms. Negotiation and mediation are about a lot more than rational arguments. You must think about the resources for each side and the future resources for each side all the while, both material resources and also face, status, prestige, reputation and community standing.

With this in mind, we will look at a few summaries of how negotiations and mediations should occur; what are the types of strategies and tactics used (also Bazerman, Curhan, Moore, & Valley, 2000; Druckman, 1977).

Feldman (1985)

Coming from one form of intergroup conflict research, Feldman (1985) provided a clear summary of different strategies for interventions to reduce conflict. This work was directed primarily towards managers in organizations who must solve intergroup and interpersonal disputes, but has wider application as a starting point to make sense of any negotiation and mediation.

Conflict-avoidance. One strategy for conflict is to avoid trying to solve anything. In the strategy Feldman calls *ignoring the conflict*, the conflict is not commented on or referred to at all. This usually leads to worse trouble, but not always. Sometimes there are conflicts that just sort themselves out and directing attention, especially public attention, onto the problem can lead to worse outcomes (Haley, 1973). This depends, of course, on the resources involved being ones that change over time and sort themselves out. Erickson seems to have found that many adolescent problems sort themselves out given time, but this always depended upon the exact social context.

With the *imposing a solution* strategy, a high power third party forces a solution upon the conflicting parties. This is what NATO and the United Nations sometimes attempt when there is deadlock on peace agreements. The difficulty is justifying the intervention by a third-party on two groups who do not want that third-party involved anyway. The justification in these cases has usually been humanitarian, that innocent people are being harmed by the conflict and it is up to the rest of the world to intervene and impose a solution.

The other problem is whether the solution maintains over time. If it is part of the normal legal or social system it might, but a heavy-handed imposition is unlikely to maintain and the conflict will arise again, perhaps in a more covert way and thus be more difficult to stop. Imposing a solution is useful when there is a time limit on the conflict, and something needs to be done quickly. Business organizations often have to make quick financial decisions that engender conflict from all sides but putting off the decision until everyone has agreed would take too long and be worse for everyone concerned.

Conflict-defusion. Conflict-defusion means to gloss over the conflict and do something to play down the fuss. *Smoothing* means to try and reduce the intensity of the conflict so it does not spread, by showing similarities between the sides or convince the sides that the issue is not really that important. This is not so silly a technique as it might sound initially, because conflicts are always going to occur in every social environment, and people can learn to just put up with a little conflict and let it pass, so long as they do not always bear the brunt of it. Nothing is ever going to be completely smooth, so directing attention to every small conflict and facing it can emphasize diversion and be counter productive in other ways.

Appealing to superordinate goals. A similar strategy is to show the sides that there are higher goals that they all share, and that putting up with a little difference or inequality can help both parties in the long run. In the extreme, if a social group is constantly in conflict over every small difference then the group as a whole is not going to work—the government will fail or the organization will go out of business.

Conflict-containment. Conflict-containment confronts the issues but controls the number and types of conflicts confronted. *Representatives* can be used to take the conflict out of the general complaint arena and keep it within strict bounds, although representatives have severe constraints put on them because they must face each of the opposing side, a mediator in some cases, and their own constituents, all of whom place limitations on what they can do. It is also possible to *limit the interaction between the groups* in some way to contain the intensity of the conflict while dealing with the issues. Both these strategies also work then with *bargaining* to make some progress on the particular issues to be tackled. This still tries to contain the conflict by negotiating over specific issues, rather than looking at the whole social context.

Conflict-confrontation. This means to confront the bigger issues, even those that do not seem relevant to the conflict in hand. *Problem-solving* is close to the strategies mentioned by the samples of Wall and colleagues earlier—talk separately to the sides and get information about what is going on, try to present the information of both sides so the other can understand, look for common points of view and possible mutual concessions that would resolve the conflict, and find an end-point that is agreeable to all sides.

Such problem-solving sometimes requires *organizational redesign* as part of the solution, structuring the allocation of resources in new ways so the conflict can not arise again. Once again, maintaining face for the sides so they can deal with the future is very important.

GRIT

A conflict resolution intervention method proposed by Osgood (1962) and developed by Lindskold and colleagues is the *Graduated and Reciprocated Initiative in Tension-reduction* (Lindskold, Betz & Walters, 1986; Lindskold & Collins, 1978; Lindskold, Han & Betz, 1986). This was in reaction to the Arm's Race by America and the USSR in the 1950s and 1960s. At that time, the main thought was that one had to either be tough and make war or else consider that you had lost, and hence it was said by patriotic Americans that they would "rather be dead than red." Osgood put forward one strategy for reducing conflict levels without weakness.

In the GRIT strategy, one side unilaterally announces that they are working towards conciliation but remain capable of retaliation (so as not to appear weak and lose face and resources). That side carries out some conciliatory actions or events, but if the other side exploits this they retaliate. But unlike a tit-for-tat strategy (Axelrod, 1984), GRIT does not mechanically match what the other side does but continues to press for conciliation (Lindskold & Collins, 1978).

The research of Lindskold and colleagues found that a formalized announcement by the conciliatory side was required by this strategy. The first side announces what it is going to do, including the use of retaliation for exploitation, and then proceeds to carry out the first conciliatory actions.

Pruitt (1995)

Dean Pruitt (1995) looked at a common principle in negotiations which he refers to as "firm flexibility." Both these components are required, and finding the right mixture of being firm and being flexible is the important part. If you are totally firm then no negotiation is likely to eventuate. If you are too flexible then the other side will take advantage and you will not get a good deal: you will also not be likely to interact with that side again and that is probably against *their* interest as well as yours. It must be remembered that if the negotiation is a one-off occurrence then you can exploit the other side for all you can get, but typically, you want to keep relations good with the other side so you can exchange in the future.

Pruitt suggested six tactics of negotiation that encompass the idea of firm flexibility:

1. Concede but only to a point
2. Hold firm to one's position while seeking a way to compensate the other

3. Hold firm on more important issues while conceding on less important issues
4. Hold firm on the interests underlying one's position while seeking novel ways to achieve these interests
5. Hold firm on more important interests while abandoning less important interests
6. Hold firm if one's interests seem stronger than those of the other party and yield if the other's interests seem stronger.

The use of "interests" here means the same as what I have meant by "allocation of resources," whether the conflict is about material water resources in the Middle-East (Drake, 1996) or more complex social resources in psychotherapies such as identities and image management (Guerin, 2004; Nezu, Nezu & Lombardo, 2003). The sixth tactic means what I have said above about protecting continuing relationships by not going all out in every negotiation to get the most from the other side.

Negotiation Maneuvers

Wall (1985) presents some nice summaries of the negotiation strategies, tactics and maneuvers. For example, there are three major maneuvers: increase your strength, reduce the other side's strength, and alter the relationships of strength. To increase one's strength one might make deals with third parties, put disclaimers on what the others are arguing, or develop new abilities and forces. To reduce the other's strength you might disrupt their relationships with third parties, reduce the trust between the other and their constituency, or lower their status. To alter the relationships of strength, you could focus on the other's weakest point, wait until a vulnerable moment, or change the negotiation to other areas of strength that favor you over them.

Many of these maneuvers are sneaky and are for use in anarchy and war, and we must be aware again of severing too much of the relationship with the other side since you will usually need to continue some sort of relationship with them in the future.

With respect to negotiation tactics, Wall (1985) breaks these down into irrational versus rational tactics, and the latter down into debating tactics and bargaining tactics (logic versus resource allocation). Bargaining is further broken into three types:

Aggressive tactics: threat and coercion
Nonaggressive tactics: conciliation and reward
Posturing tactics: tough, soft and neutral

For anyone interested in the more specifics of these categories, pages 52ff has tables of more detailed tactics (also cf. Lawler & Ford, 1995). For example, under threat tactics, there are 11 tactics listed:

ask for commitment
use 'trip wire'
show force in side area
use overkill in one negotiation facet
claim opponent abuse to hint retaliation
claim opponent abuse and specify retaliation
claim opponent irrationality and hint retaliation
hint about declining patience
make claims about tension production
make claims of opponent's deliberate misunderstanding
claim opponent is dragging feet

In any negotiation you can find elements of these, although threats will be lessened if the parties need to remain friendly and trusting afterwards. If you follow any of the major international conflicts and their negotiations you will find these tactics present. At present, as I write this, the Serbs and Albanian Serbs are negotiating with international mediators but the Serbs are being very threatening, coercive, nonconciliatory, and are acting tough. It is likely that within hours of my writing this, NATO forces will begin bombing Serb positions in and around Kosovo.

Training Negotiation as a Social Skill

Some studies have intervened to train negotiation as a social skill. To do this we break it down into component skills and train them individually (Hazel, Schumaker, Sherman, & Sheldon-Wildgen, 1981; Quinn, Sherman, Sheldon, Quinn & Harchik, 1992). The component behaviors used by the last-named authors were these, in their model that also included responding to destructive criticism (see Chapter 5):

Nonverbal Components
    face the other person during negotiation
    keep eye-contact with the other person
    keep a neutral facial expression
    keep a straight posture
Specific Verbal Components
    ask if they can talk to the person
    state what they want
    give a reason for what they want
    if answer is negative, ask for a solution
    if answer is negative, propose a compromise solution
    thank the person
General Verbal Components
    maintain a normal voice tone
    do not interrupt when other person is talking

These are some component behaviors to train negotiation skills in people who lack such skills, using the intervention methods from Chapter 3 to 5. They are obviously not the complete set of negotiation behaviors but they provide a generic basis.

Quinn, Sherman, Sheldon, Quinn and Harchik (1992) made videotapes of actors performing such component behaviors well or poorly in a realistic setting and asked judges to rate how well they handled the situation, how pleasant was the interaction, how acceptable was their behavior, how much they would like to respond to such a person, and how likely they would respond in this way to the person. In all cases they found the most positive ratings on these questions for the videos with all components performed well, the lowest ratings on videos with all the components performed poorly, and middling ratings when only some of the components were performed poorly.

The problem with training negotiation as a social skill is that the skills needed will change depending upon the types of social relationships between the parties (Table 3 of Chapter 1). Mediating in a close and remote community is very different from mediation between strangers in a western neighborhood. More will be said of this at the end of the chapter, but be critical of the sorts of studies I have reported which assume one best way to negotiate and base it entirely on what works with western forms of social relationships.

Mediation

Mediation involves a person or group extraneous to the conflict, although such persons or groups must have some involvement or they would not be mediating. An arbitrator has some power to make a decision about the conflict whereas a mediator tries to solve the problem between the two (or more) sides (Wall, Stark & Standifer, 2001).

Most of the strategies of mediation are similar to those given above for negotiation—to gather information, present the sides of the arguments, persuade the sides to make concessions, keep the peace while this is occurring, and discover solutions that neither side has considered (Wall, 1981, 1993). Wall (1981) identified over 100 techniques that mediators can use to carry out these points.

The independence of the mediator allows new properties not found with negotiation, so long as the mediator is thought to be independent (Richmond, 1998). One strategy for sides in a dispute is to claim that the mediator is favoring the other side, and thereby gain concessions. Of course, this can backfire and lead to the breakdown of all talk. Being independent means that the mediator can stand back from the history of conflict and find outcomes not previously tried. Perhaps the greatest benefit of the mediator's independence is concerned with judging that both sides can keep face and reputation for their future interactions. When sides are negotiating face-to-face they cannot afford to "drop their guard" for a moment; with a mediator they can have unilateral talks and be more frank about the possible outcomes to which they would agree. This is the origin of the "shuttle diplomacy" of international negotiations.

Richmond (1998) points out some problems for mediators, first, that they can be used by the disputants. Mediators need to be aware of this. Using mediators can increase delays, which might be to the advantage of one side, mediators can give respectability to the sides which might be to their advantage, or one side might see the mediator as a chance to advertise their position and thereby gain more allies and force their demands.

One other property of mediation is that powerless victims of the dispute can have an advocate. Two key examples of this are the innocent refugees caught in the middle of a conflict between two countries or ethnic groups, and children caught in the middle of a dispute within a family, especially a divorce between the parents (Roberts, 1997). Not only can a mediator work to resolve the conflict but they can protect the innocent victims and protect the future interests of those victims, which neither side would do alone.

Negotiation and Mediation between Individuals: The Worlds of Therapy

We saw at the start of this chapter a study looking at everyday negotiation and mediation mainly between individuals (McCall, Ngeva & Mbebe, 1997). Those examples were from communities with many close ties and this is reflected in the number of disputes going to family and elders for resolution, although there were many other forums listed for disputes between non-family members (see earlier for these). When we get to fully westernized communities (see the infamous Table 3 of Chapter 1), a whole range of strangers are brought in to resolve conflicts and problems, and these were outlined in Chapter 2–psychiatrists, psychologists, social workers, therapists, consultants, lawyers, ombudsmen, and tribunals.

Most of these disputes look like any other mediation or negotiation–there are resource inequalities or "perceived" (verbal, Chapter 5) inequalities and the parties need to problem solve, find out what is really happening, and then come up with compromises for the resources (see *Intervention Analysis 15*). For example, a lot of couples therapy in western countries is about having the couple see what each other is giving or contributing and then get the other to accept or cope with this (Hayes, Jacobson, Follette & Dougher, 1994), or if resources are a true source of conflict then change the resourcs to suit. This could mean giving the persons new skills (Chapters 3 and 4) to obtain the resources needed (Nezu, Nezu & Lombardo, 2003). If one party is not getting what they want then they and the other might be taught some communication skills or some social skills, depending upon the context. They might be taught other skills such as employment skills, life skills or health skills, to reduce stress or local problems.

A lot of this is fairly straightforward and some simple systems such as motivation interviewing (Miller & Rollnick, 1991) give fairly simple problem solving and advice-giving as their "therapy" and in a lot of cases this is enough. For many western couples and families, time management is the problem since western societies are built around fairly intensive time scheduling of jobs and life. Most

***Intervention Analysis 16*: Three Problem Cases for Negotiation and Mediation between Individuals**

1. Cases in which a larger extended families or communities are inherently involved (see Chapter 6)

2. Cases in which there is a long history of problems which might have started from simple strategic adjustments to a bad situation but which has now become entrenched

3. Cases for which the resources in conflict are:

   symbolic

   religious

   dealing with status

   concerning reputation

   ritual

western "therapies" do these steps of negotiation but they are often disguised behind a whole lot of other things. There are also three cases that are trickier.

There are three other cases, then, in which things are more difficult to deal with. First, there are resource problems between individuals that need a larger extended family or community to change and not just the individuals involved. This was mentioned in Chapter 2 and dealt with a bit more in Chapter 6, at least to the extent of giving you some skills to learn for this sort of work. Here the resource conflicts spread out through many people and usually through a longer history. They need time to work through all this. Negotiation and mediation are very different here than between strangers.

The second case is in which a situation has gone on for a long time and while the original problem might have been simple, the chronic nature itself now leads to conflict. I am thinking here of cases such as chronic "mental illness", poverty, drug use or unemployment. These cases usually need a broader approach since so many other people (originally irrelevant to the problem situation) are now involved and since so many situations are now involved. The sorts of interventions that can be tried are given in Chapter 4 (*"Training Decision Making, "Life" Skills and Changing Whole Systems"*).

The third problem case concerns situations in which the "resources" being negotiated or mediated are ones that we call symbolic, religious, status, reputation, or ritual (Guerin, 2004). For example, an adolescent girl has to maintain a certain image to get status or reputation amongst peers (and all that goes with that in terms of more direct resources, Guerin, 2004), but her parents want her to have another image because of their concerns. A therapist or other intervention agent (social worker, priest) working with this family is really mediating resources as we saw in *Intervention Analysis 15* but the resources are generalized social resources and have all the difficult properties of being hidden, having effects over many people, coming into audience conflicts, etc. (Guerin, 2001c, d, 2004). Much of this is to do with how one images or talks about these abstract (but very real in consequences) resources of status, reputation, etc., so the methods of Chapter 5 become important.

Using the social properties of such generalized consequences (Table 4 and Analysis 3 of Guerin, 2004) into account, we need to work through the following procedures for interventions: change the resource balance knowing that different audiences are having an influence; take seriously the concerns even though they are spread out in consequences and cannot be seen or touched; work on status repair or image management; involve all audiences if possible; look seriously at what would happen if things changed; if things are changed make sure there are more immediate outcomes to offset the "potentially available" outcomes 'promised' by generalized consequences; and take any irrational behaviors seriously as having a hidden social pressure from another audience not present.

More analysis is needed of these cases, but once the social contexts are understood, any 'strange' aspects of therapy can be seen as negotiation or mediation of generalized exchanges that are difficult to see in the immediate situation but which are very real in their consequences.

Negotiation and Mediation in International Conflicts

Conflict reduction methods have a long history in solving international problems through non-military intervention (Bercovitch & Schneider, 2000; Kriesberg, 1997; Lederach, 1997; Zartman & Rasmussen, 1997). National groups typically have forms of government or central control that can adjudicate disputes and settle things. Early settling of countries, however, show the anarchy of conflicts (e. g., Brown, 1994; Waller, 1988). The international scene, however, is basically anarchic with little real control by one country over another (Kaplan, 1996). There are treaties and United Nations initiatives, but international law prohibits one country intervening on another except in extreme conditions such as a humanitarian disaster (Bellamy, 1997). A lot of this is interesting but all I can do here is to review just a few facets of how countries negotiate and the conflicts and cooperations that arise (Spanier, 1972).

Dixon (1996) reviewed some of the third-party intervention techniques both for preventing an international dispute from escalating and for bringing about a peaceful settlement. Of the major techniques some were ones we have already seen– communication, mediation, observation, intervention, adjudication– and other were particular to international affairs–public appeals and humanitarian aid. He also carried out analyses on the results of 688 interstate disputes and found that mediation to either open or maintain communications between the countries was the most effective technique, although all techniques had some successes.

Given the anarchy at the level of relations between countries, how can there be more cooperation? One solution we have already seen in looking at other negotiations—that countries rely on each other in the long term for trade, resources, and protection against others. They need to negotiate and cooperate to face the future—no country can go it alone. Fearon (1998), however, points out how facing the future is a two-edged sword. He argues for a two-step model in which long-term cooperation controls the enforcement of deals and treaties, but because there are long-term consequences which might be difficult to change, this inhibits cooperation in deciding exactly what each country wants to commit to. If they get it wrong it can have poor long-term effects. So Fearon argues for a difference between negotiating for the particular bargain or deal, and negotiating for enforcing that deal afterwards.

A more specific example of international conflict resolution has been presented by Kelman (1983, 1997, 1998; cf. Doob, 1970; Hubbard, 1999; Knox, 1994). Kelman's idea is to work at an individual level of intervention but think long-term solutions. He argues that settlement of a conflict is not the goal but finding long-term ways of accommodating the parties to cooperative living:

> An important implication of the intersocietal view of conflict is that negotiations and third-party efforts should ideally be directed not merely to a *settlement* of the conflict in the form of a brokered political agreement, but to its *resolution*. Conflict resolution in this deeper and more lasting sense implies arrangements and accommodations that emerge out of the interaction between representatives of the parties themselves, that address the basic needs of both parties, and to which the parties are committed. (Kelman, 1998, p. 10)

It can be argued, of course, that unless the larger political solutions are there the "basic needs" will not be available to one or other party, and that the word "deeper" merely begs this question, but the overall aim is commendable because it does not try to be the complete solution. Kelman's work is done outside of any formal peace negotiations or peace deals, and covers ground that many political solutions leave in the air—how to guarantee some longer lasting conflict reduction.

To make this happen, Kelman has run workshops for many years, mostly concentrating on Middle East conflicts but also giving some consideration to Cyprus and other conflict areas. The workshops involve high-ranking people from both sides of a dispute but ones who are not there in any official capacity at all. In the best case, these people would be politically influential or perhaps younger people who are likely to become influential in future years. There are third parties present to facilitate but who do not interfere. The workshops run for three or four days.

One of the key features of these workshops is that it is entirely confidential and nothing can be cited outside of the forum. No notes are taken and there is no audience or publicity. There is an attempt to make this a safe place to air ideas and views counter to the norms of each side. The two parties talk to each other rather than to the third-party, and the focus is problem-solving rather than competition or debate. There is nothing binding decided during the workshops and no commitments are made. What is hoped for is that the parties learn about the other's view and transfer that knowledge back into their own society in many little ways in the future. The people who have attended workshops can be thought of as seeds put back into their own societies that will hopefully grow later into something useful. Some might be involved in the more formal political negotiations and they might have an impact more immediately.

We can see some of the same intervention techniques in Kelman's workshops as for the other negotiation and mediations strategies dealt with here, but the main differences are in running the workshops in parallel to the formal negotiations, in keeping complete confidentiality, and in thinking mostly of the long-term outcomes rather than the immediate settlement of the current conflict crisis. Each of these differences is important, and the same could be tried for other forms of conflict management, perhaps especially for organizational and family conflicts.

With more conflicts requiring mediation by the United Nations or individual countries, examples of negotiations can be found in both journals and bookstores. An example of an account of the peace efforts in Bosnia-Herzegovina from 1992 to 1995 is in Beriker Atiyas (1995), while Owen (1995) is a popular book account of David Owen's major role in the early part of those talks.

Negotiation and Mediation with Terrorists and Hostage-Takers

There are only a few research based accounts of interventions with hostage-takers or "terrorists." In both cases a person or a group has taken people hostage and threatened to kill or hurt them unless something is done—a ransom is given, political prisoners released or some other demand met. Many of the accounts are probably very good but not based on systematic research; they are accounts of what a hostage mediator has done and what seemed to work. These should by no means be discounted, especially if the person has a long history of mediating with hostage-takers, but their explanations are not reliable even if what they did worked consistently. I can ride a bike but not tell you how I did it. There is also a problem that research is difficult to carry out, case-controls are needed rather than control groups, and so these reports are often all there is for groups to train new mediators. The final problem is that many techniques of intervention are not published but written in police training manuals or unpublished special government department reports that are difficult to get hold of to read. So the literature is probably flawed, but it is all we have.

To give the flavor, without the detail or the final answers, I will rely on just two sources. The first is on negotiating with hostage-takers by two research psychologists and the other is about re-examining the evidence at a policy level for negotiating with terrorists. We must also note somewhere here that the term "terrorist" is a loaded one—one person's terrorist is another person's savior or hero. Most "terrorist" groups claim that worse injury is being done to the people they are attempting to save and the small number of deaths or injuries is justified in the longer term since other interventions are not working.

I shall not consider such ethical issues further, because case-by-case details would be required and there probably is no answer anyway. What is very relevant, however, is that thinking of "terrorists" as crazy or madmen, giving dispositional attributions for them, is counter-productive to mediating or negotiating. If one can see where the "terrorist" is coming from that will help the intervention, whether or not what is being done is justified in the long-term. The main analysis to make sense, therefore, is game theory, in the way we saw for police interrogations in Chapter 5 (Douglas & Mars, 2003; Guerin, 2004; Leo, 1996). We need to know the resources conflicts driving the trouble. One does not have to agree with the solution taken, but it will help your understanding and negotiations.

Interventions in Hostage Situations

The situation of negotiating with a hostage-taker is built on all the techniques dealt within this chapter, with the additions of safety considerations for the hostages, the complex and often unknown social context of the situation, and the other regard that giving in to all demands is likely to encourage others to also take hostages in similar situations (but see Clutterbuck below). The procedures given by Miron and Goldstein (1979) reflect this, with safety given first, gathering information next, the negotiator next, and followed by the different strategies used to contain such situations. Except for the safety concerns, the rest follows the suggestions of Wall and others above.

The overall strategy for negotiation is one of problem-solving and compromise, according to Miron and Goldstein. Being too forceful or too soft backfires. The general conditions to set, then, is one of solving a problem, not the problem of shooting people but the problem that caused the situation in the first place. *The overall aim is to get the hostage-taker to release the hostages so that the problem can then be worked on properly.* In this way, future concessions can be made for the final problem-solving even though nothing is settled on the spot.

Some other general conditions are interesting. They recommend that a low rank be used for police negotiating. This emphasizes a general condition that all decisions must appear to be made at a higher level than the negotiator, even if they are not. This gives the negotiator a lever that they must check everything with the authority, thus giving some delays and ways of stalling for time. Also, access should be limited and people close by clearly identifiable in case shooting begins or something happens quickly. Demands should be stalled or politely refused, and the situation kept in the same location. There should be no show of force designed to intimidate the person into submission—they point out how easily this backfires when the person realizes that they have nothing to lose. *Intervention Analysis 17* gives some more of the specific strategies recommended by Miron and Goldstein (1979).

Miron and Goldstein (1979) also list different intervention methods to *calm the hostage-taker*, to *build rapport*, to *gather information*, and to *persuade the hostage-taker*.

> ***Intervention Analysis 17*: Strategies for Intervening with Hostage-takers**
>
> 1. Contain and stabilize the situation; do not force events or rush anything; calm them down as possible
>
> 2. Establish a problem-solving atmosphere; emphasizing that you are there to help them work through the problem; find alternative (peaceful) solutions; develop rapport; focus upon fighting the problem rather than each other; all the time stalling so that the anxiety or intensity reduces; gather as much information as possible
>
> 3. Develop an atmosphere of compromise; give and take; this is the same as the "firm flexibility" we saw earlier from Pruitt (1995)
>
> 4. Avoid the use of force or coercion
>
> 5. Avoid being too soft; do not worry about being liked
>
> 6. Match the negotiation to what you know about the hostage-taker and the situation; criminals more likely to bargain and compromise; psychotics less likely; with psychotics reflect feelings and restate content and show you are tracking the person; the terrorist is a mixture of these
>
> 7. Plan for force but use only in the last resort
>
> Drawn from Miron and Goldstein (1979)

The other useful suggestions made by Miron and Goldstein (1979) are about training people (police mainly) to carry out such negotiations (in their Chapter 8). These are a mixture of all the techniques we have seen so far in this book: structured situations where there is presentation of material containing the steps and procedures; many opportunities for modeling and role-playing so the trainees can learn and rehearse; reinforcement for good work; training of transfer (generalization) to the real situation; and feedback. They also have a component for dealing with trainees who are resisting the procedures as taught. These will be, for example, seasoned police officers who believe they already know how to negotiate and resist the steps trained. None of this should be new or magical for diligent readers of this book.

An interesting exercise for the reader at this point would be to look at the steps I have listed from Miron and Goldstein (1979) and see if you can design a training program for them. Perhaps try a role-play with a friend. I do this as an exercise in my teaching classes; in groups of four with one person a hostage, one the hostage-taker, one as the negotiator, and the other an observer who can learn and comment to the others. Try this before looking up Chapter 8 of Miron and Goldstein's book, where they outline how they run their training programs. Their long experience brings out points and issues that you might not think of initially. Trying to do it would be great training for you.

Interventions with Terrorists

Clutterbuck (1992; also Bolz, Dudonis & Schulz, 2001) presents a masterly overview of the terrorist attacks and hostage taking since the 1960s. Most importantly, attention is given to the responses by governments and other concerned parties and the consequences of those responses. For example, he recommends against a complete "no negotiation" stance, since this breaks off dialogue and information gathering and can lead to the terrorists having nothing to lose. The negotiations do not have to follow the demands made, however, and some examples are given of trading political demands such as releasing prisoners for publicity or money instead. The evidence seems to be that giving in to demands leads to further attacks, although this pattern has not always occurred.

There are many dilemmas in negotiating with terrorists. For example, it is unethical to prohibit families and corporations from trying to pay ransoms for their loved ones or employees even if this interferes with future negotiations with future terrorists. Companies cannot afford to sit back and watch an employee be killed because of the effect this would have on the rest of the company staff in the future.

Details of handling terrorist crises (p. 280ff in Clutterbuck, 1992) are remarkably similar to the hostage-taking negotiations given above, except for a greater concentration of force. Interestingly, Clutterbuck writes that the British personnel almost always include a psychiatrist. Compare the following to what was taken from Miron and Goldstein earlier:

> ...the British police have developed a highly skilled team of police negotiators. These officers are experts in keeping terrorists or criminals talking—and hoping. They are of middle rank, so that they can avoid being rushed into decisions ('I will have to refer that to my boss'), and frequently succeed in establishing a cordial working relationship with the terrorist negotiator. This, however distasteful to them, can be an important factor in saving the lives of the hostages.
> (Clutterbuck, 1992, p. 282)

> Dutch experience has been that the first two days of a siege are highly dangerous, when terrorists are volatile and excitable, and liable to use violence if they feel thwarted. The aim of crisis management during the next three to five days is to allow a fragile equilibrium to develop between terrorists and hostages and also between terrorists and negotiators.
> (Clutterbuck, 1992, p. 283)

Specific problems occur with terrorists that can hamper negotiations:

One of the biggest problems experienced by the Dutch has been to prevent the media from prejudicing the success of siege and rescue operations. Though many journalists do have some conscience about putting Dutch hostages' lives at risk, others–especially some foreign journalists–have no such scruples, and will stop at nothing to get the sensational stories they want. The police normally operate two concentric cordons, the outer one admitting residents only and the inner one admitting no unauthorized persons at all. There is, however, no Dutch law to prevent a resident from accepting huge fees for the use of his house and its windows, and the media are willing to spend unlimited money to get round the police controls. (Clutterbuck, 1992, p. 283)

In all, interventions with hostage-takers and terrorists are fraught with difficulties. The main idea is to calm them down and keep a dialogue going, while stalling on any decisions and negotiating the person to another demand. International agreements over terrorists have not been successful (Clutterbuck, 1992) because loopholes have always been used to break these agreements when the crunch comes. Remaining firm against demands has worked but only with some flexibility in shifting to other lesser demands. The best intervention has been preparing ahead of time for such events and having a chain of command and procedures to follow (Clutterbuck, 1992). Just having such precautions in place has deterred some would-be hostage-takers and terrorists.

Ethical and Cultural Concerns with Negotiation

We have already considered Wall's research showing different negotiation strategies between Japanese, Korean and Chinese groups, as well as differences between rural and urban living persons (e. g., Arunachalam, Chan & Wall, 1998; Callister & Wall, 1997; Goldman, 1994). Among smaller groups and communities (the 3rd type in Table 3 of Chapter 1), the strategies will also change because we have seen that negotiation cannot be separated from the social and community organization, and from the resource allocation procedures of those groups (Kowalsky, Verhoef, Thurston & Rutherford, 1996; Montville, 1991; Nader, 1995). Negotiation does not work by just making good arguments like a debate, but requires the social organization to be flexible and to adapt. Interventions are adjustments to social relationships, we must remember (from Chapter 1).

The main cultural consideration in negotiating has already been said: that negotiation is about intervening in a social or community organization. One cannot expect a group to adapt to arguments when there are outstanding obligations and consequences throughout the entire population to be considered. Racing into negotiations with the main goal being to find the point at which the group will concede is not what it is all about. Negotiation should be about finding out how the other side functions and organizes itself, where its resource allocations flow, and how there might be other ways of doing this that could benefit both sides. This needs to be done slowly and carefully or the effects could be felt for decades or centuries to come (Kaplan, 1993; Kowalsky, Verhoef, Thurston & Rutherford, 1996; Orange, 1987; Waitangi Tribunal, 1988, 1998a, b; Ward, 1993; Williams, 1969).

This point was given a new twist by Nader (1995) who argued that the whole idea of negotiation is one that favors the more powerful groups, and that it has been promoted particularly by the United States of America in poorer countries for this reason—to have a measure of control over them. Negotiation is talked about as the *only* method of resolving conflict although many other methods can be used if the social organization is utilized. But Nader's point is that imposing the negotiation procedure imposes a change of social organization unwittingly on the smaller groups, and it can only be done if there is powerful pressure—that is, hegemony or imperialism.

I referred to this earlier when pointing out that the key social skills for negotiation were very much based on western negotiation, as defined by the properties in Table 3 of Chapter 1. They involve relative strangers who have little in relationship beyond the specific dispute. This means that concessions and compromise tend to focus on the conflict situation itself because there might not be much in common beyond that.

When dealing with close communities and extended families on the other hand, probably the majority of personkind, the obligations and consequences (social properties) are very different. This is why Nader has argued that the standard forms of negotiation are not standard, but their being imposed on other groups puts the imposer at a distinct advantage in the negotiation. This in turn goes back to the point I made in Chapter 1 that it is often the conditions for setting up an intervention that really contains the main force of the intervention. In this case, being able to impose your form of negotiation on others, and making it appear to be the only form of negotiation, is to have already won the competition.

Example. An example of intercultural mediation is found summarized in Parker and King (1987). Anthropologist Parker was doing fieldwork on the Pacific island of Truk, having learned the language and set her work up. It was suddenly announced that the airport which had been built by the Japanese and more recently run by the American Military was to be expanded, and this included dredging fishing areas up to 40 feet and cutting off access to several commonly used beaches. It also meant closing the one spot where people could urinate and not cause public health problems. Because she was present and spoke the language, Parker became involved in mediation between the people and the US Government (who had not consulted the people at all).

King (Parker's husband) was appointed to the Trust Territory to work on preserving the culturally significant sites. He tried to point out to the US the issues and problems that were brewing over the destruction of fishing grounds and sacred areas, but that resulted in an effort to have him removed from the position. But after much negotiation he remained and was given the job of meditating between the locals and the government. Parker had no official duties but continued to help mediate with her knowledge of the language and people.

We next have a statement about the negotiation and mediation that is very typical and with themes that have recurred through this chapter (*Intervention Analysis 15*):

> Clearly, the first step was to get the villagers to present their concerns in a way that the government could easily understand. Their deeply felt, but not very systematically expressed, outrage over what they believed the project would do to them had to be developed into a bill of particulars that could serve as a basis for negotiation. The government knew what it wanted: the airport. For an amicable solution to the conflict, the villagers' objections had to be broken down into a list of wants that could perhaps be met. To avoid charges by the government that the villagers were adding to their list of grievances as the negotiations proceeded, the list had to be as comprehensive as possible at the outset.
> (Parker & King, 1987, p. 164)

The interesting thing here, linking cultural specific conditions to what Nader (1995) was arguing, is that the manner of getting these grievances and list of wants was very different for different groups of the villagers. Some had councils of senior people who did the work; some had meetings of the whole village at which Parker and King were in attendance; and some had full meetings but (politely) excluded the anthropologists. The western model of negotiation, where parties are forced to sit around a table on opposite sides and contest points, does not always need to be followed. Different methods can even be used within a negotiation. It all depended on the social relationships and social organizations of these different groups.

King found himself in the middle of the conflict, having to tell the government that certain of their suggestions would not be acceptable to the people, and having to tell the people that some of their wants would not get through the government's committees. This part, like most negotiations, took time. The same occurs in international negotiations and is called "shuttle diplomacy," and the authors even write that "King shuttled back and forth every few weeks" (p. 164).

In the end, with shuttling mediation, solutions were found for each of the problems caused by building up the airport. For example, a new sewerage system was to be installed so public health could be maintained; fishing and agricultural cooperatives were established. Parker and King also give a very good summary of the issues involved in the post-negotiation settling down. As I have stressed, working negotiations into the longer term settlement is very important, or else the same conflicts will appear again with more and more resentment as time goes by. This is not always necessary for negotiations between strangers in western contexts, but is almost always required otherwise.

Parker and King report that the villagers were in general satisfied, although there was resentment still about the whole affair, and how it was unilaterally planned to go ahead with absolutely no consultation at all. They write that the success will probably depend upon how well the fishing and agricultural cooperatives work out; if they fail then the villagers will become resentful again about the whole business.

The government people are of course happy to have the airport extended, but some claimed to Parker and King that it was too costly with all the economic deals and compensations. Others said that without such a settlement the eventual end would have been costly litigation brought by the villagers that the government would have lost, and that would have entailed much higher compensation figures.

This is a good example of the common negotiation principles being adapted to specific social context. In particular, the manner of consultation (not initially of course!) proceeded in the manner to which the people were accustomed. The two anthropologists were well suited to this task as cultural brokers because they were open to observation of what was happening, and had already learned a lot about the life of the villagers by spending a great deal of time with them and speaking their language. Having the trust of both the villagers and the government, and maintaining that, helped enormously. Notice that trust from the government (the US Navy) side was just as important as the trust from the villagers; King wrote that the government even tried to throw him out of the job at one point, but he managed to resolve that.

A final comment about negotiations with close communities. A common situation for negotiation is with researchers who are working in a community. To gain access to peoples' lives and have them tell you about themselves can be just as important and intrusive as building an extension to an airport. Research also needs to be carefully negotiated and follow the organization of the communities who are being approached to participate. This means that a lot of "indigenous" research has become tied to negotiating with the people involved, since the intrusiveness must be worked out. Most versions of this have similar negotiating and mediating principles to those we have seen in this chapter and the last (Durie, 1994; Fundación Sabiduría Indígena & Kothari, 1997; García & Zea, 1997; Kowalsky, Verhoef, Thurston & Rutherford, 1996; Lichtenstein, Lopez, Glasgow, Gilbert-McRae & Hall, 1996; Manderson, Kelaher, Williams & Shannon, 1998; Marin, 1993; Murchie, 1984; Smith, 1999).

Conclusions

There is a simple story with negotiation and mediation. The main goals are to get the parties communicating in a peaceful way, get them to state their positions in a way that the other party can at least understand, have them find new solutions to their problems, and work out a solution to implement. If one negotiating side does not intend any further interaction with the other side then their goal can be to do all this so as to maximize their own gains and reduce their concessions. In almost all instances, however, future interaction will be required so long-term peace must be built into the negotiation situation. The case of Maori in New Zealand is instructive. After a Treaty was pushed through by the colonials in 1840 and then continually broken, to allow land to be bought by colonizers, this has now been brought back to the negotiation and arbitration table 150 years later as a fresh debate to solve the long-term resolutions that the colonialists did not think about.

These are the basic processes of negotiation and mediation, and the changes you must make depend upon the local conditions and social contexts. Negotiating peace in the Balkans is extremely similar in the principles to mediating between a Union and an employer, but there are many on-the-ground differences because of the social histories, the resources involved, and the future consequences of any resolution.

To intervene with negotiation or mediation you need to keep these main principles in mind while struggling to understand the conditions that apply to each side of the dispute. That is where all negotiators start from, and their success or not depends upon how well they learn the local conditions (Zartman & Berman, 1982). You must join the principles of this chapter with a thorough social analysis of the contexts as outlined at the start of this book (and more in Guerin, 2004).

Chapter 8

Family Planning Interventions: An Extended Example

One of the longest-running community intervention campaigns is that of family planning. Family planning aims to intervene to have people think about and actively decide whether, how, and when they have children. The most common aim is to reduce the number of children in over-populated areas of the world by planning and contraception, rather than parents having pregnancy after pregnancy.

I have included a chapter on this topic for two reasons. First, the interventions used in family planning cover a wide range of types, of the sorts we have seen in this book. Second, this area has two special features of its own that would be very useful for other areas of intervention to adapt: acceptability of interventions, and program effort. These have not been coved in the book but I would like to see them used more widely. Few intervention agents will have read about them except those in the family planning literature.

Family planning interventions have been happening for many years across many countries with much success. While the message they are selling has many obvious benefits, unlike trying to sell the latest fashions, they have been successful in thinking through many of the problems and solutions we have found with the interventions dealt with in this book. Another reason for considering such interventions in more detail is that they cover a broad spectrum of interventions from individual training of contraceptive techniques or counselling to large community campaigns with media presentation to changing laws and policies of governments. Anyone interested in interventions should look at the history and details of family planning interventions (Ross & Frankenberg, 1993, and Cuca and Pierce, 1977, are good places to start). There is a considerable amount of social science input already (Freedman, 1987) but more would be useful.

There are also two additional elements emphasized in family planning interventions that are not found in other intervention areas but which those other areas would do well to emulate: First, checking the acceptability of intervention methods before beginning the intervention; and second, measuring "program efforts" as a key indicator. While traditional family planning studies have been on large groups of people and looking at demographic level changes, there has been a lot of research in the last twenty years on micro- or individual-level effects of family planning campaigns.

Measuring Acceptability of Family Planning Interventions

A broad scheme for introducing contraceptives is given by Simmons et al. (1997). As part of this they suggest the need for field trials and acceptability research before introducing any new methods of birth control. Just because medical personnel know that a new method is superior does not mean that doctors and clients will accept it, that it will be properly catered for in terms of service delivery and after-care, and that it will replace older methods. An example comes from a study by Stash (1999), in which families from Nepal were interviewed and many factors that influenced their contraceptive use were found. Poor families, for example, were not just concerned about the cost of birth control; they were also very concerned about any possible health side-effects that often result from contraceptive use, because they could not afford to get sick even for a short while. Although the medical side-effects of new birth control methods might seem small for us, perhaps a half-day of feeling sick, the poorer people in that study said they could not afford such sickness if they were to meet their daily needs.

Acceptability studies help ascertain these sorts of considerations, and collaboration with clients is a large component of the Simmons et al. (1997) model of intervention. Such a model is useful for all intervention agents to read, regardless of the area of intervention.

New methods of contraception are now typically having their acceptability tested before going on the market. For example, a few published reports exist of acceptability testing of the NORPLANT® contraceptive (Darney et al., 1990; Ping et al., 1997; Zimmerman et a., 1990). Here are other examples.

Example 1. Severy (1999) gives a good account of acceptability trials conducted on a new form of contraception: the Unipath System of Contraception. Women are required to take small urine samples and a monitor keeps track of whether they can get pregnant that day or not. After initial adjustments by the monitor, they only need do this 8 times a month. Severy outlines the European tests, which were reported to be highly successful, but it is unclear how independent they were from the company making the product. He also outlines in detail the design of the (impending) American trials, providing all the measures and procedures that were planned to be used.

Example 2. Bernhart and Uddin (1990) interviewed 106 men who were reported by their wives to be opposed to family planing on religious grounds. They found that very few, once questioned, actually opposed family planning. Only one quarter gave the common Islamic reasons for opposition. While the authors conclude that opposition might not be as great as reported, it is very unclear still how much the interviews – with both the husbands and wives – were valid. Independent evidence and further research would be useful to pinpoint where these discrepancies were coming from. So rather than assuming unacceptability by males, or relying on just females' reports, the acceptability trials with the men themselves proved most valuable.

Measuring Family Planning Program Effort

Another interesting measure used within this topic area is that of program effort (Ross & Frankenberg, 1993; Ross & Maudlin, 1996). What this means is getting an indication of how much, how hard and to what extent the programs have been working. The methodology is interesting and perhaps unique in interventions. Questionnaires are sent out to specified persons who are knowledgeable about a country's family planning situation. Many of the questions are factual, and other safeguards are in place to protect against biased responding (see Ross & Maudlin, 1996). For each of 30 questions the respondent is asked to give a rating of 0 to 4 on the strength of the family planning programs in that country. This indicates whether the country had no program efforts in that regard, weak program efforts, etc. The 30 questions are given in Table 6.

While such a measure might seem a bit weak to some in the social sciences, there are some very useful findings it generates. Ross and Maudlin (1996), for example, found that programs which had become stronger between 1972 and 1994 had improved on most of the criteria, rather than become a lot stronger on a subset of criteria. Those with the lowest ratings in the 1980s improved mostly through policy changes and least through availability of contraceptives. They also showed that over the 22-year period studied, the association between strength of program and socioeconomic situation has declined. Other results can be found in Ross and Frankenberg (1993).

One reason that such a measure is interesting is precisely because this is not done in other intervention areas. For example, a similar list could be assembled for smoking and tobacco. How much good effort is happening in a country to reduce alcohol abuse and tobacco smoking? If nothing else, it would get people in the area thinking about how they would even judge good and bad outcomes of interventions. For example, trying to judge the total program efforts in a country for dealing with persons with intellectual disabilities would be extremely difficult, ranging from availability of trainers within institutions or community homes, insurance or government costing, human rights for persons with intellectual disabilities, or school services available. While everyone might not agree on certain outcomes, the task itself of developing 30 questions to answer this, would be a useful one.

Education and Contraceptive Use

Most studies show a strong negative correlation between women's education levels and fertility (e. g., Ainsworth, Beegle & Nyamete, 1995; Hogan, Berhanu, & Hailemariam, 1999). That is, the more schooling females have the more use is made of contraception, although Ainsworth, Beegle, and Nyamete (1995) found that the correlation was not linear and it is also known to differ for different methods of contraceptives (Ross & Frankenberg, 1993). The problem with this finding is that it does not necessarily help with interventions. We do not know that the schooling *caused* the use of contraception, just that it was correlated. It could be that the factors that allowed women to partake of more schooling, which is uncommon in many of

Table 6. The 30 Measures of Family Planning Program Effort
Adapted from Ross and Maudlin (1996)

Policy and Stage-Setting Activities

    1. Policy on fertility reduction and family planning
    2. Statements by leaders
    3. Level of program leadership
    4. Policy on age at marriage
    5. Import laws and legal regulations
    6. Advertising of contraceptives allowed
    7. Involvement of other ministries and public agencies
    8. Proportion of in-country funding of family planning budget

Services and Service-Related Activities

    9. Involvement of private-sector agencies and groups
    10. Involvement of civil bureaucracy
    11. Community-based distribution
    12. Social marketing
    13. Postpartum program
    14. Home-visiting workers
    15. Administrative structure
    16. Training program
    17. Personnel completion of assigned tasks
    18. Logistics and transport
    19. Supervision system
    20. Mass media used for information, education, and communication
    21. Incentives and disincentives

Record-Keeping and Evaluation

    22. Record-keeping
    23. Evaluation
    24. Management's use of evaluation findings

Availability and Accessibility of contraceptive Supplies and Services

    25. Male sterilization
    26. Female sterilization
    27. Pills and injectables
    28. Condoms, spermicides, foam, diaphragms
    29. IUDs
    30. Abortion

the countries studied, also caused the change in contraceptive use rather than anything about the schooling itself. Women in more westernised areas might have both the opportunity to continue education longer and also more use of contraceptives. The schooling might not have caused the increase in contraceptive use. If true, this would mean that merely increasing schooling for women (while in itself an admirable goal for many other reasons) might not cause any change in contraceptive use unless other conditions are also put in place. [This is a good example of a subtle point made way back in Chapter 1, about studying actual interventions versus studying factors affecting a phenomenon. See the sections "*What is Included as an Intervention?*" and "*Analyzing the Contexts is more important than Finding the Causes*".]

There is some evidence, however, of a more causal role for education on contraceptive use, although other conditions still needed to be in place (Gertler & Molyneaux, 1994; Martin, 1995). There is also much more to women's gender role than level of education, and Govindasamy and Malhotra (1996) suggested that for Egyptian women that education and employment not be used as the sole indicators of women's position in society, since in Egyptian society the role of interaction and negotiation are more indicative than autonomy through education and employment.

Other Contexts Influencing Contraceptive Use

Clearly, the issues in changing contraceptive use are complex and more work needs to be done. Other studies have found that information and advice through informal social networks play roles in contraceptive use, and they need to be considered in family planning interventions (Rutenberg & Watkins, 1997; Watkins & Danzi, 1995). Other studies have interviewed families and found a lack of adequate knowledge about contraceptive use (Goldberg & Toros, 1994). An interesting study by Bawah et al. (1999) found that a very effective family planning project in northern Ghana seemed to produce conflict between the genders and the extended families. They thought this probably arose from traditional expectations that paying bridewealth meant obligations that the woman would produce a certain number of children, and contraception meant that this was not being met. This is clearly something that could have been picked up through acceptability studies before the program began so counter measures to this had not been pre-tested.

Obstacles to family planning include development, politics, religion and law, and these also limit contraceptive use (Basu, 1990; Krull & Pierce, 1997; Ntozi & Kabera, 1991; Obermeyer, 1994; Sai, 1993). In line with what was written in Chapter 1, however, we must beware of labelling these events "obstacles' since that is only taking one perspective on them. For example, Ntozi and Kabera (1991) found that in the Ankole region of Uganda there has been a low level of contraception use, and this might be thought to be related to the use of traditional contraceptive methods. Traditional methods include the use of herbs, herb cuts in the body, withdrawal, prolonged breastfeeding, and rituals involving the first born child. They found, though, that the low use of modern contraceptives was not related to traditional methods but to lack of knowledge of modern methods and poor supplies and services. It is also not wise to discredit traditional doctors as bbstacles since a study mentioned in Chapter 2 found that traditional doctors could be trained to deliver modern contraceptives (also Nazzar et al., 1995).

A review of many studies found only "plausible" evidence that increasing the use of contraceptives decreases the desire for more children; families might use contraception but still "want" more children than they have (Freedman, 1997; also Dharmalingam, 1996). Finally, a study in Bangladesh found no evidence that a strong birth control program decreased fertility preferences compared to a control area (Koenig et al. (1987).

Types of Family Planning Interventions

I mentioned earlier that family planning is interesting because so many of the interventions have been tried in this area—from macro, large scale efforts to micro, personal efforts. Below are some of the methods which should be quite familiar to you. You can see how they have been adapted from the uses made of them elsewhere, and explained throughout this book, to be directed at family planning.

Home Visitations

Many programs use a clinic worker or home visitation method (Cuco & Pierce, 1977, p. 59). The example below shows one study in which this was clearly one of the most important facets of increasing contraceptive use. Mita and Simmons (1995) led women in focus groups and found that many had first been impressed by the family planning worker before marriage, and had learned a lot that way. So there is some evidence that even before needing contraception, the home visitations can provide a useful service.

Example. Hotchkiss et al. (1999) looked at some of the factors that worked in a family planning intervention in Morocco. They had a large survey done in both 1992 and 1995 on the same women, and coded the interviews for a number of factors. In the period from 1979 to 1995, contraceptive use in Morocco had steadily increased from 19.4% to 50.3% among married women, and the fertility rate had dropped from 5.9 children to 3.3 children. The results showed that a few factors were significant in promoting modern contraceptive use, especially trained nurses at health facilities and improvements to the facilities' infrastructure. A remaining problem was a still high rate of use of oral contraceptives instead of more modern methods.

Mass Media Campaigns

Family planning has been an area in which large mass media campaigns have been trialled, and experiments attempted to see the effects over large groups of people (Cuco & Pierce, 1977, p. 54). As noted earlier, the typical finding is that mass media alone might work to an extent, but the addition of home visits or clinics makes a significant advance on mass media alone. The types of mass media events has been varied, including funny skits put into already popular shows on television (Piotrow et al., 1990), radio soap operas (Rogers et al., 1999), and magazine advertising (Foreit et al., 1989).

Example. Kane et al. (1998) studied a family planning multimedia campaign in Mali. The campaign was a highly saturated exposure to the 900,000 people of a city. Messages were broadcast on radio and television, using traditional music and theater and some details of these are given in Table 1 of their paper. The main messages were those of modern contraceptive methods, male responsibility for contraception, communication between spouses, and that Islam does not oppose family planning.

The overall results showed a dramatic increase in knowledge about contraceptives and more positive attitudes towards them. The use of contraceptive methods, at least that reported in a survey, was noticeable but relatively small. However, the authors went further than this and looked at current use of contraceptives as a function of exposure to the media campaign. It was found quite strongly that the more exposure to the media campaign (the more advertisements seen, etc.), the higher the percentage of current contraceptive use (also Cohen, 2000). Strong differences were also found between those exposed to the media campaign and those not exposed. However, it could be that people pre-disposed to watch these programs were the ones more likely to use contraceptives anyway: correlations do not mean cause. This needs checking in further research.

Integrated Health Approach

Other interventions treat family planning as a wider health issue and integrate family planning into already extant medical or health services (Cuco & Pierce, 1977, p. 56; Ross & Frankenberg, 1993, p. 34). This has several advantages, although people who slip through the medical and health systems might not be approached if this is the only approach. Studies have looked at integrating family planning into western medical services as well as the existing traditional health services (Debpuur, Phillips, Jackson, Nazzar, Ngom & Binka, 2002; Kambo et al., 1994). Integration has frequently been done combining maternal care and nutrition with family planning.

Example. Diaz and Croxatto (1993) report on a program that integrated contraceptive planning with post partum maternal care. Instead of approaching people in a random context to promote contraception, this program cared for women after a baby was born and integrated contraceptive use, information exchange, health care for both mother and child, breast feeding management, and maternal care for mother and child. Although the outcome was a high usage of contraception (98%), the authors write that in the first interview it was made clear that going to the clinic involved contraceptive trials so women might have left if they were really opposed to contraception.

Incentives

Incentives have been used to pay both those who accept contraceptive measures and those who recruit "acceptors" (Cuco & Pierce, 1977, p. 61; Ross & Frankenberg, 1993, p. 40). As mentioned previously, both schemes can have ethical and practical problems, with bribery and unethical coercion being possible outcomes. Other schemes can be managed though, such as the Taiwanese plans of giving education certificates for parents with less than three children, or free delivery costs for a second baby if there is a large enough spacing between the two children (Cuco & Pierce, 1977, p. 220; Finnigan & Sun, 1972; Wang & Chen, 1973).

Example. Sunil, Pillai and Pandey (1999) looked at whether incentives for sterilization or contraceptive use were effective over and above "motivational" attempts to have people comply. The context was that incentives had been used in India but there was some ethical opposition because it was claimed to amount to bribery for getting people to accept sterilization, whereas other replied that the incentives were to offset costs involved. The Ammanpettai Family Welfare Program studied was not about sterilization but having women attend clinics to learn about contraceptive methods, and to encourage spacing of children.

There were four conditions. In the Bonus and CP (contact person) condition women were given a small payment for using any temporary contraceptive method, and they had a contact person. The CPs were well trained and from a village also, and talked to them about information and methods. A second condition had the contact person but no incentive. Third, there was a group that received the bonus but no CP, and finally, there was a control group that received neither bonus nor CP visits. The program was introduced in 1989 and stopped in 1991. The actual research or evaluation study was carried out in 1994 by interviewing 1600 women who had been in the trials.

The results relevant here were that the CPs made a difference whereas the bonus did not. The two CP groups reported 37.6% and 33.2% of women never having taken contraceptives while the no CP groups reported 56.1% and 51.8%. Clearly the bonus had no effect (only 4.4% difference with a CP and 5.7% without). Of the women who were still using contraceptives after the 3/4-year period, those with a CP reported 22.0% and 26.0% use while those with no CP reported 7.1% and 9.5%. Again, the CP made a difference but not the bonus. In the case of both measures, even adding a bonus to the CP visits did not improve the measures, and adding a bonus when there was no CP contact also did not help.

In summary, then, and thinking back to Chapter 2 on the use of others in interventions, having a trained contact person visit the households and talk to women had a strong impact on past and present contraceptive use. The use of a cash bonus had little or no effect, even when some socio-economic variables were taken into account (but also see Stevens & Stevens, 1992).

Community Involvement

Most family planning interventions involve a whole community, and contact and action is taken through that community (Ross & Frankenberg, 1993). Askew and Khan (1990) present an example of this, reviewing the role and extent of community participation in a variety of campaigns from around the world. They report that this mainly consists of involving leaders of the community, and that community participation in management or planning are much weaker. This requires such programs to make their campaigns more directly useful or relevant to the community. Many of the studies using home visitations (see above) also involve strong community support and leadership.

Example. A study finding interesting support for community-based distribution of contraceptives is that of Vernon, Ojeda and Townsend (1988). They compared community distribution with the introduction of social marketing through pharmacies and other commercial outlets. They found that both were effective although the social marketing made more profit. The problem, however, was that the government changed the controls over pricing and this made the social marketing unprofitable, and so the programs running these closed down altogether. The authors point out that if the community-based distributions had been totally replaced then there would have been a period of no contraceptive availability. They therefore caution against replacing one with the other. Since social marketing is based on making some profit, it is always possible for it to collapse.

Mobile Units and Telephones

Coeytaux et al. (1989) report an intervention in which mobile family planning units were used in Tunisia. They were very effective, covered a large percentage of the total country service, and were cost effective. Telephone information services have also been tried and are generally successful. An ICARP trial in the Philippines in 1975 had many calls and 42% were from men who were led into discussions of vasectomies (Cuco & Pierce, 1977, p. 196). They also found a large percentage of calls were from public phones, which either meant that the poorer people who did not have a phone in the house were phoning in or else that people wanted anonymity by using a public phone. A phone service in Taipei, Taiwan also had 43% male callers and 50% of the calls from public phones (Cernada, Lee & Lin, 1974).

Inundation

Inundation refers to moving a great number of supplies into the area. In family planning this refers to stopping bottlenecks in government-supplied contraceptives and making cheap forms of contraception readily available (Cuco & Pierce, 1977, p. 64). Supply has always been a problem for family planning since education and information are no use at all if the contraceptives are not readily available to people, both in terms of accessibility and in cost. Typically, prices are subsidized or the contraceptives are made free, but sometimes new outlets are established. One caution; a new report I read claimed that an Indian state gave free contraceptives for family planning but when they started going through many hundreds of thousands it was found that some people were using the condoms as materials in wares they made. The free condoms apparently were quickly stopped which is unfortunate.

Example. An example of inundation is reported in an unpublished paper by Chow and Yen (see Cuco & Pierce, 1977, p. 210). Twenty four towns with a poor history of family planning were selected and twelve received the intervention and twelve were controls. At first, postpartum women were given free contraceptives and had follow-up checks. Later all women between 20 and 24 years were approached and offered the contraceptives. Supply depots gave easy access. Results found that contraceptive use increased by 75% for the experimental groups and only 30% in control areas. They also report that about 70% of those who used the supplies had never used contraceptives before.

Law and Political Change

We have already seen that many of the changes in family planning come through government laws (Cuco & Pierce, 1977; Finkle & McIntosh, 1994; Ross & Frankenberg, 1993). These have been a key feature of the measure of family planning program effort, how far a country's government is willing to support family planning and legislate for it. China, for example, has been almost heroic in making strong effort to keep to a one-child family plan. While there is religious and political opposition to this, the huge growths in population predicted for China seem to warrant strong measures (White, 1994). Governments have also legislated for free hospital charges for the first two children only, free contraceptives, allowance for nurses to insert IUD instead of doctors only, increasing education for women, making family planning a national human right, and even building or reinforcing roads leading to main centers with family planning clinics.

As discussed throughout this book, the way to legislation is not easy, and political parties rely on organization and popular support. In countries with strong Roman Catholic groups or other political pressure, governments will steer a careful path whatever their private views might be. In some ways, the path has been made easier with the spread of AIDS viruses, as nasty as that sounds, since some contraception and safe sex programmes can be reframed in this light rather than as family planning.

Example. Gertler and Molyneaux (1994) reported on changes in Indonesian fertility that were primarily prompted by the government establishment of a National Family Planning Coordinating Board that coordinated between government ministries, local governments and volunteers. It had a wide and flexible mandate, and mostly acted to promote rather than punish; by developing local networks, improving distribution networks, encouraging postponement of pregnancy, and increasing education and information availability.

Family Planning as a Crucible of Interventions

As someone interested in interventions, reading the family planning interventions literatures is fascinating. We sometimes strive to get interventions done with maybe ten people and research what might be the effects. In the family planning literature you come across studies with many thousands of participants, and huge intervention designs. Witness the Chow and Yen study mentioned above, with twenty four towns selected and twelve receiving the intervention and twelve acting as controls. This must have affected the lives and futures of many thousands of people.

As I have tried to show in this chapter also, the majority of methods from Chapters 2, 3, 4, 5, and 6 have been used in these interventions, and a lot can be learned from reading family planning interventions about how to go about these interventions and the practical problems when doing them. If you are interested, there is a lot more you can find out and the journals I have cited have much more in them to excite.

References

Action Research Reader. (1988). Melbourne: Deakin University Press.

Adkins, V. K., & Mathews, R. M. (1997). Prompted voiding to reduce incontinence in community-dwelling older adults. *Journal of Applied Behavior Analysis, 30,* 153-156.

Aguirre-Molina, M., & Gorman, D. M. (1996). Community-based approaches for the prevention of alcohol, tobacco, and other drug use. *Annual Review of Public Health, 17,* 337-358.

Ainsworth, M., Beegle, K., & Nyamete, A. (1995). *The impact of female schooling on fertility and contraceptive use: A study of fourteen Sub-Saharan countries.* Washington, DC: The World Bank.

Akillas, E., & Efran, J. S. (1995). Symptom prescription and reframing: Should they be combined? *Cognitive Therapy and Research, 19,* 263-279.

Akwabi-Ameyaw, K. (1990). The political economy of agricultural resettlement and rural development in Zimbabwe: The performance of family farms and producer cooperatives. *Human Organization, 49,* 320-338.

Albee, G. W., & Gullotta, T. P. (Eds.). (1997). *Primary prevention works.* London: Sage.

Alberto, P. A., & Troutman, A. C. (1986). *Applied behavior analysis for teachers.* Columbus, Ohio: Merrill.

Alemán, M. W. (2001). Complaining among the elderly: Examining multiple dialectical oppositions to independence in a retirement community. *Western Journal of Communication, 65,* 89-112.

Alford, B. A. (1986). Behavioral treatment of schizophrenic delusions: A single-case experimental analysis. *Behavior Therapy, 17,* 637-644.

Alicke, M. D., Braun, J. C., Glor, J. E., Klotz, M. L., Magee, J., Sederholm, H., & Siegel, R. (1992). Complaining behavior in social interaction. *Personality and Social Psychology Bulletin, 18,* 286–295.

Alinsky, S. D. (1971). *Rules for radicals: A pragmatic primer for realistic radicals.* New York: Vintage.

Allan, A., & Allan, M. M. (2000). The South African Truth and Reconciliation Commission as a therapeutic tool. *Behavioral Sciences and the Law, 18,* 459-477.

Allen, J. P., & Philliber, S. (2001). Who benefits most from a broadly targeted prevention program? Differential efficacy across populations in the Teen Outreach Program. *Journal of Community Psychology, 29,* 637-655.

Allen, K. D., & Fuqua, R. W. (1985). Eliminating selective stimulus control: A comparison of two procedures for teaching mentally retarded children to respond to compound stimuli. *Journal of Experimental Child Psychology, 39,* 55-71.

Allport, F. H., & Lepkin, M. (1945). Wartime rumors of waste and special privilege: Why some people believe them. *Journal of Abnormal and Social Psychology, 40,* 3-36.

American Psychological Association. (1992). Ethical principles of psychologists and code of conduct. *American Psychologist, 47,* 1597-1611.

Anderson, R. (2000). How multilateral development assistance triggered the conflict in Rwanda. *Third World Quarterly, 21,* 441-456.

Andrade, S. J., & Burnstein, A. G. (1973). Social congruence and empathy in paraprofessional and professional mental health workers. *Community Mental Health Journal, 9,* 388-397.

Andrasik, F., & Heimberg, J. S. (1982). Self-management procedures. In L. W. Frederiksen. (Ed.), *Handbook of organizational behavior management* (pp. 219-247). New York: Wiley.

Andrasik, F., Heimberg, J. S., & McNamara, J. R. (1981). Behavior modification of work and work-related problems. In M. Hersen, R. M. Eisler & P. M. Miller (Eds.), *Progress in behavior modification* (Vol. 11, pp. 117-161). New York: Academic Press.

Andreasen, A. R. (1995). *Marketing social change: Changing behavior to promote health, social development, and the environment.* San Francisco, CA: Jossey-Bass.

Andrewes, D. G., O'Connor, P., Mulder, C., McLennan, J., Derham, H., Weigall, S., & Say, S. (1996). Computerised psychoeducation for patients with eating disorders. *Australian and New Zealand Journal of Psychiatry, 30,* 492-497.

Antaki, C., Condor, S., & Levine, M. (1996). Social identities in talk: Speakers' own orientations. *British Journal of Social Psychology, 35,* 473-492.

Arblaster, L., Lambert, M., Entwistle, V., Forster, M., Fullerton, D., Sheldon, T., & Watt, I. (1996). A systematic review of the effectiveness of health service interventions aimed at reducing inequalities in health. *Journal of Health Service Research and Policy, 1,* 93-103.

Arcury, T. A. (1997). Occupational injury prevention knowledge and behavior of African-American farmers. *Human Organization, 56,* 167-173.

Arends-Kuenning, M., Hossain, M. B., & Barkat-e-Khuda. (1999). The effects of family planning workers' contact on fertility preferences: Evidence from Bangladesh. *Studies in Family Planning, 30,* 183-192.

Aronson, E., Blaney, N., Stephan, C., Sikes, J., & Snapp, M. (1978). *The Jigsaw classroom.* London: Sage.

Aronson, E., & Patnoe, S. (1997). *The Jigsaw classroom. 2nd ed.* New York: Longman.

Arunachalam, V., Chan, C., & Wall, J. A. (1998). Hong Kong versus U.S. negotiations: Effects of culture, alternatives, outcomes scales, and mediation. *Journal of Applied Social Psychology, 28,* 1219-1244.

Askew, I., & Khan, A. R. (1990). Community participation in national family planning programs: Some organizational issues. *Studies in Family Planning, 21,* 127-142.

Austin, D. (2003). Community-based collaborative team ethnography: A community-university-agency partnership. *Human Organization, 62,* 143-152.

Awabi-Ameyaw, K. (1990). The political economy of agricultural resettlement and rural development in Zimbabwe: The performance of family farms and producer cooperatives. *Human Organization, 49,* 320-338.

Axelrod, R. (1984). *The evolution of cooperation.* New York: Basic Books.

Azar, E. E. (1990). *The management of protracted social conflict.* Aldershot, England: Dartmouth Publishing.

Babor, T. F. (1994). Avoiding the horrid and beastly sin of drunkenness: Does dissuasion make a difference? *Journal of Consulting and Clinical Psychology, 62,* 1127-1140.

Baer, J. S., Marlatt, G. A., Kivlahan, D. R., Fromme, K., Larimer, M. E., & Williams, E. (1992). An experimental test of three methods of alcohol risk reduction with young adults. *Journal of Consulting and Clinical Psychology, 60,* 974-979.

Bakewell, O. (2000). Uncovering local perspectives on humanitarian assistance and its outcomes. *Disasters, 24,* 103-116.

Bank, L., Patterson, G. R., & Reid, J. B. (1987). Delinquency prevention through training parents in family management. *The Behavior Analyst, 10,* 75-82.

Banks, S. (2001). *Ethics and values in social work.* London: Palgrave.

Bardach, E. (1980). On designing implementable programs. In G. Majone & E. S. Quado (Eds.), *Pitfalls of analysis* (pp. 138-15). New York: Wiley.

Barnard, R. (2002). Peer tutoring in the primary classroom: A sociocultural interpretation of classroom interaction. *New Zealand Journal of Educational Studies, 37,* 57-72.

Barnes, H. M. (2000). Collaboration in community action: A successful partnership between indigenous communities and researchers. *Health Promotion International, 15,* 17-25.

Baron, R. A. (1988). Negative effects of destructive criticism: Impact on conflict, self-efficacy, and task performance. *Journal of Applied Psychology, 73,* 199-207.

Baron, R. A. (1990). Countering the effects of destructive criticism: The relative efficacy of four interventions. *Journal of Applied Psychology, 75,* 235-245.

Barrett, P. M., Moore, A. F., & Sonderegger, R. (2000). The FRIENDS Program for young former-Yugoslavian refugees in Australia: A pilot study. *Behaviour Change, 17,* 124-133.

Barton, E. J. (1986). Modification of children's prosocial behavior. In P. S. Strain, M. J. Guralnick, & H. M. Walker (Eds.), *Children's social behavior: Development, assessment and modification* (pp. 331-372). London: Academic Press.

Basu, A. M. (1990). Cultural influences on health care use: Two regional groups in India. *Studies in Family Planning, 21,* 275-286.

Baum, F., Kalucy, E., Lawless, A., Barton, S., & Steven, I. (1998). Health promotion in different medical settings: Women's health, community health and private practice. *Australian and New Zealand Journal of Public Health, 22,* 200-205.

Baum F., Sanderson, C., & Jolley, G. (1997). Community participation in action: An analysis of the South Australian Health and Social Welfare Councils. *Health Promotion International, 12,* 125-134.

Baumann, J. F., Seifert-Kessell, N., & Jones, L. A. (1992). Effect of think-aloud instruction on elementary students' comprehension monitoring abilities. *Journal of Reading Behavior, 24,* 143-172.

Baumann, K. E., & Ennett, S. T. (1994). Peer influence on adolescent drug use. *American Psychologist, 49,* 820-822.

Baumeister, R. F., Bratslavsky, E., Finkenauer, C., & Vohs, K. D. (2001). Bad is stronger than good. *Review of General Psychology, 5,* 23-370.

Bawah, A. A., Akweongo, P., Simmons, R., & Phillips, J. F. (1999). Women's fears and men's anxieties: The impact of family planning on gender relations in Northern Ghana. *Studies in Family Planning, 30,* 54-66.

Bay-Hinitz, A. K., Peterson, R. F., & Quilitch, H. R. (1994). Cooperative games: A way to modify aggressive and cooperative behaviors in young children. *Journal of Applied Behavior Analysis, 27,* 435-446.

Bazerman, M. H., Curhan, J. R., Moore, D. A., & Valley, K. L. (2000). Negotiation. *Annual Review of Psychology, 51,* 279-314.

Becker, H. A., & Vanclay, F. (Eds.). (2003). *The international handbook of social impact assessment: Conceptual and methodological advances.* Cheltenham, UK: Edward Elgar.

Becoña, E., & Vázquez, F. L. (2001). Effectiveness of personalized written feedback through a mail intervention for smoking cessation: A randomized-controlled trial in Spanish smokers. *Journal of Consulting and Clinical Psychology, 69,* 33-40.

Behavior analysis and safety. (1988). [Special Issue]. *Journal of Applied Behavior Analysis, 21* (3).

Bell, S. K., Boggs, S. R., & Eyberg, S. M. (2003). Positive attention. In W. O'Donohue, J. E. Fisher & S. C. Hayes (Eds.), *Cognitive behavior therapy: Applying empirically supported techniques in your practice* (pp. 294-300). New York: Wiley.

Bellamy, C. (1997). *Knights in white amour: The new art of war and peace.* London: Pimlico.

Belloni, R. (2001). Civil society and peacebuilding in Bosnia and Herzegovina. *Journal of Peace Research, 38,* 163-180.

Benfari, R. C., Eaker, E., & Stoll, J. G. (1981). Behavioral interventions and compliance to treatment regimes. *Annual Review of Public Health, 2,* 431-471.

Bentley, A. F. (1935). *Behavior knowledge fact.* Bloomington, Indiana: Principia Press.

Bentley, A. F. (1954/1910). Knowledge and society. In A. F. Bentley, *Inquiry into inquiries: Essays in social theory* (pp. 3-26). Boston: Beacon Press.

Bercovitch, J., & Schneider, G. (2000). Who mediates? The political economy of international conflict management. *Journal of Peace Research, 37,* 145-165.

Beresford, Q., & Partington, G. (Eds.). (2003). *Reform and resistance in Aboriginal education: The Australian experience.* Perth: University of Western Australia Press.

Berger, P. L., & Luckmann, T. (1967). *The social construction of reality.* Harmondsworth, Middlesex: Penguin.

Berg-Smith, S. M., Stevens, V. J., Brown, K. M., Van Horn, L., Gernhofer, N., Peters, E., Greenberg, R., Snetselaar, L., Ahrens, L., & Smith, K. (1999). A brief motivational intervention to improve dietary adherence in adolescents. *Health Education Research, 14,* 399-410.

Beriker Atiyas, N. (1995). Mediating regional conflicts and negotiating flexibility: Peace efforts in Bosnia-Herzegovina. *Annals of the American Academy of Political and Social Science, 542,* 185-201.

Bernhart, M. H., & Uddin, M. M. (1990). Islam and family planning acceptance in Bangladesh. *Studies in Family Planning, 21,* 287-292.

Biegel, D. E., & Schulz, R. (1999). Caregiving and caregiver interventions in aging and mental illness. *Family Relations, 48,* 345-354.

Bierman, K. L., Greenberg, M. T., & the Conduct Problems Prevention Research Group. (1996). Social skills training in the Fast Track Program. In R. DeV. Peters & R. J. McMahon (Eds.), *Preventing childhood disorders, substance abuse, and delinquency* (pp. 65- 89). London: Sage.

Biglan, A. (1995). *Changing cultural practices.* Reno, NV: Context Press.

Biglan, A., Ary, D., Yudelson, H., Duncan, T. E., Hood, D., James, L., Koehn, V., Wright, Z., Black, C., Levings, D., Smith, S., & Gaiser, E. (1996). Experimental evaluation of a modular approach to mobilizing antitobacco influences of peers and parents. *American Journal of Community Psychology, 24,* 311-339.

Biglan, A., & Taylor, T. K. (2000). Why have we been more successful in reducing tobacco use than violent crime? *American Journal of Community Psychology, 28,* 269-287.

Binder, C. (1996). Behavioral fluency: Evolution of a new paradigm. *The Behavior Analyst, 19,* 163-197.

Bingham, R. D., & Felbinger, C. L. (2001). *Evaluation in practice: A methodological approach.* New York: Seven Bridges Press.

Birnbrauer, J. S., & Leach, D. J. (1993). The Murdoch Early Intervention Program after 2 years. *Behaviour Change, 10,* 63-74.

Birnie-Selwyn, B., & Guerin, B. (1997). Teaching children to spell: Decreasing consonant cluster errors by eliminating selective stimulus control. *Journal of Applied Behavior Analysis, 30,* 69-91.

Black, D. R., Blue, C. L., Kosmoski, K., & Coster, D. C. (2000). Social marketing: Developing a tailored message for a physical activity program. *American Journal of Health Behavior, 24,* 323-337.

Black, D. R., Tobler, N. S., & Sciacca, J. P. (1998). Peer helping/involvement: An efficacious way to meet the challenge of reducing alcohol, tobacco, and other drug use among youth? *Journal of School Health, 68,* 87-93

Blanchard, F. A., Crandell, C. S., Brigham, J. C., & Vaughn, L. A. (1994). Condemning and condoning racism: A social context approach to interracial settings. *Journal of Applied Psychology, 79,* 993-997.

Blinn-Pike, L., Kuschel, D., McDaniel, A., Mingus, S., & Mutti, M. P. (1998). The process of mentoring pregnant adolescents: An exploratory study. *Family Relations, 47,* 119-127.

Bloom, G. A., Crumpton, R., & Anderson, J. E. (1999). A systematic observation study of the teaching behaviors of an expert basketball coach. *The Sports Psychologist, 13,* 157-170.

Bloom, G. A., Durand-Bush, N., & Salmela, J. H. (1997). Pre- and postcompetition routines of expert coaches of team sports. *The Sports Psychologist, 11,* 127-141.

Bogat, G. A., Sullivan, L. A., & Grober, J. (1993). Applications of social support to preventive interventions. In D. S. Glenwick & L. A. Jason (Eds.), *Promoting health and mental health in children, youth, and families* (pp. 205-232). New York: Springer.

Bolz, F., Dudonis, K. J., & Schulz, D. P. (2001). *The counterterrorism handbook: Tactics, procedures, and techniques.* London: CRC Press.

Booth, M., Bauman, A., Oldenburg, B., Owen, N., & Magnus, P. (1992). Effects of a national mass-media campaign on physical activity participation. *Health Promotion International, 7,* 241-247.

Borland, R., Chapman, S., Owen, N., & Hill, D. (1990). Effects of workplace smoking bans on cigarette consumption. *American Journal of Public Health, 80,* 178-180.

Borsari, B., & Carey, K. B. (2000). Effects of a brief motivational intervention with college student drinkers. *Journal of Consulting and Clinical Psychology, 68,* 728-733.

Boton, G., Howlett, S., Lago, C., & Wright, J. K. (Eds.). (2004). *Writing cures: An introductory handbook of writing in counseling and therapy.* NY: Bruner-Routledge.

Botsford, A. L., & Rule, D. (2004). Evaluation of a group intervention to assist aging parents with permanency planning for an adult offspring with special needs. *Social Work, 49,* 423-431.

Botvin, G. J. (1996). Substance abuse prevention through life skills training. In R. DeV. Peters & R. J. McMahon (Eds.), *Preventing childhood disorders, substance abuse, and delinquency* (pp. 215-240). London: Sage.

Brady, N. C., Saunders, K. J., & Spradlin, J. E. (1994). A conceptual analysis of request teaching procedures for individuals with severely limited verbal repertoires. *The Analysis of Verbal Behavior, 12,* 43-52.

Branwhite, A. B. (1983). Boosting reading skills by direct instruction. *British Journal of Educational Psychology, 53,* 291-298.

Brawley, L. R., Rejeski, W. J., & Lutes, L. (2000). A group-mediated cognitive-behavioral intervention for increasing adherence to physical activity in older adults. *Journal of Applied Biobehavioral Research, 5,* 47-65.

Brem, S., & Rutherford, K. (2001). Walking together or divided agenda? Comparing landmines and small-arms campaigns. *Security Dialogue, 32,* 169-186.

Brewer, D. D. (1992). Hip Hop graffiti writers' evaluations of strategies to control illegal graffiti. *Human Organization, 51,* 188-196.

Briggs, H. E., & Paulson, R. I. (1996). Racism. In M. A. Mattaini & B. A. Thyer (Eds.), *Finding solutions to social problems: Behavioral strategies for change* (pp. 147-177). Washington, DC: American Psychological Association.

Brown, D. (1994). *The American West.* New York: Simon & Schuster.

Brown, J. H., & Kreft, I. G. G. (1998). Zero effects of drug education programs: Issues and solutions. *Evaluation Review, 22,* 3-14.

Brown, K. G. (2001). Using computers to deliver training: Which employees learn and why? *Personnel Psychology, 54,* 271-296

Brownell, K. D., Marlatt, G. A., Lichtenstein, E., & Wilson, G. T. (1986). Understanding and preventing relapse. *American Psychologist, 41,* 765-782.

Brubaker, R., & Laitin, D. D. (1998). Ethnic and nationalistic violence. *Annual Review of Sociology, 24,* 423-452.

Brug, J., Steenhuis, I., van Assema P., Glanz, K., & De Vries, H. (1999). Computer-tailored nutrition education: Differences between two interventions. *Health Education Research, 14,* 249-256.

Brzuzy, S. (1998). Public policy interventions for prejudice. In M. L. Hecht (Ed.), *Communicating prejudice* (pp. 326-333). London: Sage.

Bryant, L. E., & Budd, K. S. (1984). Teaching behaviorally handicapped preschool children to share. *Journal of Applied Behavior Analysis, 17,* 45-56.

Budd, K. S., Green, D. R., & Baer, D. M. (1976). An analysis of multiple misplaced parental social contingencies. *Journal of Applied Behavior Analysis, 9,* 459-470.

Burns, B. J., Hoagwood, K., & Mrazek, P. J. (1999). Effective treatment for mental disorders in children and adolescents. *Clinical Child and Family Psychology Review, 2,* 199-254.

Burton, J. W. (1996). *Conflict resolution: Its language and processes.* Lanham, MD: Scarecrow Press.

Busch, R., & Robertson, N. (1993). "What's love got to do with it?": An analysis of an intervention approach to domestic violence. *Waikato Law Review (Taumauri), 1,* 109-140.

Byles, J. E., & Sanson-Fisher, R. W. (1996). Mass mailing campaigns to promote screening for cervical cancer: Do they work, and do they continue to work? *Australian and New Zealand Journal of Public Health, 20,* 254-260.

Callister, R. R., & Wall, J. A. (1997). Japanese community and organizational mediation. *Journal of Conflict Resolution, 41,* 311-328.

Camarata, S. (1993). The application of naturalistic conversation training to speech production in children with speech disabilities. *Journal of Applied Behavior Analysis, 26,* 173-182.

Campbell, D. T. (1969). Reforms as experiments. *American Psychologist, 24,* 409-429.

Campbell, D. T., & Stanley, J. C. (1963). *Experimental and quasi-experimental designs for research.* Chicago, IL: Rand-McNally.

Campos, R., Raffaelli, M., Ude, W., Greco, M., Ruff, A., Rolf, J., Antunes, C., Halsey, N., & Greco, D. (1994). Social networks and daily activities of street youth in Belo Horizonte, Brazil. *Child Development, 65,* 319-330.

Capafóns, J. I., Sosa, C. D., & Viña, C. M. (1999). A reattributional training program as a therapeutic strategy for fear of flying. *Journal of Behavior Therapy and Experimental Psychiatry, 30,* 259-272.

Capp, K., Deane, F. P., & Lambert, G. (2001). Suicide prevention in Aboriginal communities: Application of community gatekeeper training. *Australian and New Zealand Journal of Public Health, 25,* 315-321.

Card, J. J. (1999). Teen pregnancy prevention: Do any programs work? *Annual Review of Public Health, 20,* 257-285.

Card, O. S. (1977). *Ender's game*. New York: Tom Doherty Associates Books.

Carlsson, L. (2000). Policy networks as collective action. *Policy Studies Journal, 28*, 502-520.

Carr, D., & Halvorsen, K. (2001). An evaluation of three democratic, community-based approaches to citizen participation: Surveys, conversations with community groups, and community dinners. *Society and Natural Resources, 14*, 107-126.

Carter, N., Holmstrom, A., Simpanen, M., & Melin, L. (1988). Theft reduction in a grocery store through product identification and graphing of losses for employees. *Journal of Applied Behavior Analysis, 21*, 385-389.

Castle, C. M., Skinner, T. C., & Hampson, S. E. (1999). Young women and sun tanning: An evaluation of a health education leaflet. *Psychology and Health, 14*, 517-527.

Ceci, S. J., & Bruck, M. (1993). Suggestibility of the child witness: A historical review and synthesis. *Psychological Bulletin, 113*, 403-439.

Cecil, H., Evans, R. I., & Stanley, M. A. (1996). Perceived believability among adolescents of health warning labels on cigarette packs. *Journal of Applied Social Psychology, 26*, 502-519.

Cernada, E. C-C., Lee, Y. J., & Lin, M. (1974). Family planning telephone services in two Asian cities. *Studies in Family Planning, 5*, 111-114.

Chadwick, P. D. J., Lowe, C. F., Horne, P. J., & Higson, P. J. (1994). Modifying delusions: The role of empirical testing. *Behavior Therapy, 25*, 35-49.

Chandler, L. K., Lubeck, R. C., & Fowler, S. A. (1992). Generalization and maintenance of preschool children's social skills: A critical review and analysis. *Journal of Applied Behavior Analysis, 25*, 415-428.

Childs, J. M. (1996). Training systems evaluation. In T. G. O'Brien & S. G. Charleton (Eds.), *Handbook of human factors testing and evaluation* (pp. 201-222). Mahwah, NJ: Erlbaum.

Cialdini, R. B. (1987). Compliance principles of compliance professionals: Psychologists of necessity. In M. P. Zanna, J. M. Olson & C. P. Herman (Eds.), *Social influence: The Ontario symposium, Volume 5* (pp. 165-184). Hillsdale, NJ: Erlbaum.

Clark, D. M. (1999). Anxiety disorders: Why they persist and how to treat them. *Behaviour Research and Therapy, 37*, S5-S27.

Clark, D. A., & Purdon, C. L. (1995). The assessment of unwanted intrusive thoughts: A review and critique of the literature. *Behaviour Research and Therapy, 33*, 967-976.

Clayton, R. R., Leukefeld, C. G., Harrington, N. G., & Cattarello, A. (1996). DARE (Drug Abuse Resistance Education): Very popular but not very effective. In C. B. McCoy, L. R. Metsch, & J. A. Inciardi (Eds.), *Intervening with drug-involved youth* (pp. 101-109). London: Sage.

Close, D. W., & Horner, R. H. (1999). Architectural design in positive behavioral support. In J. R. Scotti & L. H. Meyer (Eds.), *Behavioral intervention: Principles, models, and practices* (pp. 251-266). London: Paul H. Brookes.

Clutterbuck, R. (1992). Negotiating with terrorists. *Terrorism and Political Violence, 4*, 263-287.

Coeytaux, F., Donaldson, D., Aloui, T., Kilani, T., & Fourati, H. (1989). An evaluation of the cost-effectiveness of mobile family planning services in Tunisia. *Studies in Family Planning, 20*, 158-169.

Cohen, B. (2000). Family planning programs, socioeconomic characteristics, and contraceptive use in Malawi. *World Development, 28*, 843-860.

Cohen, S., Lichtenstein, E., Prochaska, J. O., Rossi, J. S., Gritz, E. R., Carr, C. R., Orleans, C. T., Schoenbach, V. J., Biener, L., Abrams, D., DiClemente, C. C., Curry, S., Marlatt, G. A., Cummings, K. M., Emont, S. L., Giovino, G., & Ossip-Klein, D. (1989). Debunking myths about self-quitting: Evidence from 10 prospective studies of persons who attempt to quit smoking by themselves. *American Psychologist, 44*, 1355-1365.

Coie, J. D. (1996). Prevention of violence and antisocial behavior. In R. DeV. Peters & R. J. McMahon (Eds.), *Preventing childhood disorders, substance abuse, and delinquency* (pp. 1-18). London: Sage.

Comer, E., Meier, A., & Galinsky, M. J. (2004). Development of innovative group work practice using the Intervention Research paradigm. *Social Work, 49*, 250-260.

Cone, J. D., & Hayes, S. C. (1980). *Environmental problems: Behavioral solutions*. Monterey, CA: Brooks/Cole.

205

Connell, M. C., Carta, J. J., & Baer, D. M. (1993). Programming generalization of in-class transition skills: Teaching preschoolers with developmental delays to self-assess and recruit contingent teacher praise. *Journal of Applied Behavior Analysis, 26,* 345-352.

Conte, J. R., Wolf, S., & Smith, T. (1989). What sexual offenders tell us about prevention strategies. *Child Abuse & Neglect, 13,* 293-301.

Cook, T. D., & Connor, R. F. (1976). The educational impact. [Sesame Street] *Journal of Communication, 26* (2), 155-164.

Cooley, C. H. (1909). *Social organization.* New York: Charles Scribner's Sons.

Cooper, J. O., Heron, T. E., & Heward, W. L. (1987). *Applied behavior analysis.* Columbus, Ohio: Merrill Publishing Company.

Copello, A., Orford, J., Hodgson, R., Tober, G., & Barrett, C. (2002). Social behaviour and network therapy: Basic principles and early experiences. *Addictive Behaviors, 27,* 345-366.

Costa, A. C. G., Kottak, C. P., & Prado, R. M. (1997). The sociopolitical context of participatory development in Northeastern Brazil. *Human Organization, 56,* 138-146.

Cotton, S. R., & Gupta, S. S. (2003). Characteristics of online and offline health information seekers and factors that discriminate between them. *Social Science & Medicine, 59,* 1795-1806.

Cowan, E. L. (1997). On the semantics and operations of primary prevention and wellness enhancement (or will the real primary prevention please stand up?). *American Journal of Community Psychology, 25,* 245-255.

Creamer, M. (1996). Treatment interventions in post-traumatic stress. In D. Paton & N. Long (Eds.), *Psychological aspects of disasters: Impact, coping and intervention* (pp. 177-192). Dunedin, New Zealand: Dunmore Press.

Cronan, T. A., Brooks, L. B., Kilpatrick, K., Bigatti, S. M., & Tally, S. (1999). The effects of a community-based literacy program: One-year follow-up findings. *Journal of Community Psychology, 27,* 431-442.

Crosbie, J., & Kelly, G. (1994). Effects of imposed postfeedback delays in programmed instruction. *Journal of Applied Behavior Analysis, 27,* 483-491.

Crowell, C. R., Anderson, D. C., Abel, D. M., & Sergio, J. P (1988). Task clarification, performance feedback, and social praise: Procedures for improving the customer service of bank tellers. *Journal of Applied Behavior Analysis, 21,* 65-71.

Cuca, R., & Pierce, C. S. (1977). *Experiments in family planning: Lessons from the developing world.* London: Johns Hopkins University Press.

Cugliari, A. M., Sobal, J., & Miller, T. (1999). Use of videotape for educating patients about advance directives. *American Journal of Health Behavior, 23,* 105-114.

Cunningham, C. E., Cunningham, L. J., Tran, A., Young, J., Zacharias, R., & Martorelli, V. (1998). The effects of primary division, student-mediated conflict resolution programs on playground aggression. *Journal of Child Psychology and Psychiatry, 39,* 653-662.

Cunningham, M. (1999). Saying sorry: The politics of apology. *The Political Quarterly, 70,* 285-293.

Dachman, R. S., Alessi, G. J., Vrazo, G. J., Fuqua, R. W., & Kerr, R. H. (1986). Development and evaluation of an infant-care training program with first-time fathers. *Journal of Applied Behavior Analysis, 19,* 221-230.

da Costa, I. G., Rapoff, M. A., Lemanek, K., & Goldstein, G. L. (1997). Improving adherence to medication regimens for children with asthma and its effect on clinical outcome. *Journal of Applied Behavior Analysis, 30,* 687-691.

Daly, E. J., Martens, B. K., Hamler, K. R., Dool, E. J., & Eckert, T. L. (1999). A brief experimental analysis for identifying instructional components needed to improve oral reading fluency. *Journal of Applied Behavior Analysis, 32,* 83-94.

Danish, S. J. (1997). Going for the Goal: A life skills program for adolescents. In G. W. Albee & T. P. Gullotta (Eds.), *Primary prevention works* (pp. 291-312). London: Sage.

Darney, P. D., Atkinson, E., Tanner, S., MacPherson, S., Hellerstein, S., & Alvarado, A. (1990). Acceptance and perceptions of NORPLANT® among users in San Francisco, USA. *Studies in Family Planning, 21,* 152-160.

Darr, A. (1999). Conflict and conflict resolution in a cooperative: The case of the Nir Taxi Station. *Human Relations, 52,* 279-301.

Darrah, C. N. (1995). Workplace training, workplace learning: A case study. *Human Organization, 54*, 31-41.

Darvall, P. (1995). Exploring simulations as a tool for adult education: The challenging racism game. In J. Collins (Ed.), *Confronting racism in Australia, Canada and New Zealand* (Vol. 1, pp. 367-379). University of Technology, Sydney: Faculty of Business.

Davidson, B. (2000). The interpreter as institutional gatekeeper: The social-linguistic role of interpreters in medical discourse. *Journal of Sociolinguistics, 4*, 379-405.

Davidson, L., Chinman, M. Kloos, B., Weingarten R., Stayner, D., & Tebes, J. K. (1999). Peer support among individuals with severe mental illness: A review of the evidence. *Clinical Psychology: Science & Practice, 6*, 165-187.

Davies, J., Mitra, S. N., & Schellstede, W. P. (1987). Oral contraception in Bangladesh: Social marketing and the importance of husbands. *Studies in Family Planning, 18*, 157-168

Davies, M. F. (1997). Belief persistence after evidential discrediting: The impact of generated versus provided explanations on the likelihood of discredited outcomes. *Journal of Experimental Social Psychology, 33*, 561-578.

Davis, J., & Whittington, D. (1998). "Participatory" research for development projects: A comparison of the community meeting and household survey techniques. *Economic Development and Cultural Change, 46*, 73-94.

Davison, G. C., & Best, J. L. (2003). Think-aloud techniques. In W. O'Donohue, J. E. Fisher & S. C. Hayes (Eds.), *Cognitive behavior therapy: Applying empirically supported techniques in your practice* (pp. 423-428). New York: Wiley.

Davison, G. C., Vogel, R. S., & Coffman, S. G. (1997). Think-aloud approaches to cognitive assessment and the articulated thoughts in simulated situations paradigm. *Journal of Consulting and Clinical Psychology, 65*, 950-958.

Davison, K. P., Pennebaker, J. W., & Dickerson, S. S. (2000). Who talks? The social psychology of illness support groups. *American Psychologist, 55*, 205-217.

De Andrade, L. L. (2000). Negotiating from the inside: Constructing racial and ethnic identity in qualitative research. *Journal of Contemporary Ethnography, 29*, 268-290.

Debpuur, C., Phillips, J. F., Jackson, E. F., Nazzar, A., Ngom, P., & Binka, F. N. (2002). The impact of the Navrongo Project on contraceptive knowledge and use, reproductive preferences, and fertility. *Studies in Family Planning, 33*, 141-164.

De Drue, C. K. W., Giebels, E., & Van de Vliert, E. (1998). Social motives and trust in integrative negotiation: The disruptive effects of punitive capability. *Journal of Applied Psychology, 83*, 408-422.

DeJong, W., & Hingson, R. (1998). Strategies to reduce driving under the influence of alcohol. *Annual Review of Public Health, 19*, 359-378.

De la Ray, C., & Parekh, A. (1996). Community-based peer groups: An intervention programme for teenage mothers. *Journal of Community and Applied Social Psychology, 6*, 373-381.

Dempster, F. N. (1988). The spacing effect. *American Psychologist, 43*, 627-634.

Deodhar, N. S., Yemul, V. L., & Banerjee, K. (1998). Plague that never was: A review of the alleged plague outbreaks in India in 1994. *Journal of Public Health Policy, 19*, 184-199.

de Silva, P. (1985). Early Buddhist and modern behavioral strategies for the control of unwanted intrusive cognitions. *The Psychological Record, 35*, 437-443.

Dharmalingam, A. (1996). The social context of family size preferences and fertility behaviour in a South India village. *Genus, 52*, 83-103.

Diaz, S., & Croxatto, H. B. (1993). Scientific aspects in family planning services. In F. Graham-Smith (Ed.), *Population–the complex reality: A report of the Population Summit of the world's scientific academies* (pp. 131-321). London: The Royal Society.

Dick, B. (1993). *So you want to do an action research thesis?* Chapel Hill, Queensland: Interchange.

Dickson, G., & Green, K. L. (2001). Participatory action research: Lessons learned with aboriginal grandmothers. *Health Care for Women International, 22*, 471-482.

Dielman, T. E., Shope, J. T., Butchart, A. T., & Campanelli, P. C. (1986). Prevention of adolescent alcohol misuse: An elementary school program. *Journal of Pediatric Psychology, 11*, 259-282.

Difonzo, N., Bordia, P., & Rosnow, R. L. (1994). Reining in rumors. *Organizational Dynamics, 23*, 47-62.

Dillard, J. P., & Pfau, M. (2002). *The persuasion handbook: Developments in theory and practice*. London: Sage.

Dillon, M. J., & Malott, R. W. (1981). Supervising masters theses and doctoral dissertations. *Teaching of Psychology, 8*, 195-202.

Dimidjian, S., & Linehan, M. M. (2003). Mindfulness practice. In W. O'Donohue, J. E. Fisher & S. C. Hayes (Eds.), *Cognitive behavior therapy: Applying empirically supported techniques in your practice* (pp. 229-237). New York: Wiley.

Dingo, S. (1998). *Dingo: The story of our mob*. Sydney: Random House.

Diprizio, R. (1999). Adverse effects of humanitarian aid in complex emergencies. *Small Wars and Insurgencies, 10*, 97-106.

Dishman, R. K. (Ed.). (1994). *Advances in exercise adherence*. Champaign, IL : Human Kinetics.

Dishion, T. J., & Andrews, D. W. (1995). Preventing escalation in problem behaviors with high-risk young adolescents: Immediate and 1-year outcomes. *Journal of Consulting and Clinical Psychology, 63*, 538-548.

Dishion, T. J., McCord, J., & Poulin, F. (1999). When interventions harm: Peer groups and problem behavior. *American Psychologist, 54*, 755-764.

Dixon, W. J. (1996). Third-party techniques for preventing conflict escalation and promoting peaceful settlement. *International Organization, 50*, 653-681.

Dixon-Woods, M. (2000). The production of printed consumer health information: Order from chaos? *Health Education Journal, 59*, 108-115.

Dixon-Woods, M. (2001). Writing wrongs? An analysis of published discourses about the use of patient information leaflets. *Social Science & Medicine, 52*, 1417-1432.

Dobbinson, S., Borland, R., & Anderson, M. (1999). Sponsorship and sun protection practices in lifesavers. *Health Promotion International, 14*, 167-176.

Dobson, K. S., & Hamilton, K. E. (2003). Cognitive restructuring: Behavioral test of negative cognitions. In W. O'Donohue, J. E. Fisher & S. C. Hayes (Eds.), *Cognitive behavior therapy: Applying empirically supported techniques in your practice* (pp. 84-88). New York: Wiley.

Dolinski, D., & Nawrat, R. (1998). "Fear-then-relief" procedure for producing compliance: Beware when the danger is over. *Journal of Experimental Social Psychology, 34*, 27-50.

Donaldson, S. I., Graham, J. W., Piccinin, A. M., & Hansen, W. B. (1995). Resistance-skills training and onset of alcohol use: Evidence for beneficial and potentially harmful effects in public schools and in private Catholic schools. *Health Psychology, 14*, 291-300.

Donovan, R. J., & Owen, N. (1993). Social marketing and mass intervention. In R. K. Dishman (Ed.), *Exercise adherence: Its impact on public health* (2nd Ed., pp. 249-290). Champaign, IL: Human Kinetics.

Doob, L. W. (1970). *Resolving conflict in Africa: The Fermeda Workshop*. London: Yale University Press.

Dougher, M. J., & Hackbert, L. (1994). A behavior-analytic account of depression and a case report using acceptance-based procedures. *The Behavior Analyst, 17*, 321-334.

Douglas, M., & Mars, G. (2003). Terrorism: A positive feedback game. *Human Relations, 56*, 763-786.

Downs, J. S., Murray, P. J., de Bruin, W. B., Penrose, J., Palmgren, C., & Fischhoff, B. (2004). Interactive video behavioral intervention to reduce adolescent females' STD risk: A randomized control design. *Social Science & Medicine, 59*, 1561-1572.

Dowswell, T., Towner, E. M. L., Simpson, G., & Jarvis, S. N. (1996). Preventing childhood unintentional injuries—what works? A literature review. *Injury Prevention, 2*, 140-149.

Drake, C. (1996). Water resource conflicts in the Middle East. *Journal of Geography, 96*, 4-12.

Drew, P., & Holt, E. (1988). Complainable matters: The use of idiomatic expressions in making complaints. *Social Problems, 35*, 398-417.

Druckman, D. (Ed.). (1977). *Negotiations: Some social-psychological perspectives*. London: Sage.

Dube, W. V., McDonald, S. J., McIlvane, W. J., & Mackay, H. A. (1991). Constructed-response matching to sample and spelling instruction. *Journal of Applied Behavior Analysis, 24*, 305-317.

DuBois, D. L., & Neville, H. A. (1997). Youth mentoring: Investigation of relationship characteristics and perceived benefits. *Journal of Community Psychology, 25,* 227-234.

Ducharme, J. M., & Holborn, S. W. (1997). Programming generalization of social skills in preschool children with hearing impairments. *Journal of Applied Behavior Analysis, 30,* 639-651.

Ducharme, J. M., & Worling, D. E. (1994). Behavioral momentum and stimulus fading in the acquisition and maintenance of child compliance in the home. *Journal of Applied Behavior Analysis, 27,* 639-647.

Duckworth, M. P. (2003). Assertiveness skills and the management of related factors. In W. O'Donohue, J. E. Fisher & S. C. Hayes (Eds.), *Cognitive behavior therapy: Applying empirically supported techniques in your practice* (pp. 16-22). New York: Wiley.

Dumas, J. E., Prinz, R. J., Smith, E. P., & Laughlin, J. (1999). The EARLY ALLIANCE Prevention Trial: An integrated set of interventions to promote competence and reduce risk for conduct disorder, substance abuse, and school failure. *Clinical Child and Family Psychology Review, 2,* 37-53.

Duncan, P. K., & Lloyd, K. E. (1982). Training format in industrial behavior modification. In R. M. O'Brien, A. M. Dickinson, & M. P. Rosnow (Eds.), *Industrial behavior modification* (pp. 387-404). New York: Pergamon.

Dunham, P. J., Hurshman, A., Litwin, E., Guesella, J., Ellsworth, C., & Dodd, P. W. D. (1998). Computer-mediated social support: Single young mothers as a model system. *American Journal of Community Psychology, 26,* 281-306.

Dunn, A. L., Marcus, B. H., Kampert, J. B. Garcia, M. E., Kohl, H. W., & Blair, S. N. (1999). Comparison of lifestyle and structured interventions to increase physical activity and cardiorespiratory fitness. *Journal of the American Medical Association, 281,* 327-334.

Dunn, J., Steginga, S. K., Occhipinti, S., & Wilson, K. (1999). Evaluation of a peer support program for women with breast cancer–Lessons for practitioners. *Journal of Community & Applied Social Psychology, 9,* 13-22.

Dunne, E. (2000). Consultation, rapport, and collaboration: Essential preliminary stages in research with urban Aboriginal groups. *Australian Journal of Primary Health-Interchange, 6,* 6-14.

Dunphy, D. C. (1981). *Organizational change by choice.* Sydney: McGraw-Hill.

Durie, M. (1994). *Whaiora: Maori health development.* New York: Oxford University Press.

Durlak, J. A. (1977). Primary prevention programs in schools. *Advances in Clinical Child Psychology, 19,* 283-318.

Durlak, J. A., & Wells, A. M. (1998). Evaluation of indicated preventive intervention (secondary prevention) mental health programs for children and adolescents. *American Journal of Community Psychology, 26,* 775-802.

Durrenberger, E. P. (1997). That'll teach you: Cognition and practice in a Chicago union local. *Human Organization, 56,* 388-392.

Dush, D. M., Hirt, M. L., & Scroeder, H. E. (1989). Self-statement modification in the treatment of child behavior disorders: A meta-analysis. *Psychological Bulletin, 106,* 97-106.

Dwyer, W. O., Leeming, F. C., Cobern, M. K., Porter, B. E., & Jackson, J. M. (1993). Critical review of behavioral interventions to preserve the environment: Research since 1980. *Environment and Behavior, 25,* 275-321.

D'Zurilla, T. J., & Goldfried, M. R. (1971). Problem-solving and behavior modification. *Journal of Abnormal Psychology, 78,* 107-126.

Edleson, J. L., & Tolman, R. M. (1992). *Intervention for men who batter: An ecological approach.* London: Sage.

Edwards, D. (1997). *Discourse and cognition.* London: Sage.

Edwards, R., Brown, J. S., Hodgson, P., Kyle, D., Reed, D., & Wallace, B. (1999). An action plan for tobacco control at regional level. *Public Health, 113,* 165-170.

Edwards, S., & Dickerson, M. (1987). On the similarity of positive and negative intrusions. *Behaviour Research and Therapy, 25,* 207-211.

Eggleston, E. J. (2000). Wilderness rehabilitation: An 18-month follow-up of the Whakapakari Youth Programme. *Social Policy Journal of New Zealand, 14,* 164-178.

Elliott, A. J., Miltenberger, R. G., Kaster-Bundgaard, J., & Lumley, V. (1996). A national survey of assessment and therapy techniques used by behavior therapists. *Cognitive and Behavioral Practice, 3*, 107-125.

Elliott, B. (1989). *Effective road safety campaigns: A practical handbook* (Report CR80). Adelaide, South Australia: South Australian Department of Transport.

Ellis, A. (2003). Cognitive restructuring of the disputing of irrational beliefs. In W. O'Donohue, J. E. Fisher & S. C. Hayes (Eds.), *Cognitive behavior therapy: Applying empirically supported techniques in your practice* (pp. 79-83). New York: Wiley.

Emmelkamp, P. M. G., & de Lange, I. (1983). Spouse involvement in the treatment of obsessive-compulsive patients. *Behaviour Research and Therapy, 21*, 341-346.

Englemann, S., & Carnine, D. W. (1982). *Theory of instruction: Principles and applications.* New York: Irvington.

Ennett, S. T., Rosenbaum, D. P., Flewelling, R. L., Beiler, G. S., Ringwalt, C. L., & Bailey, S. L. (1994). Long-term evaluation of drug abuse resistance education. *Addictive Behaviors, 19*, 113-125.

Epstein, L. H. (1996). Family-based behavioral intervention for obese children. *International Journal of Obesity, 20*, S14-S21.

Epstein, L. H., & Masek, B. J. (1978). Behavioral control of medicine compliance. *Journal of Applied Behavior Analysis, 11*, 1-9.

Epstein, L. H., Wing, R. R., Koeske, R., & Valoski, A. (1987). Long-term effects of family-based treatment of childhood obesity. *Journal of Consulting and Clinical Psychology, 55*, 91-95.

Erickson, M. H. (1980a). *Hypnotic alteration of sensory, perceptual and psychophysical processes. The collected papers of Milton H. Erickson on hypnosis, Volume II.* New York: Irvington Publishers.

Erickson, M. H. (1980b). *Innovative hypnotherapy. The collected papers of Milton H. Erickson on hypnosis, Volume IV.* New York: Irvington Publishers.

Ernst, C. C., Grant, T. M., Streissguth, A. P., & Sampson, P. D. (1999). Intervention with high-risk alcohol and drug-abusing mothers: II. Three-year findings from the Seattle Model of paraprofessional advocacy. *Journal of Community Psychology, 27*, 19-38.

Evans, I. M., & Ave, K. T. (2000). Mentoring children and youth: Principles, issues, and policy implications for community programmes in New Zealand. *New Zealand Journal of Psychology, 29*, 41-49.

Evans, I. M., & Okifuji, A. (1992). Home-school partnerships: A behavioral community approach to childhood behavior disorders. *New Zealand Journal of Psychology, 21*, 14-24.

Evans, I. M., Meyer, L. M., Kurkjian, J. A., & Kushi, G. S. (1988). An evaluation of behavioral interrelationships in child behavior therapy. In J. C. Witt, S. N. Elliott, & F. M. Gresham (Eds.), *Handbook of behavior therapy in education* (pp. 189-215). New York: Plenum Press.

Evans, I. M., & Moltzen, N. L. (2000). Defining effective community support for long-term psychiatric patients according to behavioural principles. *Australian and New Zealand Journal of Psychiatry, 34*, 637-644.

Fairbank, J. A., & Prue, D. M. (1982). Developing performance feedback systems. In L. W. Frederiksen. (Ed.), *Handbook of organizational behavior management* (pp. 281-299). New York: Wiley.

Fearon, J. D. (1998). Bargaining, enforcement, and international cooperation. *International Organization, 52*, 269-305.

Fearon, J. D., & Laitin, D. D. (1996). Explaining interethnic cooperation. *American Political Science Review, 90*, 715-735.

Febbraro, G. A. R., Clum, G. A., Roodman, A. A., & Wright, J. H. (1999). The limits of bibliotherapy: A study of the differential effectiveness of self-administered interventions in individuals with panic attacks. *Behavior Therapy, 30*, 209-222.

Feldman, D. C. (1985). A taxonomy of intergroup conflict-resolution strategies. *The 1985 Annual: Developing Human Resources*, 169-175.

Fellner, D. J., & Sulzer-Azaroff, B. (1984). A behavioral analysis of goal setting. *Journal of Organizational Behavior Management, 6*, 33-51.

Fengqin, L. (1999). Rural poverty alleviation in China. In J. Mullen (Ed.), *Rural poverty, empowerment and sustainable livelihoods* (pp. 52-58). Aldershot: Ashgate.

Ferguson, K. E. (2003). Shaping. In W. O'Donohue, J. E. Fisher & S. C. Hayes (Eds.), *Cognitive behavior therapy: Applying empirically supported techniques in your practice* (pp. 374-383). New York: Wiley.

Fetterman, D. M. (Ed.). (1993). *Speaking the language of power: Communication, collaboration and advocacy (translating ethnography into action)*. New York: Falmer Press.

Findlayson, J. ((2001-2002). Anthropology's contribution to public policy formulation: The imagined other? *Australian Aboriginal Studies*, 18-26.

Finkle, J. L., & McIntosh, C. A. (Eds.). (1994). *The new politics of population: Conflict and consensus in family planning*. New York: Oxford University Press.

Finnigan, O. D., & Sun, T. H. (1972). Planning, starting, and operating an educational incentives project. *Studies in Family Planning, 3,* 1-7.

Fisher, P. A., & Ball, T. J. (2003). Tribal participatory research: Mechanisms of a collaborative model. *American Journal of Community Psychology, 32,* 207-216.

Fiske, S., & Chambers, E. (1996). The inventions of practice. *Human Organization, 55,* 1-12.

Fo, W. S. O., & O'Donnell, C. R. (1974). The buddy system: Relationship and contingency conditions in a community intervention program for youth with nonprofessionals as behavior change agents. *Journal of Consulting and Clinical Psychology, 42,* 163-169.

Foa, E. B., Steketee, G., Grayson, J. B., Turner, R. M., & Latimer, P. R. (1984). Deliberate exposure and blocking of obsessive-compulsive rituals: Immediate and long-term effects. *Behavior Therapy, 15,* 450-472.

Fontaine, G. (1986). Roles of social support systems in overseas relocation: Implications for intercultural training. *International Journal of Intercultural Relations, 10,* 361-378.

Forbat, L. (2003). Concepts and understandings of dementia by 'gatekeepers' and minority ethnic 'service users'. *Journal of Health Psychology, 8,* 645-655.

Forehand, R. (1977). Child compliance to parental requests: Behavior analysis. In M. Hersen, R. M. Eisler & P. M. Miller (Eds.), *Progress in behavior modification* (Vol. 5, pp. 111-147). New York: Academic Press.

Forehand, R., & Kotchick, B. A. (1996). Cultural diversity: A wake-up call for parent training. *Behavior Therapy, 27,* 187-206.

Foreit, K. G., de Castro, M. P. P., & Franco, E. F. D. (1989). The impact of mass media advertising on a voluntary sterilization program in Brazil. *Studies in Family Planning,20,* 107-116.

Foster, M. (1972). The theory and practice of action research in work organisations. *Human Relations, 25,* 529-556.

Foucault, M. (1973). *The birth of the clinic*. London: Tavistock.

Foucault, M. (1977). *Discipline and punish*. London: Allen Lane.

Foucault, M. (1978). *The history of sexuality: Vol. 1. An introduction*. New York: Vintage Books.

Fowler, S. A., Dougherty, B. S., Kirby, K. C., & Kohler, F. W. (1986). Role reversals: An analysis of therapeutic effects achieved with disruptive boys during their appointments as peer monitors. *Journal of Applied Behavior Analysis, 19,* 437-444.

Foxx, R. M. (1996). Twenty years of applied behavior analysis in treating the most severe problem behavior: Lessons learned. *The Behavior Analyst, 19,* 225-235.

Foxx, R. M., & Rubinoff, A. (1979). Behavioral treatment of caffeinism: Reducing excessive coffee drinking. *Journal of Applied Behavior Analysis, 12,* 335-344.

Frank, R. G., Bouman, D. E., Cain, K., & Watts, C. (1992). Primary prevention of catastrophic injury. *American Psychologist, 47,* 1045-1049.

Frankel, F., & Simmons, J. Q. (1992). Parent behavioral training: Why and when some parents drop out. *Journal of Clinical Child Psychology, 21,* 322-330.

Frederiksen, L. W. (Ed.). (1982). *Handbook of organizational behavior management*. New York: Wiley.

Freedman, R. (1987). The contribution of social science research to population policy and family planning program effectiveness. *Studies in Family Planning, 18,* 57-82.

Freedman, R. (1997). Do family planning programs affect fertility preferences? A literature review. *Studies in Family Planning, 28,* 1-13.

Freeston, M. H., & Ladouceur, R. (1997). What do patients do with their obsessive thoughts? *Behaviour Research and Therapy, 35,* 335-348.

Freeston, M. H., Ladouceur, R., Gagnon, F., Thibodeau, N., Rhéaume, J., Letarte, H., & Bujold, A. (1997). Cognitive-behavioral treatment of obsessive thoughts: A controlled study. *Journal of Consulting and Clinical Psychology, 65,* 405-413.

Freitas, M. F. Q. (1998). Models of practice in community in Brazil: Possibilities for the psychology-community relationship. *Journal of Community Psychology, 26,* 261-268.

Friman, P. C., & Finney, J. W. (2003). Time-out (and time-in). In W. O'Donohue, J. E. Fisher & S. C. Hayes (Eds.), *Cognitive behavior therapy: Applying empirically supported techniques in your practice* (pp. 429-435). New York: Wiley.

Fruzzetti, A. R., & Fruzzetti, A. E. (2003). Dialectics in cognitive and behavior therapy. In W. O'Donohue, J. E. Fisher & S. C. Hayes (Eds.), *Cognitive behavior therapy: Applying empirically supported techniques in your practice* (pp. 121-128). New York: Wiley.

Fruzzetti, A. E., Shenk, C., Mosco, E., & Lowry, K. (2003). Emotion regulation. In W. O'Donohue, J. E. Fisher & S. C. Hayes (Eds.), *Cognitive behavior therapy: Applying empirically supported techniques in your practice* (pp. 152-159). New York: Wiley.

Fundación Sabiduría Indígena (FSI) and Kothari, B. (1997). Rights to the benefits of research: Compensating indigenous peoples for their intellectual contribution. *Human Organization, 56,* 127-137.

Gaertner, S. L., Dovidion, J. F., Rust, M. C., Nier, J. A., Banker, B. S., Ward, C. M., Mottola, G. R., & Houlette, M. (1999). Reducing intergroup bias: Elements of intergroup competition. *Journal of Personality and Social Psychology, 76,* 388-402.

Gaetz, S. (1995). 'Youth development'—Conflict and negotiations in an urban Irish youth club. In P. Caplan (Ed.), *Understanding disputes: The politics of argument* (pp. 181-201). Oxford, Providence: Berg.

García, J. G., & Zea, M. C. (Eds.). (1997). *Psychological interventions and research with Latino populations.* London: Allyn and Bacon.

Gardner, R., Sainato, D. M., Cooper, J. O., Heron, T. E., Heward, W. L., Eschleman, J. W., & Grossi, T. A. (1994). *Behavior analysis in education: Focus on measurably superior instruction.* Pacific Grove, CA: Brooks/Cole.

Garven, S., Wod, J. M., & Malpass, R. S. (2000). Allegations of wrongdoing: The effects of reinforcement on children's mundane and fantastic claims. *Journal of Applied Psychology, 85,* 38-49.

Gatmon, D., Jackson, D., Koshkarian, L., Martos-Perry, N., Molina, A., Patel, N., & Rodolfa, E. (2001). Exploring ethnic, gender, and sexual orientation variables in supervision: Do they really matter? *Journal of Multicultural Counseling and Development, 29,* 102-113.

Gawron, V. J., Dennison, T. W., & Biferno, M. A. (1996). Mockups, physical and electronic models, and simulations. In T. G. O'Brien & S. G. Charleton (Eds.), *Handbook of human factors testing and evaluation* (pp. 43-80). Mahwah, NJ: Erlbaum.

Gaylord-Ross, R. J., Haring, T. G., Breen, C., & Pitts-Conway, V. (1984). The training and generalization of social interaction skills with autistic youth. *Journal of Applied Behavior Analysis, 17,* 229-247.

Gebhardt, D. L., & Crump, C. E. (1990). Employee fitness and wellness programs in the workplace. *American Psychologist, 45,* 262-272.

Geller, E. S., Winett, R. A., & Everett, P. B. (1982). *Preserving the environment: New strategies for behavior change.* New York: Pergamon.

Gena, A., Krantz, P. J., McClannahan, L. E., & Poulson, C. L. (1996). Training and generalization of affective behavior displayed by youth with autism. *Journal of Applied Behavior Analysis, 29,* 291-304.

Gepkens, A., & Gunning-Schepers, L. J. (1996). Intervention to reduce socioeconomic health differences: A review of the international literature. *European Journal of Public Health, 6,* 218-226.

Gertler, P. J., & Molyneaux, J. W. (1994). How economic development and family planning programs combined to reduce Indonesian fertility. *Demography, 31,* 33-63.

Gilbert, T. F. (1978). *Human competence: Engineering worthy performance.* New York: McGraw-Hill.

Girgis, A., Doran, C. M., Sanson-Fisher, R. W., & Walsh, R. A. (1995). Smoking by adolescents: Large revenue but little for prevention. *Australian Journal of Public Health, 19,* 29-33.

Glasgow, R. E., & Terborg, J. R. (1988). Occupational health promotion programs to reduce cardiovascular risk. *Journal of Consulting and Clinical Psychology, 56,* 365-373.

Glick, B., & Goldstein, A. P. (1999). Aggression replacement training: A comprehensive approach for assultive, violent, and ganging youth. In J. R. Scotti & L. H. Meyer (Eds.), *Behavioral intervention: Principles, models, and practices* (pp. 195-211). London: Paul H. Brookes.

Glynn, T., & McNaughton, S. (1985). The Mangere home and school remedial reading procedures: Continuing research on their effectiveness. *New Zealand Journal of Psychology, 14,* 66-77.

Goldberg, H. I., & Toros, A. (1994). The use of traditional methods of contraception among Turkish couples. *Studies in Family Planning, 25,* 122-128.

Goldblat, J. (1999). Anti-personnel mines: From mere restrictions to a total ban. *Security Dialogue, 30,* 9-23.

Goldman, A. (1994). The centrality of "Ningensei" to Japanese negotiating and interpersonal relationships: Implication for U.S.–Japanese communication. *International Journal of Intercultural Relationships, 18,* 29-54.

Goldstein, A. P., & Sorcher, M. (1974). *Changing supervisor behavior.* New York: Pergamon.

Goltz, S. M., Citera, M., Jensen, M., Favero, J., & Komaki, J. L. (1989). Individual feedback: Does it enhance effects of group feedback? *Journal of Organizational Behavior Management, 10,* 77-92.

Gonsalves, C. J. (1992). Psychological stages of the refugee process: A model for therapeutic interventions. *Professional Psychology: Research and Practice, 23,* 382-389.

Goodnow, J. J. (1980). Differences in popular theories of instruction. In J. R. Kirby and J. B. Biggs (Eds.), *Cognition, development, and instruction* (pp. 187-197). New York: Academic Books.

Gordon, D. (1978). *Therapeutic metaphors.* Cupertino, CA: Meta Publications.

Gorman, D. M., & Speer, P. W. (1996). Preventing alcohol abuse and alcohol-related problems through community interventions: A review of evaluation studies. *Psychology and Health, 11,* 95-131.

Gotlib, I. H., & Krasnoperova, E. (1998). Biased information processing as a vulnerability factor for depression. *Behavior Therapy, 29,* 603-617.

Gould, D., Damarjian, N., & Medbery, R. (1999). An examination of mental skills training in junior tennis coaches. *The Sports Psychologist, 13,* 127-143.

Govindasamy, P., & Malhotra, A. (1996). Women's position and family planning in Egypt. *Studies in Family Planning, 27,* 328-340.

Grant, T. M., Ernst, C. C., & Streissguth, A. P. (1999). Intervention with high-risk alcohol and drug-abusing mothers: I. Administrative strategies of the Seattle Model of paraprofessional advocacy. *Journal of Community Psychology, 27,* 1-18.

Greenspoon, J. (1997). Compliance, health service, and behavior analysis. In P. Lamal (Ed.), *Cultural contingencies: Behavior analytic perspectives on cultural practices* (pp. 31-52). London: Praeger.

Greenwood, C. R. et al. (1992). Out of the laboratory and into the community: 26 years of applied behavior analysis as the Juniper Gardens Children's Project. *American Psychologist, 47,* 1464-1474.

Greenwood, C. R., Dinwiddie, G., Bailey, V., Carta, J. J., Dorsey, D., Kohler, F. W., Nelson, C., Rotholz, D., & Schulte, D. (1987). Field replication of classwide peer tutoring. *Journal of Applied Behavior Analysis, 20,* 151-160.

Greer, R. D. (1996). The education crisis. In M. A. Mattaini & B. A. Thyer (Eds.), *Finding solutions to social problems: Behavioral strategies for change* (pp. 113-146). Washington, DC: American Psychological Association.

Grossman, J. B., & Tierney, J P. (1998). Does mentoring work? An impact study of the Big Brothers Big Sisters Program. *Evaluation Review, 22,* 401-426.

Grote, I., Rosales, J., & Baer, D. M. (1996). A task analysis of the shift from teacher instructions to self-instructions in performing an in-common task. *Journal of Experimental Child Psychology, 63,* 339-357.

Grote, I., Rosales, J., Morrison, K., Royer, C., & Baer, D. M. (1997). A use of self-instruction to extend the generalization of a self-instructed in-common discrimination. *Journal of Experimental Child Psychology, 66,* 144-162.

Guerin, B. (1994). *Analyzing social behavior: Behavior analysis and the social sciences.* Reno, NV: Context Press.

Guerin, B. (1997). How things get done: Socially, non-socially; with words, without words. In L. J. Hayes & P. Ghezzi (Eds.), *Investigations in behavioral epistemology* (pp. 219-235). Reno, NV: Context Press.

Guerin, B. (2001a). What makes human social behavior look so special? Putting psychology into the social sciences. *Mexican Journal of Behavior Analysis, 27,* 263-284.

Guerin, B. (2001b). Explanations of bereavement, grief, and trauma: The misuse of both mental and foundational terms. *European Journal of Behaviour Analysis, 2,* 154-161.

Guerin, B. (2001c). Individuals as social relationships: 18 ways that acting alone can be thought of as social behavior. *Review of General Psychology, 5,* 406-428.

Guerin, B. (2001d). Replacing catharsis and uncertainty reduction theories with descriptions of the historical and social context. *Review of General Psychology, 5,* 44-61.

Guerin, B. (2003a). Language use as social strategy: A review and an analytic framework for the social sciences. *Review of General Psychology, 7,* 251-298.

Guerin, B. (2003b). Putting a radical socialness into consumer behaviour analysis. *Journal of Economic Psychology, 24,* 697-718.

Guerin, B. (2004). *Handbook for analyzing the social strategies of everyday life.* Reno, Nevada: Context Press.

Guerin, B. (2005a). *Handbook of interventions for changing people and communities.* Reno, Nevada: Context Press.

Guerin, B. (2005b). *Arthur F. Bentley, social Scientist: His relevance to the contemporary social sciences.* Book in progress.

Guerin, B., Guerin, P. B., Diiriye, R. O., & Abdi, A. (2004). Living in a close community: The everyday life of Somali refugees. *Network: Journal of the Australian College of Community Psychologists, 16,* 7-17.

Guerin, B., Guerin, P. B., Diiriye, R. O., & Yates, S. (2004). Somali conceptions and expectations of mental health: Some guidelines for mental health professionals. *New Zealand Journal of Psychology, 33,* 59-67.

Guerin, P. B., & Elmi, F. H. (2004). The analysis of female circumcision stories: The uses and abuses of oral histories. *Oral History in New Zealand, 16,* 9-16.

Gumpel, T. P., & Frank, R. (1999). An expansion of the peer-tutoring paradigm: Cross-age peer tutoring of social skills among socially rejected boys. *Journal of Applied Behavior Analysis, 32,* 115-118.

Gunthorpe, W., & Guerin, B. (1996). Conversational expansions and initiations form a response class for adults with intellectual handicaps. *Japanese Journal of Behavior Analysis, 9,* 2-10.

Guyall, M., Spoth, R. L., Chao, W., Wickrama, K. A. S., & Russell, D. (2004). Family-focused preventive interventions: Evaluating parental risk moderation of substance use trajectories. *Journal of Family Psychology, 18,* 293-301.

Gwynne, M. A. (2003). *Applied anthropology: A career-oriented approach.* New York: Pearson Education.

Hackenberg, R. A. (1999). Strategic and game plans. *Human Organization, 58,* 105-107.

Hackenberg, R. A. (2002). Closing the gap between anthropology and public policy: The route through cultural heritage development. *Human Organization, 61,* 288-298.

Hackenberg, R. A., & Hackenberg, B. H. (1999). You CAN do something! Forming policy from applied projects, then and now. *Human Organization, 58,* 1-15.

Haines, K., & Case, S. (2005). Promoting prevention: Targeting family-based risk and protective factors for drug use and youth offending in Swansea. *British Journal of Social Work, 35,* 169-187.

Haley, J. (1973). *Uncommon therapy: The psychiatric techniques of Milton H. Erickson, M.D.* London: Norton.

Hall, B. L. (1982). Strategic planning for employee productivity improvement. In L. W. Frederiksen. (Ed.), *Handbook of organizational behavior management* (pp. 301-328). New York: Wiley.

Handmer, J., Keys, C., & Elliott, J. (1999). Achieving lasting change in multi-organizational tasks: The case of flood warnings in Australia. *Applied Geography, 19,* 179-197.

Hankin, J. R., Sloan, J. J., & Sokol, R. J. (1998). The modest impact of the alcohol beverage warning label on drinking during pregnancy among a sample of African-American women. *Journal of Public Policy & Marketing, 17,* 61-69.

Hansen, J., & Pearson, P. D. (1983). An instructional study: Improving the inferential comprehension of good and poor fourth-grade readers. *Journal of Educational Psychology, 75,* 821-829.

Hansen, W. B., & McNeal, R. B. (1997). How D.A.R.E. works: An examination of program effects on mediating variables. *Health Education & Behavior, 24,* 165-176.

Haring, T. G. (1993). Research basis of instructional procedures to promote social interaction and integration. In R. A. Gable & S. F. Warren (Eds.), *Strategies for teaching students with mild to severe mental retardation* (pp. 129-164). London: Jessica Kingsley Publishers.

Harpham, T., Burton, S., & Blue, I. (2001). Healthy cities projects in developing countries: The first evaluation. *Health Promotion International, 16,* 111-125.

Harré, N., & Field, J. (1998). Safe driving education programs at school: Lessons from New Zealand. *Australian and New Zealand Journal of Public Health, 22,* 447-450.

Harris, N. (1995). *The new untouchables: Immigration and the new world worker.* London: Penguin Books.

Harris, S. (1984). *Culture and learning: Tradition and education in north-east Arnhem Land.* Canberra: Australian Institute of Aboriginal Studies.

Harris, S. (1990). *Two-way Aboriginal schooling: Education and cultural survival.* Canberra: Aboriginal Studies Press.

Harrison, D. F., Thyer, B. A., & Wodarski, J. S. (1996). *Cultural diversity and social work practice.* Springfield, IL: Charles C. Thomas.

Hawkins, J. D., Catalano, R. F., & Miller, J. Y. (1992). Risk and protective factors for alcohol and other drug problems in adolescence and early adulthood: Implications for substance abuse programs. *Psychological Bulletin, 112,* 64-105.

Hawkins, R. P., Mathews, J. R., & Hamdan, L. (1999). *Measuring behavioral health outcomes: A practical guide.* New York: Plenum.

Hawton, K., Salkovskis, P. M., Kirk, J., & Clark, D. M. (1989). *Cognitive behavior therapy for psychiatric problems: A practical guide.* New York: Oxford University Press.

Hayes, S. C., Follette, V. M., & Linehan, M. M. (Eds.). (2004). *Mindfulness and acceptance: Expanding the cognitive-behavioral tradition.* NY: Guilford Press.

Hayes, S. C., Jacobson, N. S., Follette, V. M., & Dougher, M. J. (Eds.). (1994). *Acceptance and change: Content and context in psychotherapy.* Reno, NV: Context Press.

Hayes, S. C., & Pankey, J. (2003). Acceptance. In W. O'Donohue, J. E. Fisher & S. C. Hayes (Eds.), *Cognitive behavior therapy: Applying empirically supported techniques in your practice* (pp. 4-9). New York: Wiley.

Hayes, S. C., Strosahl, K. D., & Wilson, K. G. (1999). *Acceptance and commitment therapy: An experiential approach to behavior change.* NY: Guilford Press.

Hayes, S. C., & Wilson, K. G. (1994). Acceptance and commitment therapy: Altering the verbal support for experiential avoidance. *The Behavior Analyst, 17,* 289-303.

Hazel, J. S., Schumaker, J. B., Sherman, J. A., & Sheldon-Wildgen, J. (1981). The development and evaluation of a group social skills training program for court-adjudicated youths. In D. Upper & S. M. Ross (Eds.), *Behavioral group therapy, 1981: An annual review* (pp. 113-152). Champaign, IL: Research Press.

Head, L. S., & Gross, A. M. (2003). Systematic desensitization. In W. O'Donohue, J. E. Fisher & S. C. Hayes (Eds.), *Cognitive behavior therapy: Applying empirically supported techniques in your practice* (pp. 417-422). New York: Wiley.

Heiby, E. M., & Frank, M. R. (2003). Compliance with medical regimens. In W. O'Donohue, J. E. Fisher & S. C. Hayes (Eds.), *Cognitive behavior therapy: Applying empirically supported techniques in your practice* (pp. 103-108). New York: Wiley.

Heidt, J. M., & Marx, B. P. (2003). Self-monitoring as a treatment vehicle. In W. O'Donohue, J. E. Fisher & S. C. Hayes (Eds.), *Cognitive behavior therapy: Applying empirically supported techniques in your practice* (pp. 361-367). New York: Wiley.

Helms, J. E., & Carter, R. T. (1991). Relationship of White and Black racial identity attitudes and demographics similarity to counselor preferences. *Journal of Counseling Psychology, 38,* 446-457.

Hempenstall, K. (1996). The gulf between educational research and policy: The example of direct instruction and whole language. *Behaviour Change, 13,* 33-46.

Henk, W. A., & Helfeldt, J. P. (1987). How to develop independence in following written instructions. *Journal of Reading, 30,* 602-607.

Herbert-Cheshire, L. (2000). Contemporary strategies for rural community development in Australia: A governmentality perspective. *Journal of Rural Studies, 16,* 203-215.

Herbinger, W., Crawshaw, B., & Shaw, J. (1999). Beneficiary participation in context: Practical experiences from a food-aided project in Ethiopia. In J. Mullen (Ed.), *Rural poverty, empowerment and sustainable livelihoods* (pp. 1-13). Aldershot: Ashgate.

Herr, P. M., Kardes, F. R., & Kim, J. (1991). Effects of word-of-mouth and product-attribute information on persuasion: An accessibility-diagnosticity perspective. *Journal of Consumer Research, 17,* 454-462.

Hess, G. A. (1993). Testifying on the Hill: Using ethnographic data to shape public policy. In D. M. Fetterman (Ed.), *Speaking the language of power: Communication, collaboration and advocacy (translating ethnography into action)* (pp. 38-49). New York: Falmer Press.

Hewstone, M. (1996). Contact and categorization: Social psychological interventions to change intergroup relations. In C. N. Macrae, C. Stangor & M. Hewstone (Eds.), *Stereotypes & stereotyping* (pp. 323-368). New York: Guilford.

Hill, D., Chapman, S., & Donovan, R. (1998). The return of scare tactics. *Tobacco Control, 7,* 5-8.

Hill, P. S. (2000). Planning and change: A Cambodian public health case study. *Social Science and Medicine, 51,* 1711-1722.

Hoberman, H. M., Clarke, G. N., & Saunders, S. M. (1996). Psychosocial interventions for adolescent depression: Issues, evidence, and future directions. In M. Hersen, R. M. Eisler & P. M. Miller (Eds.), *Progress in behavior modification* (Vol. 30, pp. 25-73). London: Brooks/Cole.

Hoffart, A. (1998). Cognitive and guided mastery therapy of agoraphobia: Long-term outcome and mechanisms of change. *Cognitive Therapy and Research, 22,* 195-207.

Hogan, B. E., Linden, W., & Najarian, B. (2002). Social support interventions: Do they work? *Clinical Psychology Review, 2,* 381-440.

Hogan, D. P., Berhanu, B., & Hailemariam, A. (1999). Household organization, women's autonomy, and contraceptive behavior in Southern Ethiopia. *Studies in Family Planning, 30,* 303-314.

Hogue, A., & Liddle, H. A. (1999). Family-based preventive intervention: An approach to preventing substance use and antisocial behavior. *American Journal of Orthopsychiatry, 69,* 278-293.

Holding, D. H. (1970a). Guidance. In D. Legge (Ed.), *Skills: Selected readings* (pp. 266-275). Harmondsworth, Middlesex: Penguin.

Holding, D. H. (1970b). Knowledge of results. In D. Legge (Ed.), *Skills: Selected readings* (pp. 249-265). Harmondsworth, Middlesex: Penguin.

Holquist, M. (1990). *Dialogism: Bakhtin and his world.* London: Routledge.

Homans, G. C. (1941). Anxiety and ritual: The theories of Malinowski and Radcliffe-Brown. *American Anthropologist, 43,* 164-172.

Hooker, J. (2003). *Working across cultures.* Stanford, CA: Stanford Business Books.

Horner, R. D., & Keilitz, I. (1975). Training mentally retarded adolescents to brush their teeth. *Journal of Applied Behavior Analysis, 8,* 301-309.

Horner, R. H., Dunlap, G., Koegel, R. L., Carr, E. G., Sailor, W., Anderson, J., Albin, R. W., & O'Neill, R. E. (1990). Toward a technology of 'nonaversive' behavioral support. *Journal of the Association for Persons with Severe Handicaps, 15,* 123-132.

Hornstein, H. A. (1975). Social psychology as social intervention. In M. Deutsch & H. A. Hornstein (Eds.), *Applying social psychology: Implications for research, practice, and training* (pp. 211-234). Hillsdale, NJ: Erlbaum.

Hotchkiss, D. R., Magnani, R. J., Lakssir, A., Brown, L. F., & Florence, C. S. (1999). Family planning program effects on contraceptive use in Morocco, 1992-1995. *Population Research and Policy Review, 18,* 545-561.

Houghton, S., & Glynn, T. (1993). Peer tutoring of below average secondary school readers using pause, prompt, and praise: The successive introduction of tutoring components. *Behaviour Change, 20,* 75-85.

Howson, A. (1999). Cervical screening, compliance and moral obligation. *Sociology of Health and Illness, 21,* 401-425.

Hubbard, A. S. (1999). Cultural and status differences in intergroup conflict resolution: A longitudinal study of a Middle East dialogue group in the United States. *Human Relations, 52,* 303-325.

Huebner, C. E. (2000). Promoting toddlers' language development through community-based intervention. *Journal of Applied Developmental Psychology, 21,* 513-535.

Hughes, C., Killian, D. J., & Fischer, G. M. (1996). Validation and assessment of a conversational interaction intervention. *American Journal on Mental Retardation, 100,* 493-509.

Hull, T. H., Hasmi, E., & Widyantoro, N. (2004). "Peer" educator initiatives for adolescent reproductive health projects in Indonesia. *Reproductive Health Matters, 12,* 29-39.

Humphries, T. L. (1999). Improving peer mediation programs: Student experiences and suggestions. *Professional School Counseling, 3,* 13-21.

Hundert, J., & Hopkins, B. (1992). Training supervisors in a collaborative team approach to promote peer integration of children with disabilities in integrated schools. *Journal of Applied Behavior Analysis, 25,* 385-400.

Hutchby, I. (1992). The pursuit of controversy: Routine skepticism on 'talk radio'. *Sociology, 26,* 673-694.

Improving social competence. (1992). [Special Issue]. *Journal of Applied Behavior Analysis, 25* (2).

Ingersoll-Dayton, B., Schroepfer, T., Pryce, J., & Waarala, C. (2003). Enhancing relationships in nursing homes through empowerment. *Social Work, 48,* 420-424.

Irvin, J. E., Bowers, C. A., Dunn, M. E., & Wang, M. C. (1999). Efficacy of relapse prevention: A meta-analytic review. *Journal of Consulting and Clinical Psychology, 67,* 563-570.

Ivancevich, J. M., Matteson, M. T., Freedman, S., & Phillips, J. S. (1990). Worksite stress management interventions. *American Psychologist, 45,* 252-261.

Iwata, B. A., Pace, G. M., Cowdery, G. E., & Miltenberger, R. G. (1994). What makes extinction work: An analysis of procedural form and function. *Journal of Applied Behavior Analysis, 27,* 131-144.

Jamison, C., & Scogin, F. (1995). The outcome of cognitive bibliotherapy with depressed adults. *Journal of Consulting and Clinical Psychology, 63,* 644-650.

Janelle, C. M. (1999). Ironic mental processes in sport: Implications for sports psychologists. *The Sports Psychologist, 13,* 201-220.

Janis, I. L. (Ed.). (1982). *Counseling on personal decisions: Theory and research on short-term helping relationships.* London: Yale University Press.

Jason, L., Billows, W., Schnopp-Wyatt, D., & King, C. (1996). Reducing the illegal sales of cigarettes to minors: Analysis of alternative enforcement schedules. *Journal of Applied Behavior Analysis, 29,* 333-344.

Jason, L. A., McMahon, S. D., Salina, D., Hedeker, D., Stockton, M., Dunson, K., & Kimball, P. (1995). Assessing a smoking cessation intervention involving groups, incentives, and self-help manuals. *Behavior Therapy, 26,* 393-408.

Joffe, J. M., & Albee, G. W. (Eds.). (1981). *Prevention through political action and social change.* London: University Press of New England.

Johnson, K. M., Lando, H. A., Schmid, L. S., & Solberg, L. I. (1997). The GAINS Project: Outcome of smoking cessation strategies in four urban Native American clinics. *Addictive Behaviors, 22,* 207-218.

Johnson, K. R., & Layng, T. V. J. (1992). Breaking the structuralist barrier: Literacy and numeracy with fluency. *American Psychologist, 47,* 1475-1490.

Jones, J. W., Barge, B. N., Steffy, B. D., Fay, L. M., Kunz, L. K., & Wuebker, L. J. (1988). Stress and medical malpractice: Organizational risk assessment and intervention. *Journal of Applied Psychology, 73,* 727-735.

Josephs, I. E., & Valsiner, J. (1998). How does autodialogue work? Miracles of meaning maintenance and circumvention strategies. *Social Psychology Quarterly, 61,* 68-83.

Juster, H. R., Heimberg, R. G., & Holt, C. S. (1996). Social phobia: Diagnostic issue and review of cognitive behavioral treatment strategies. In M. Hersen, R. M. Eisler & P. M. Miller (Eds.), *Progress in behavior modification* (Vol. 30, pp. 74-98). London: Brooks/Cole.

Kagitcibasi, C., Sunar, D., & Bekman, S. (2001). Long-term effects of early intervention: Turkish low-income mothers and children. *Applied Developmental Psychology, 22*, 333-361.

Kaluza, G. (2000). Changing unbalanced coping profiles–A prospective controlled intervention trial in worksite health promotion. *Psychology and Health, 15*, 423-433.

Kambo, I. P., Gupta, R. N., Kundu, A. S., Dhillon, B. S., Saxena, H. M., & Saxena, B. N. (1994). Use of traditional medical practitioners to deliver family planning services in Uttar Pradesh. *Studies in Family Planning,25*, 32-40.

Kamps, D. M., Barbetta, P. M., Leonard, B. R., & Delquadri, J. (1994). Classwide peer tutoring: An integration strategy to improve reading skills and promote peer interactions among students with autism and general education peers. *Journal of Applied Behavior Analysis, 27*, 49-61.

Kane, T. T., Gueye, M., Speizer, I., Pacque-Margolis, S., & Baron, D. (1998). The impact of a family planning multimedia campaign in Bamako, Mali. *Studies in Family Planning, 29*, 309-323.

Kanfer, R., Ackerman, P. L., Murtha, T. C., Dugdale, B., & Nelson, L. (1994). Goal setting, conditions of practice, and task performance: A resource allocation perspective. *Journal of Applied Psychology, 79*, 826-835.

Kantor, J. R. (1969). *The scientific evolution of psychology.* Chicago: Principia Press.

Kaplan, R. D. (1993). *Balkan ghosts: A journey through history.* New York: Vintage Books.

Kaplan, R. D. (1996). *The ends of the earth: From Togo to Turkmenistan, from Iran to Cambodia–A journey to the frontiers of anarchy.* New York: Vintage Books.

Karwowski, W. (Ed.). (2001). *International encyclopedia of ergonomics and human factors* (3 Vols). London: Taylor & Francis.

Kassin, S. M., & McNall, K. (1991) Police interrogation and confessions: Communicating promises and threats by pragmatic implication. *Law and Human Behavior, 15*, 233-251.

Katz, P. A., & Zalk, S. R. (1978). Modification of children's racial attitudes. *Developmental Psychology, 14*, 447-461.

Kaufmann, F. X., Majone, G., & Ostrom, V. (1986). *Guidance, control, and evaluation in the public sector.* Berlin: De Gruyter.

Kazdin, A. E. (1987). Treatment of antisocial behavior in children: Current status and future directions. *Psychological Bulletin, 102*, 187-203.

Keen, I. (2004). *Aboriginal economy and society: Australia at the threshold of colonisation.* Oxford: Oxford University Press.

Keller, J. J. (1991). The recycling solution: How I increased recycling on Dilworth Road. *Journal of Applied Behavior Analysis, 24*, 617-619.

Keller, P. A. (1999). Converting the unconverted: The effects of inclination and opportunity to discount health-related fear appeals. *Journal of Applied Psychology, 84*, 403-415.

Kellermann, A. L., Fuqua-Whitley, D. S., Rivara, F. P., & Mercy, J. (1998). Preventing youth violence: What works? *Annual Review of Public Health, 19*, 271-292.

Kelley, M. L. ((2003). Daily report cards: Home-school contingency management procedures. In W. O'Donohue, J. E. Fisher & S. C. Hayes (Eds.), *Cognitive behavior therapy: Applying empirically supported techniques in your practice* (pp. 114-120). New York: Wiley.

Kelly, A. E. (2000). Helping construct desirable identities: A self-presentational view of psychotherapy. *Psychological Bulletin, 126*, 475-494.

Kelley, J. G., Snowden, L. R., & Muñoz, R. F. (1977). Social and community interventions. *Annual Review of Psychology, 28*, 323-361.

Kelman, H. C. (1983). Conversation with Arafat: A social-psychological assessment of the prospects for Israeli-Palestinian peace. *American Psychologist, 38*, 203-216.

Kelman, H. C. (1997). Group processes in the resolution of international conflicts: Experiences from the Israeli-Palestinian case. *American Psychologist, 52*, 212-220.

Kelman, H. C. (1998). Social-psychological contributions to peacemaking and peacebuilding in the Middle East. *Applied Psychology: An International Review, 47*, 5-28.

Kerr, J., Eves, F. F., & Carroll, D. (2001). Getting more people on the stairs: The impact of a new message format. *Journal of Health Psychology, 6*, 495-500.

Kim, C. S. (1990). The role of the non-western anthropologist reconsidered: Illusion versus reality. *Current Anthropology, 31*, 196-201.

Kirby, K. C., & Bickel, W. K. (1988). Toward an explicit analysis of generalization: A stimulus control interpretation. *The Behavior Analyst, 11*, 115-129.

Kirby, K. C., Fowler, S. A., & Baer, D. M. (1991). Reactivity in self-recording: Obtrusiveness of recording procedure and peer comments. *Journal of Applied Behavior Analysis, 24*, 487-498.

Kirigin, K. A. (2001). The Teaching-Family model: A replicable system of care. In S. I. Pfeiffer & L. A. Reddy (Eds.), *Innovative mental health interventions for children: Programs that work* (pp. 99-110). London: The Haworth Press.

Kitzinger, C. (2000). How to resist an idiom. *Research on Language and Social Interaction, 33*, 121-154.

Know, C. (1994). Conflict resolution at the microlevel: Community relations in Northern Ireland. *Journal of Conflict Resolution, 38*, 595-619.

Koegel, L. K., Koegel, R. L., Hurley, C., & Frea, W. D. (1992). Improving social skills and disruptive behavior in children with autism through self-management. *Journal of Applied Behavior Analysis, 25*, 341-353.

Koegel, R. L., & Frea, W. D. (1993). Treatment of social behavior in autism through the modification of pivotal social skills. *Journal of Applied Behavior Analysis, 26*, 369-377.

Koenig, M. A., Phillips, J. F., Simmons, R. S., & Khan, M. A. (1987). Trends in family size preferences and contraceptive use in Matlab, Bangladesh. *Studies in Family Planning, 18*, 117-127.

Komaki, J. L. (1986). Toward effective supervision: An operant analysis and comparison of managers at work. *Journal of Applied Psychology, 71*, 270-279.

Komaki, J. L. (1998). When performance improvement is the goal: A new set of criteria for criteria. *Journal of Applied Behavior Analysis, 31*, 263-280.

Komaki, J. L., & Collins, R. L. (1982). In R. M. O'Brien, A. M. Dickinson, & M. P. Rosnow (Eds.), *Industrial behavior modification* (pp. 243-265). New York: Pergamon.

Komaki, J. L., Collins, R. L., & Penn, P. (1982). The role of performance antecedents and consequences in work motivation. *Journal of Applied Psychology, 67*, 334-340.

Komaki, J. L., Collins, R. L., & Temlock, S. (1987). An alternative performance measurement approach: Applied operant measurement in the service sector. *Applied Psychology: An International Review, 36*, 71-89.

Komaki, J. L., Desselles, M. L., & Bowman, E. D. (1989). Definitely not a breeze: Extending an operant model of effective supervision to teams. *Journal of Applied Psychology, 74*, 522-529.

Komaki, J., Waddell, W. M., & Pearce, M. G. (1977). The applied behavior analysis approach and individual employees: Improving performance in two small businesses. *Organizational Behavior and Human Performance, 19*, 337-352.

Kowalsky, L. O., Verhoef, M. J., Thurston, W. E., & Rutherford, G. E. (1996). Guidelines for entry into an aboriginal community. *Canadian Journal of Native Studies, 14*, 267-282.

Krasnegor, N. A., Epstein, L., Johnson, S. B., & Yaffe, S. J. (1993). *Developmental aspects of health compliance behavior.* Hillsdale, NJ: Erlbaum.

Kriesberg, L. (1997). The development of the conflict resolution field. In I. W. Zartman & J. L. Rasmussen (Eds.), *Peacemaking in international conflict: Methods & techniques* (pp. 51-77). Washington, DC: United States Institute of Peace Press.

Krull, C., & Pierce, D. W. (1997). Behavior analysis and demographics: Government control of reproductive behavior and fertility in the province of Quebec, Canada. In P. A. Lamal (Ed.), *Cultural contingencies: Behavior analytic perspectives on cultural practices* (pp. 107-131). London: Praeger.

Kumpfer, K. L., Molgaard, V., & Spoth, R. (1996). The strengthening families program for the prevention of delinquency and drug use. In R. DeV. Peters & R. J. McMahon (Eds.), *Preventing childhood disorders, substance abuse, and delinquency* (pp. 241-267). London: Sage.

Kurfman, D. G. (Ed.). (1977). *Developing decision-making skills.* Arlington, VA: National Council for the Social Studies.

Laabs, J. L. (1992). Corporate anthropologists. *Personnel Journal, 71,* 81-91.

Ladouceur, R., Freeston, M. H., Rhéaume, J., Dugas, M. J., Gagnon, F., Thibodeau, N., & Fournier, S. (2000). Strategies used with intrusive thoughts: A comparison of OCD patients with anxious and community controls. *Journal of Abnormal Psychology, 109,* 179-187.

Lai, P., & Biggs, J. (1994). Who benefits from mastery learning? *Contemporary Educational Psychology, 19,* 13-23.

Laird, R. S., & Metalsky, G. I. (2003). Attribution change. In W. O'Donohue, J. E. Fisher & S. C. Hayes (Eds.), *Cognitive behavior therapy: Applying empirically supported techniques in your practice* (pp. 23-27). New York: Wiley.

Lake, D. A., & Rothchild, D. (1996). Containing fear: The origins and management of ethnic conflict. *International Security, 21,* 41-75.

Lalli, J. S., Livezey, K., & Kates, K. (1996). Functional analysis and treatment of eye poking with response blocking. *Journal of Applied Behavior Analysis, 29,* 129-132.

Landis, D., Bennett, J. M., & Bennett, M. J. (Eds.). (2004). *Handbook of intercultural training* (3rd Ed.). CA: Sage.

Lange, A., Richard, R., Gest, A., de Vries, M., & Lodder, L. (1998). The effects of positive self-instruction: A controlled trial. *Cognitive Therapy and Research, 22,* 225-236.

Langford, G. (1978). Persons as necessarily social. *Journal of the Theory of Social Behaviour, 8,* 263-283.

Langford, T. (1999). Orchestrating peace operations: The PDD-56 process. *Security Dialogue, 30,* 137-149.

Latham, G. P., & Saari, L. M. (1982). The importance of union acceptance for productivity improvement through goal setting. *Personnel Psychology, 35,* 781-787.

Latham, G. P., Erez, M., & Locke, E. A. (1988). Resolving scientific disputes by the joint design of crucial experiments by the antagonists: Application to the Erez-Latham dispute regarding participation in goal setting. *Journal of Applied Psychology, 73,* 753-772.

Lawler, E. J., & Ford, R. (1995). Bargaining and influence in conflict situations. In K. S. Cook, G. A. Fine & J. S. House (Eds.), *Sociological perspectives on social psychology* (pp. 236-256). Boston: Allyn and Bacon.

Leach, D. J. (1996). Applying behavioural psychology in education: Contribution and barriers to the implementation of effective instruction. *Behaviour Change, 13,* 3-19.

Lederach, J. P. (1997). *Building peace: Sustainable reconciliation in divided societies.* Washington, DC: United States Institute of Peace Press.

Lee, M. R. (2000). The social dimension of interpersonal dispute resolution: A test of a general theoretical framework with survey data. *Sociological Inquiry, 70,* 1376-156.

Leermakers, E. A., Perri, M. G., Shigaki, C. L., & Fuller, P. R. (1999). Effects of exercise-focused versus weight-focused maintenance programs on the management of obesity. *Addictive Behaviors, 24,* 219-227.

Leo, R. A. (1996). *Miranda's* revenge: Police interrogation as a confidence game. *Law & Society Review, 30,* 259-288.

Lerman, D. C., Iwata, B. A., & Wallace, M. D. (1999). Side effects of extinction: Prevalence of bursting and aggression during the treatment of self-injurious behavior. *Journal of Applied Behavior Analysis, 32,* 1-8.

Levensky, E. R. (2003). Motivational interviewing. In W. O'Donohue, J. E. Fisher & S. C. Hayes (Eds.), *Cognitive behavior therapy: Applying empirically supported techniques in your practice* (pp. 252-260). New York: Wiley.

Levin, M. (1993). Creating networks for rural economic development in Norway. *Human Relations, 46,* 193-218.

Levine, E. (1993). *Freedom's children: Young civil rights activists tell their own stories.* New York: Avon Books.

Levine, M. (2000). The Family Group Conference in the New Zealand Children, Young Persons, and their Families Act of 1989 (CYP&F): Review and evaluation. *Behavioral Sciences and the Law, 18,* 517-556.

Levine, M. (1988). An analysis of mutual assistance. *American Journal of Community Psychology, 16*, 167-183.

Levine, M., & Perkins, D. V. (1997). *Principles of community psychology: Perspectives and applications.* New York: Oxford University Press,

Lévi-Strauss, C. (1949). *The elementary structures of kinship.* Boston: Beacon Press.

Lévi-Strauss, C. (1966). *The savage mind.* London: Weidenfeld & Nicolson.

Lewin, K. (1947). Group decision and social change. In T. M. Newcomb & E. L. Hartley (Eds.), *Readings in social psychology.* NY: Holt.

Lichtenstein, E., Lopez, K., Glasgow, R. E., Gilbert-McRae, S., & Hall, R. (1996). Effectiveness of a consultation intervention to promote tobacco control policies in Northwest Indian tribes: Integrating experiential evaluation and service delivery. *American Journal of Community Psychology, 24*, 639-655.

Liebert, R. M. (1976). Evaluating the evaluators. [Sesame Street] *Journal of Communication, 26* (2), 165-171.

Liebkind, K., & McAlister, A. L. (1999). Extended contact through peer modeling to promote tolerance in Finland. *European Journal of Social Psychology, 29*, 765-780.

Limbrick, E., McNaughton, S., & Glynn, T. (1985). Reading gains for underachieving tutors and tutees in a cross-age tutoring programme. *Journal of Child Psychology and Psychiatry, 26*, 939-953.

Lindskold, S., Betz, B., & Walters, P. S. (1986). Transforming competitive or cooperative climates. *Journal of Conflict Resolution, 30*, 99-114.

Lindskold, S. & Collins, M. G. (1978). Inducing cooperation by groups and individuals: Applying Osgood's GRIT strategy. *Journal of Conflict Resolution, 22*, 679-690.

Lindskold, S., Han, G., & Betz, B. (1986). The essential elements of communication in the GRIT strategy. *Personality and Social Psychology Bulletin, 12*, 179-186.

Lindsley, S. L. (1998). Organizational interventions to prejudice. In M. L. Hecht (Ed.), *Communicating prejudice* (pp. 302-310). London: Sage.

Litton, I., & Potter, J. (1985). Social representations in the ordinary explanation of 'riot'. *European Journal of Social Psychology, 15*, 371-388.

Lochman, J. E., Coie, J. D., Underwood, M. K., & Terry, R. (1993). Effectiveness of a social relations intervention program for aggressive and nonaggressive, rejected children. *Journal of Consulting and Clinical Psychology, 61*, 1053-1058.

Locke, E. A. (1980). Latham versus Komaki: A tale of two paradigms. *Journal of Applied Psychology, 65*, 16-23.

Lofland, J. (1971). *Analyzing social settings: A guide to qualitative observation and analysis.* Belmont, CA: Wadsworth.

Lodhi, S., & Greer, R. D. (1989). The speaker as listener. *Journal of the Experimental Analysis of Behavior, 51*, 353-360.

Ludwig, T. D., & Geller, E. S. (1999). Behavior change among agents of a community safety program: Pizza deliverers advocate community safety belt use. *Journal of Organizational Behavior Management , 19*, 3-24.

Lumley, V. A., Miltenberger, R. G., Long, E. S., Rapp, J. T., & Roberts, J. A. (1998). Evaluation of a sexual abuse prevention program for adults with mental retardation. *Journal of Applied Behavior Analysis, 131*, 91-101.

Lumpe, L. (1999). Curbing the proliferation of small arms and light weapons. *Security Dialogue, 30*, 151-164.

Luoma, J. B., & Hayes, S. C. (2003). Cognitive defusion. In W. O'Donohue, J. E. Fisher & S. C. Hayes (Eds.), *Cognitive behavior therapy: Applying empirically supported techniques in your practice* (pp. 71-78). New York: Wiley.

Lusk, M. W. (1989). Street children programs in Latin America. *Journal of Sociology and Social Welfare, 16*, 55-77.

Luthans, F. (1982). Improving performance: A behavioral problem-solving approach. In L. W. Frederiksen. (Ed.), *Handbook of organizational behavior management* (pp. 249-279). New York: Wiley.

Lynam, D. R., Milich, R., Zimmerman, R., Novak, S. P., Logan, T. K., Martin, C., Leukefeld, C., & Clayton, R. (1999). Project DARE: No effects at 10-year follow-up. *Journal of Consulting and Clinical Psychology, 67,* 590-593.

Lloyd, A. (2003). Urge surfing. In W. O'Donohue, J. E. Fisher & S. C. Hayes (Eds.), *Cognitive behavior therapy: Applying empirically supported techniques in your practice* (pp. 451-455). New York: Wiley.

Ma, R. (1992). The role of unofficial intermediaries in interpersonal conflicts in the Chinese culture. *Communication Quarterly, 40,* 269-278.

MacCoun, R. J. (1993). Drugs and the law: A psychological analysis of drug prohibition. *Psychological Bulletin, 113,* 497-512.

Mace, F. C., Hock, M. L., Lalli, J.S, West, B. J., Belfiore, P., Pinter, E., & Brown, D. K. (1988). Behavioral momentum in the treatment of noncompliance. *Journal of Applied Behavior Analysis, 21,* 123-142.

Mace, F. C., & Lalli, J. S. (1991). Linking descriptive and experimental analyses in the treatment of bizarre speech. *Journal of Applied Behavior Analysis, 24,* 553-562.

MacQueen, K. M., McLellan, E., Metzger, D. S., Kegeles, S., Strauss, R. P., Scotti, R., Blanchard, L., & Trotter, R. T. (2001). What is a community? An evidence-based definition for participatory public health. *American Journal of Public Health, 91,* 1929-1938.

Mager, R. F., & Pipe, P. (1984). *Analyzing performance problems.* 2nd Ed. Belmont, CA: Lake.

Mahmood, C. K. (1996). Asylum, violence, and the limits of advocacy. *Human Organization, 55,* 493-498.

Mair, J. S., & Mair, M. (2003). Violence prevention and control through environmental modifications. *Annual Review of Public Health, 24,* 209-225.

Manderson, L., Kelaher, M., Williams, G., & Shannon, C. (1998). The politics of community: Negotiation and consultation in research on women's health. *Human Organization, 57,* 222-229.

Manne, S. L. (1999). Intrusive thoughts and psychological distress among cancer patients: The role of spouse avoidance and criticism. *Journal of Consulting and Clinical Psychology, 67,* 539-546.

Mantwill, M., Köhnken, G., & Aschermann, E. (1995). Effects of cognitive interview on the recall of familiar and unfamiliar events. *Journal of Applied Psychology, 80,* 68-78.

Marcenko, M. O., & Spence, M. (1994). Home visitation services for at-risk pregnant and postpartum women: A randomized trial. *American Journal of Orthopsychiatry, 64,* 468-478.

Marin, G. (1993). Defining culturally appropriate community interventions: Hispanics as a case study. *Journal of Community Psychology, 21,* 149-161.

Markowitz, H. (1978). Engineering environments for behavioral opportunities in the zoo. *The Behavior Analyst, 1,* 34-47.

Markowitz, H. (1979). Environmental enrichment and behavioral engineering for captive primates. In J. Erwin, T. L. Maple, & G. Mitchell (Eds.), *Captivity and behavior* (pp. 217-238). New York: Van Nostrand Reinhold.

Marrs, R. W. (1995). A meta-analysis of bibliotherapy studies. *American Journal of Community Psychology, 23,* 843-870.

Marshall, S. (2000). *How to grow a backbone: 10 strategies for gaining power and influence at work.* Lincolnwood, IL: Contemporary Books.

Marsiglia, F. F., & Hecht, M. L. (1998). Personal and interpersonal interventions. In M. L. Hecht (Ed.), *Communicating prejudice* (pp. 287-301). London: Sage.

Martin, K. A., Moritz, S. E., & Hall, C. R. (1999). Imagery use in sport: A literature review and applied model. *The Sports Psychologist, 13,* 245-268.

Martin, T. C. (1995). Women's education and fertility: Results from 26 demographic and health surveys. *Studies in Family Planning, 26,* 187-202.

Marx, K. (1961). *Karl Marx: Selected writings in sociology and social philosophy.* Harmondsworth, Middlesex: Penguin.

Mathews, C., Ellison, G., Guttmacher, S., Reisch, N., & Goldstein, S. (1999). Can audiovisual presentations be used to provide health education at primary health care facilities in South Africa? *Health Education Journal, 58,* 146-156.

Mattaini, M. A., & Thyer, B. A. (Eds.). (1996). *Finding solutions to social problems: Behavioral strategies for change.* Washington, DC: American Psychological Association.

Mattaini, M. A., Twyman, J. S., Chin, W., & Lee, K. N. (1996). Youth violence. In M. A. Mattaini & B. A. Thyer (Eds.), *Finding solutions to social problems: Behavioral strategies for change* (pp. 75-111). Washington, DC: American Psychological Association.

May, S., & West, R. (2000). Do social support interventions ("buddy systems") aid smoking cessation? A review. *Tobacco Control, 9,* 415-422.

McAndrew, J. F. (1989). Obsessive-compulsive disorder: A behavioral case formulation. *Journal of Behavior Therapy and Experimental Psychiatry, 20,* 311-318.

McBride, N., Midford, R., & Cameron, I. (1999). An empirical model for school health promotion: The Western Australian school health project model. *Health Promotion International, 14,* 17-25.

McCall, G. J., Ngeva, J., & Mbebe, M. (1997). Mapping conflict cultures: Interpersonal disputing in a South African Black township. *Human Organization, 56,* 71-78.

McCallum, S. (1967). Dispute settlement in an American shopping center: A preliminary view. In P. Bohannan (Ed.), *Law and warfare* (pp. 291-299). New York: Natural History Press.

McCauley, M. R., & Fisher, R. P. (1995). Facilitating children's eyewitness recall with the revised cognitive interview. *Journal of Applied Psychology, 80,* 510-516.

McComas, J. J., Wacker, D. P., & Cooper, L. J. (1998). Increasing compliance with medical procedures: Application of the high-probability request procedure to a toddler. *Journal of Applied Behavior Analysis, 31,* 287-290.

McComas, K. A. (2003). Trivial pursuits: Participant views of public meetings. *Journal of Public Relations Research, 15,* 91-115.

McCrady, B. S. (1994). Alcoholics Anonymous and behavior therapy: Can habits be treated as diseases? Can diseases be treated as habits? *Journal of Consulting and Clinical Psychology, 62,* 1159-1166.

McCurry, S. M., & Hayes, S. C. (1992). Clinical and experimental perspectives on metaphorical talk. *Clinical Psychology Review, 12,* 763-785.

McGarry, J. (1998). 'Demographic engineering': The state-directed movement of ethnic groups as a technique of conflict regulation. *Ethnic and Racial Studies, 21,* 613-638.

McGoldrick, M., & Carter, B. (2001). Advances in coaching: Family therapy with one person. *Journal of Marital and Family Therapy, 27,* 281-300.

McGovern, P. M., Gerbeerich, S. G., Kochevar, L. K., Nachreiner, N. M., & Wingert, D. A. (1998). A survey of community-based violence prevention and control efforts in Minnesota. *Journal of Public Health Policy, 19,* 219-231.

McKinlay, E., Plumridge, L., McBain, L., McLeod, D., Pullon, S., & Brown, S. (2004). "What sort of health promotion are you talking about?": A discourse analysis of the talk of general practitioners. *Social Science and Medicine, 60,* 1099-1106.

McMahon, M. (1995). False confessions and police deception: The interrogation, incarceration and release of an innocent veteran. *American Journal of Forensic Psychology, 13,* 5-43

McMahon, R. J., Slough, N. M., and the Conduct Problems Prevention Research Group. (1996). Family-based intervention in the Fast-Track Program. In R. DeV. Peters & R. J. McMahon (Eds.), *Preventing childhood disorders, substance abuse, and delinquency* (pp. 90-110). London: Sage.

McTaggart, R. (Ed.). (1997). *Participatory action research: International contexts and consequences.* NY: State University of New York Press.

Mead, G. H. (1922). A behavioristic account of the significant symbol. *Journal of Philosophy, 19,* 157-163.

Mead, G. H. (1924/1925). The genesis of the self and social control. *International Journal of Ethics, 35,* 251-277.

Mead, G. H. (1934). *Mind, self, and society from the standpoint of a social behaviorist.* Chicago: University of Chicago Press.

Meichenbaum, D. (Ed.). (1987). *Facilitating treatment adherence : A practitioner's guidebook.* New York : Plenum Press.

Melton, G. B., & Barry, F. D. (1994). *Protecting children from abuse and neglect: Foundations for a new national strategy.* London: Guildford Press.

Mendelsohn, H. Some reasons why information campaigns can succeed. *Public Opinion Quarterly,* *32*, 50-61.

Mermelstein, R., Cohen, S., Lichtenstein, E., Baer, J. S., & Kamarck, T. (1986). Social support and smoking cessation and maintenance. . *Journal of Consulting and Clinical Psychology, 54*, 447-453.

Merrell, J. (2000). Ambiguity: Exploring the complexity of roles and boundaries when working with volunteers in well women clinics. *Social Science & Medicine, 51*, 93-102.

Meyer, H. H., & Raich, M. S. (1983). An objective evaluation of a behavior modeling training program. *Personnel Psychology, 36*, 755-761.

Meyer, L. H., & Evans, I. M. (1989). *Nonaversive intervention for behavior problems: A manual for home and community.* Baltimore, MA: Brookes.

Meyer, L. H., Evans, I. M., Wuerch, B. B., & Brennan, J. M. (1985). Monitoring the collateral effects of leisure skill instruction: A case study in multiple-baseline methodology. *Behaviour Research and Therapy, 23*, 127-138.

Meyers, A. W., Whelan, J. P., & Murphy, S. M. (1996). Cognitive behavioral strategies in athletic performance enhancement. In M. Hersen, R. M. Eisler & P. M. Miller (Eds.), *Progress in behavior modification* (Vol. 30, pp. 137-164). London: Brooks/Cole.

Michael, J. (1991). A behavioral perspective on college teaching. *The Behavior Analyst, 14*, 229-239.

Michael, M. (1997). Individualistic humans: Social constructionism, identity and change. *Theory & Psychology, 7*, 311-336.

Michaels, S., Mason, R. J., & Solecki, W. D. (2001). Participatory research on collaborative environmental management: Results from the Adirondack Park. *Social and Natural Resources, 14*, 251-255.

Miller, G. E., & Printz, R. J. (1990). Enhancement of social learning family interventions for childhood conduct disorders. *Psychological Bulletin, 108*, 291-307.

Miller, N., & Brewer, M. B. (1984). *Groups in contact: The psychology of desegregation.* New York: Academic Press.

Miller, P., & Rose, N. (1994). On therapeutic authority: Psychoanalytical expertise under advanced liberalism. *History of the Human Sciences, 7*, 29-64.

Miller, P. J., Potts, R., Fung, H., Hoogstra, L., & Mintz, J. (1990). Narrative practices and the social construction of self in childhood. *American Ethnologist, 17*, 292-311.

Miller, R., & Pfohl, W. F. (1982). Management of job-related stress. In R. M. O'Brien, A. M. Dickinson, & M. P. Rosnow (Eds.), *Industrial behavior modification* (pp. 224-242). New York: Pergamon.

Miller, W., & Rollnick, S. (1991). *Motivational interviewing: Preparing people to change addictive behaviors.* New York: Guildford Press.

Miller, W. R., Meyers, R. J., & Tonigan, J. S. (1999). Engaging the unmotivated in treatment for alcohol problems: A comparison of three strategies for intervention through family members. *Journal of Consulting and Clinical Psychology, 67*, 688-697.

Milne, E., English, D. R., Johnston, R., Cross, D., Borland, R., Costa, C., & Giles-Corti, B. (2000). Improved sun protection behaviour in children after two years of the Kidskin intervention. *Australian and New Zealand Journal of Public Health, 24*, 481-487.

Mimeault, V., & Morin, C. M. (1999). Self-help treatment for insomnia: Bibliotherapy with and without professional guidance. *Journal of Consulting and Clinical Psychology, 67*, 511-519.

Miron, M. S., & Goldstein, A. P. (1979). *Hostage.* New York: Pergamon Press.

Mita, R., & Simmons, R. (1995). Diffusion of the culture of contraception: Program effects on young women in rural Bangladesh. *Studies in Family Planning, 26*, 1-13.

Modra, A. K., & Black, D. R. (1999). Peer-led minimal intervention: An exercise approach for elderly women. *American Journal of Health Behavior, 23*, 52-60.

Molgaard, V., & Spoth, R. (2001). The Strengthening Families program for young adolescents: Overview and outcomes. In S. I. Pfeiffer & L. A. Reddy (Eds.), *Innovative mental health interventions for children: Programs that work* (pp. 15-29). London: The Haworth Press.

Montville, J. V. (Ed.). (1991). *Conflict and peacemaking in multiethnic societies.* New York: Lexington Books.

Moon, L. T., Wagner, W. G., & Kazelskis, R. (2000). Counseling sexually abused girls: The impact of sex of counselor. *Child Abuse & Neglect, 24*, 753-765.

Moore, K. J., & Patterson, G. R. (2003). Parent training. In W. O'Donohue, J. E. Fisher & S. C. Hayes (Eds.), *Cognitive behavior therapy: Applying empirically supported techniques in your practice* (pp. 280-287). New York: Wiley.

Moore, M. (2002). *Stupid white men… and other sorry excuses for the state of the nation.* London: Penguin Books.

Moore, M. (2003). *Dude, where's my country?* New York: Warner Books.

Moore, M., & Glynn, K. (1998). *Adventures in a TV nation.* NY: HarperPerennial.

Morgenstern, J., Labouvie, E., McCrady, B. S., Kahler, C. W., & Frey, R. M. (1997). Affiliation with Alcoholics Anonymous after treatment: A study of its therapeutic effects and mechanisms of action. *Journal of Consulting and Clinical Psychology, 65,* 768-777.

Morrill, C., Buller, D. B., Buller, M. K., & Larkey, L. L. (1999). Toward an organizational perspective on identifying and managing formal gatekeepers. *Qualitative Sociology, 22,* 51-72.

Morrison, B., & Lilford, R. (2001). How can action research apply to health services? *Qualitative Health Research, 11,* 436-449.

Morrow, B. H. (1999). Identifying and mapping community vulnerability. *Disasters, 23,* 1-18.

Moser, C. O. N. (1998). The asset vulnerability framework: Reassessing urban poverty reduction strategies. *World Development, 26,* 1-19.

Muchinsky, P. M. (1990). *Psychology applied to work: An introduction to industrial and organizational psychology (3rd Ed.).* Pacific Grove, CA: Brooks/Cole.

Muehrer, P. (2000). Research on adherence, behavior change, and mental health: A workshop overview. *Health Psychology, 19,* 304-307.

Mullins, R., Livingstone, P., & Borland, R. (1999). A strategy for involving general practitioners in smoking control. *Australian and New Zealand Journal of Public Health, 23,* 249-251.

Munford, R., & Nash, M. (Eds.). (1994). *Social work in action.* Auckland: Dunmore Press.

Munroe, K. J., Giacobbi, P. R., Hall, C., & Weinberg, R. (2000). The four Ws of imagery use: Where, when, why, and what. *The Sports Psychologist, 14,* 119-137.

Murchie, E. (1984). *Rapuora: Health and Maori women.* Wellington: Maori Women's Welfare League.

Murphy, T. J., Pagano, R. R., & Marlatt, G. A. (1986). Lifestyle modification with heavy alcohol drinkers: Effects of aerobic exercise and meditation. *Addictive Behaviors, 11,* 175-186.

Murray, M. (2000). Social capital formation and healthy communities: Insights from the Colorado Healthy Communities Initiative. *Community Development Journal 35,* 99-108.

Murray, S. A., Tapson, J., Turnbull, L., McCallum, J., & Little, A. (1994). Listening to local voices: Adapting rapid appraisal to assess health and social needs in general practice. *British Medical Journal, 308,* 698-700.

Murrell, S. A. (1973). *Community psychology and social systems: A conceptual framework and intervention guide.* New York: Behavioral Publications.

Nadelmann, E. A. (1989). Drug prohibition in the United States: Costs, consequences, and alternatives. *Science, 245,* 939-947.

Nader, L. (1995). Civilization and its negotiations. In P. Caplan (Ed.), *Understanding disputes: The politics of argument* (pp. 39-63). Oxford, Providence: Berg.

Nagel, J., & Snipp, C. M. (1993). Ethnic reorganization: American Indian social, economic, political, and cultural strategies for survival. *Ethnic and Racial Studies, 16,* 203-235.

Nagy, R. (2002). Reconciliation in post-commission South Africa: Thick and thin accounts of solidarity. *Canadian Journal of Political Science, 35,* 323-346.

Naugle, A. E., & Maher, S. (2003). Modeling and behavioral rehearsal. In W. O'Donohue, J. E. Fisher & S. C. Hayes (Eds.), *Cognitive behavior therapy: Applying empirically supported techniques in your practice* (pp. 238-246). New York: Wiley.

Nazzar, A., Adongo, P. B., Binka, F. N., Phillips, J. F., & Debpuur, C. (1995). Developing a culturally appropriate family planning program for the Navrongo experiment. *Studies in Family Planning, 26,* 307-324.

Neef, N. A., Lensbower, J., Hockersmith, I., DePalma, V., & Gray, K. (1990). In vivo versus simulation training: An interactional analysis of range and type of training exemplar. *Journal of Applied Behavior Analysis, 23,* 447-458.

Neumark-Sztainer, D., Martin, S. L., & Story, M. (2000). School-based programs for obesity prevention: What do adolescents recommend? *American Journal of Health Promotion, 14*, 232-235.

Newell, S., Girgis, A., & Sanson-Fisher, R. W. (1995). Recall, retention, utilisation and acceptability of written health education material. *Australian Journal of Public Health, 19*, 368-374.

Newman, C. F. (2003). Cognitive restructuring: Identifying and modifying maladaptive schemas. In W. O'Donohue, J. E. Fisher & S. C. Hayes (Eds.), *Cognitive behavior therapy: Applying empirically supported techniques in your practice* (pp. 89-95). New York: Wiley.

Nezu, A. M., Nezu, C. M., & Lombardo, E. (2003). Problem-solving therapy. In W. O'Donohue, J. E. Fisher & S. C. Hayes (Eds.), *Cognitive behavior therapy: Applying empirically supported techniques in your practice* (pp. 301-307). New York: Wiley.

Ninness, H. A. C., Fuerst, J., Rutherford, R. D., & Glenn, S. S. (1991). Effects of self-management training and reinforcement on the transfer of improved conduct in the absence of a supervisor. *Journal of Applied Behavior Analysis, 24*, 499-508.

Nolan, R. W. (2003). *Anthropology in practice: Building a career outside the academy.* London: Lynne Rienner Publishers.

Ntozi, J. P. M., & Kabera, J. B. (1991). Family planning in rural Uganda: Knowledge and use of modern and traditional methods in Ankole. *Studies in Family Planning, 22*, 116-123.

Obermeyer, C. M. (1994). Reproductive choice in Islam: Gender and state in Iran and Tunisia. *Studies in Family Planning, 25*, 41-51.

O'Brien, R. M., Dickinson, A. M., & Rosnow, M. P. (Eds.). (1982). *Industrial behavior modification.* New York: Pergamon.

O'Brien, T. G., & Charleton, S. G. (Eds.). (1996). *Handbook of human factors testing and evaluation.* Mahwah, NJ: Erlbaum.

O'Connor, P. J., & Innes, J. M. (1990). Audio-visual information on child illness prevention in hospital waiting rooms: An experimental evaluation. *Health Promotion International, 5*, 3-8.

O'Donohue, W., Fisher, J. F., & Hayes, S. C. (Eds.). (2003). *Cognitive behavior therapy: Applying empirically supported techniques in your practice.* Hoboken, NJ: John Wiley & Sons.

O'Halloran, P., Lazovich, D., Patterson, R. E., Harnack, L., French, S., Curry, S. J., & Beresford, S. A. A. (2001). Effect of health lifestyle pattern on dietary change. *American Journal of Health Promotion, 16*, 27-33.

Okafor, F. U. (1997). *New strategies for curbing ethnic & religious conflicts in Nigeria.* Enugu, Nigeria: Fourth Dimension Publishers.

Oldenburg, B. F., Sallis, J. F., Ffrench, M. L., & Owen, N. (1999). Health promotion research and the diffusion and institutionalization of interventions. *Health Education Research, 14*, 121-130.

Oldham, G. R., Cummings, A., Mischel, L. J., Schmidtke, J. M., & Zhou, J. (1995). Listen while you work? Quasi-experimental relations between personal-stereo headset use and employee work responses. *Journal of Applied Psychology, 80*, 547-564.

Olds, D., Henderson, C., Kitzman, H., Eckenrode, J., Cole, R., & Tatelbaum, R. (1998). The promise of home visitation: Results of two randomized trials. *Journal of Community Psychology, 26*, 5-21.

O'Leary-Kelly, A. M. (1998). The influence of group feedback on individual group member response. *Research in Personnel and Human Resources Management, 16*, 255-294.

Oliver, P. H., & Margolin, G. (2003). Communication/ Problem-solving skills training. In W. O'Donohue, J. E. Fisher & S. C. Hayes (Eds.), *Cognitive behavior therapy: Applying empirically supported techniques in your practice* (pp. 96-102). New York: Wiley.

Olson-Buchanan, J. B., Drasgow, F., Moberg, P. J., Mead, A. D., Keenan, P. A., & Donovan, M. A. (1998). Interactive video assessment of conflict resolution skills. *Personnel Psychology, 51*, 1-24.

Omidian, P. A., & Lipson, J. G. (1996). Ethnic coalitions and public health: Delights and dilemmas with the Afghan Health Education Project in Northern California. *Human Organization, 55*, 355-360.

Orange, C. (1987). *The Treaty of Waitangi.* Sydney, Australia: Allen & Unwin.

O'Reilly, M. F., Green, G., & Braunling-McMorrow, D. (1990). Self-administered written prompts to teach home accident prevention skills to adults with brain injuries. *Journal of Applied Behavior Analysis, 23*, 431-446.

Orlandi, M. A. (1996). Prevention technologies for drug-involved youth. In C. B. McCoy, L. R. Metsch, & J. A. Inciardi (Eds.), *Intervening with drug-involved youth* (pp. 81-100). London: Sage.

Orleans, C. T., & Cummings, K. M. (1999). Population-based tobacco control: Progress and prospects. *American Journal of Health Promotion, 14,* 83-91

Osgood, C. E. (1962). *An alternative to war or surrender.* Urbana, IL: University of Illinois Press.

Oskamp, S. (1984). *Applied social psychology.* Englewood Cliffs, NJ: Prentice Hall.

Out, J. W., & Laffreniere, K. D. (2001). Baby think it over®: Using role-play to prevent teen pregnancy. *Adolescence, 36,* 571-582.

Page, B. J., Delmonico, D. L., Walsh, J., L'Amoreaux, N. A., Danninhirsh, C., Thompson, R. S., Ingram, A. I., & Evans, A. D. (2000). Setting up on-line support groups using the Palace software. *Journal for Specialists in Group Work, 25,* 133-145.

Paine, A. L., Suarez-Balcazar, Y., Fawcett, S. B., & Borck-Jameson, L. (1992). Supportive transactions: Their measurement and enhancement in two mutual-aid groups. *Journal of Community Psychology, 20,* 163-180.

Palmer, K. (2001-2002). 'Never ask a question unless you know the answer': Anthropology and the formation of public policy. *Australian Aboriginal Studies,* 4-11.

Pálsson, G., & Helgason, A. (1999). Schooling and skipperhood: The development of dexterity. *American Anthropologist, 100,* 908-923.

Parker, L., & Langley, B. (1993). Protocol and policy-making systems in American Indian tribes. In D. M. Fetterman (Ed.), *Speaking the language of power: Communication, collaboration and advocacy (translating ethnography into action)* (pp. 70-75). New York: Falmer Press.

Parker, P. L., & King, T. F. (1987). Intercultural mediation at Truk International Airport. In R. M. Wulff & S. J. Fiske (Eds.), *Anthropological praxis: Translating knowledge into action* (pp. 160-173). Boulder, CO: Westview Press.

Parkinson, L., & Rachman, S. (1980). Are intrusive thoughts subject to habituation? *Behaviour Research and Therapy, 18,* 409-418.

Parra, G. R., DuBois, D. L., Neville, H. A., Pugh-Lilly, A. O., & Povinelli, N. (2002). Mentoring relationships for youth: Investigation of a process-oriented model. *Journal of Community Psychology, 30,* 367-388.

Parsons, M. B., Schepis, M. M. Reid, D. H., McCarn, J. E., & Green, C. W. (1987). Expanding the impact of behavioral staff management: A large-scale long-term application in schools serving severely handicapped students. *Journal of Applied Behavior Analysis, 20,* 139-150.

Paton, D. (1996). Preparing relief workers for disaster work. In D. Paton & N. Long (Eds.), *Psychological aspects of disasters: Impact, coping and intervention* (pp. 108-125). Dunedin, New Zealand: Dunmore Press.

Patton, M. Q. (2002). *Qualitative research and evaluation methods.* London: Sage.

Paul, L., Johnson, A. O., & Cranston, G. M. (2000). A successful videoconference satellite program: Providing nutritional information on dementia to rural caregivers. *Educational Gerontology, 26,* 415-425.

Pease, B., & Fook, J. (Eds.). (1999). *Transforming social work practice: Postmodern critical perspectives.* London: Allen & Unwin.

Pentz, M. A. (2000). Institutionalizing community-based prevention through policy change. *Journal of Community Psychology, 28,* 257-270.

Pérez-Cuevas, R., Reyes, H., Pego, U., Tomé, P., Ceja, K., Flores, S., & Gutiérrez, G. (1999). Immunization promotion activities: Are they effective in encouraging mothers to immunize their children? *Social Science & Medicine, 49,* 921-932.

Perlman, M., & Ross, H. S. (1997). The benefits of parent intervention in children's disputes: An examination of concurrent changes in children's fighting styles. *Child Development, 64,* 690-700.

Perri, M. G., McAllister, D. A., Gange, J. J., Jordan, R. C., McAdoo, W. G., & Nezu, A. M. (1988). Effects of four maintenance programs on the long-term management of obesity. *Journal of Consulting and Clinical Psychology, 56,* 529-534.

Perry, C. L., Sellers, D. E., Johnson, C., Pedersen, S., Bachman, K. J., Parcel, G. S., Stone, E. J., Luepker, R. V., Wu, M., Nader, P. R., & Cook, K. (1997). The Child and Adolescent Trial for

Cardiovascular Health (CATCH): Intervention, implementation, and feasibility for elementary schools in the United States. *Health Education & Behavior, 24,* 716-735.

Peterson, L., & Brown, D. (1994). Integrating child injuries and abuse-neglect research: Common histories, etiologies, and solutions. *Psychological Bulletin, 116,* 293-315.

Peterson, L., Gable, S., Doyle, C., & Ewigman, B. (1997). Beyond parenting skills: Battling barriers and building bonds to prevent child abuse and neglect. *Cognitive and Behavioral Practice, 4,* 53-74.

Peterson, L., Zink, M., & Downing, J. (1993). Childhood injury prevention. In D. S. Glenwick & L. A. Jason (Eds.), *Promoting health and mental health in children, youth, and families* (pp. 51-73). New York: Springer.

Pettigrew, T. F. (1969). Racially separate or together. *Journal of Social Issues, 28,* 43-70.

Philip, K., & Hendry, L. B. (2000). Making sense of mentoring or mentoring making sense? Reflections on the mentoring process by adult mentors with young people. *Journal of Community & Applied Social Psychology, 10,* 211-223.

Piazza, C. C., Hanley, G. P., Bowman, L. G., Tuyter, J. M., Lindauer, S. E., & Saiontz, D. M. (1997). Functional analysis and treatment of elopement. *Journal of Applied Behavior Analysis, 30,* 653-672.

Pierce, K. L., & Schreibman, L. (1994). Teaching daily living skills to children with autism in unsupervised settings through pictorial self-management. *Journal of Applied Behavior Analysis, 27,* 471-481.

Pierce, K. L., & Schreibman, L. (1995). Increasing complex social behaviors in children with autism: Effects of peer-implemented pivotal response training. *Journal of Applied Behavior Analysis, 28,* 285-295.

Pierce, L. H., & Shields, N. (1998). The Be A Star community-based after-school program: Developing resiliency factors in high-risk preadolescent youth. *Journal of Community Psychology, 26,* 175-183.

Ping, T., Shuhua, Q., Huimain, F., & Smith, H. L. (1997). Acceptance, efficacy, and side effects of NORPLANT® implants in four counties in North China. *Studies in Family Planning, 28,* 122-131.

Pinkley, R. L., Brittain, J., Neale, M. A., & Northcraft, G. B. (1995). Managerial third-party dispute intervention: An inductive analysis of intervener strategy selection. *Journal of Applied Psychology, 80,* 386-402.

Pinto, P. R., & Noah, S. L. (1980). Internal vs. external consultants: Background and behaviors. *Academy of Management Proceedings, 40,* 75-79.

Piotrow, P. T., Rimon, J. G., Winnard, K., Kincaid, D. L., Huntington, D., & Convisser, J. (1990). Mass media family planning promotion in three Nigerian cities. *Studies in Family Planning, 21,* 265-274.

Platt, J. J. (1995). Vocational rehabilitation of drug users. *Psychological Bulletin, 117,* 416-433.

Poche, C., Yoder, P., & Miltenberger, R. (1988). Teaching self-protection to children using television techniques. *Journal of Applied Behavior Analysis, 21,* 253-261.

Podolefsky, A. M. (1985). Rejecting crime prevention programs: The dynamics of program implementation in high need communities. *Human Organization, 44,* 33-40.

Podolefsky, A. M. & Brown, P. J. (Eds.). (1994). *Applying cultural anthropology: An introductory reader.* London: Mayfield.

Porter, D. J. (2002). Citizen participation through mobilization and the rise of political Islam in Indonesia. *The Pacific Review, 15,* 201-224.

Potvin, L., Cargo, M., McComber, A. M., Delormier, T., & Macaulay, A. C. (2003). Implementing participatory intervention and research in communities: Lessons from the Kahnawake Schools Diabetes Prevention Project in Canada. *Social Science & Medicine, 56,* 1295-1305.

Preston, D. (1994). Rapid household appraisal: A method for facilitating the analysis of household livelihood strategies. *Applied Geography, 14,* 203-213.

Prilleltensky, I., & Nelson, G. (2000). Promoting child and family wellness: Priorities for psychological and social interventions. *Journal of Community and Social Psychology, 10,* 85-105.

Prince, R., & Geissler, P. W. (2001). Becoming "One who treats": A case study of a Luo healer and her grandson in Western Kenya. *Anthropology and Education Quarterly, 32,* 447-471.

Prinz, R. J., & Miller, G. E. (1996). Parental engagement in interventions for children at risk for conduct disorder. In R. DeV. Peters & R. J. McMahon (Eds.), *Preventing childhood disorders, substance abuse, and delinquency* (pp. 161-183). London: Sage.

Pruitt, D. G. (1995). Flexibility in conflict episodes. *Annals of the American Academy of Political and Social Science, 542,* 100-115.

Pryor, K. (1984). *Don't shoot the dog! The new art of teaching and training.* New York: Bantam Books.

Pulido, L. (2000). Rethinking environmental racism: White privilege and urban development in Southern California. *Annals of the Association of American Geographers, 90,* 12-40.

Quinn, J. M., Sherman, J. A., Sheldon, J. B., Quinn, L. M., & Harchik, A. E. (1992). Social validation of component behaviors of following instructions, accepting criticism, and negotiating. *Journal of Applied Behavior Analysis, 25,* 401-413.

Quinones, M. A. (1995). Pretraining context effects: Training assignment as feedback. *Journal of Applied Psychology, 80,* 226-238.

Rabbit, P., & Banerji, N. (1989). How does very prolonged practice improve decision speed? *Journal of Experimental Psychology: General, 118,* 338-345.

Rachman, S. J. (1981). Unwanted intrusive cognitions. *Advances in Behavior Research and Therapy, 3,* 89-99.

Ralph, A. (1997). The heterogeneity of children's social difficulties and the need for multiple assessment measures. *Behaviour Change, 14,* 166-173.

Raphael, B., & Wilson, J. P. (Eds.). (2000). *Psychological debriefing: Theory, practice and evidence.* Cambridge: Cambridge University Press.

Rappaport, J., & Seidman, E. (Eds.). (2000). *Handbook of community psychology.* New York: Kluwer Academic.

Rassin, E., Merckelbach, H., & Muris, P. (2000). Paradoxical and less paradoxical effects of thought suppression: A critical review. *Clinical Psychology Review, 20,* 973-995.

Ratcliffe, J., Cairns, J., & Platt, S. (1997). Cost effectiveness of a mass media-led anti-smoking campaign in Scotland. *Tobacco Control, 6,* 104-110.

Redd, W. H. (1996). Behavioral intervention in cancer treatment. In D. M. Baer & E. M. Pinkston (Eds.), *Environment and behavior* (pp. 155-162). Boulder, CO: Westview Press.

Rehm, L. P., & Adams, J. H. (2003). Self-management. In W. O'Donohue, J. E. Fisher & S. C. Hayes (Eds.), *Cognitive behavior therapy: Applying empirically supported techniques in your practice* (pp. 354-360). New York: Wiley.

Renaud, L., & Suissa, S. (1989). Evaluation of the efficacy of simulation games in traffic safety education of kindergarten children. *American Journal of Public Health, 79,* 307-309.

Reppucci, N. D., Woolard, J. L., & Fried, C. S. (1999). Social, community, and preventive interventions. *Annual Review of Psychology, 50,* 387-418.

Rhodes, J. E., Grossman, J. B., & Resch, N. L. (2000). Agents of change: Pathways through which mentoring relationships influence adolescents' academic adjustment. *Child Development, 71,* 1662-1671.

Rice, J. M., & Lutzker, J. R. (1984). Reducing noncompliance to follow-up appointment keeping at a family practice center. *Journal of Applied Behavior Analysis, 17,* 303-311.

Richman, G. S., Riordan, M. R., Reiss, M. L., Pyles, D. A. M., & Bailey, J. S. (1988). The effects of self-monitoring and supervisor feedback on staff performance in a residential setting. *Journal of Applied Behavior Analysis, 21,* 401-409.

Richman, O. (1998). Devious objectives and the disputants' view of international mediation: A theoretical framework. *Journal of Peace Research, 35,* 707-722.

Richmond, R. L., Kehoe, L., Heather, N., Wodak, A., & Webster, I. (1996). General practitioners' promotion of healthy life styles: What patients think. *Australian and New Zealand Journal of Public Health, 20,* 195-200.

Richmond, R. L., G-Novak, K., Kehoe, L., Calfas, G., Mendelsohn, C. P., & Wodak, A. (1998). Effect of training on general practitioners' use of a brief intervention for excessive drinkers. *Australian and New Zealand Journal of Public Health, 22,* 206-209.

Rimal, R., & Flora, J. A. (1998). Bidirectional familial influences in dietary behavior: Test of a model of campaign influences. *Human Communication Research, 24*, 610-637.

Rimke, H. M. (2000). Governing citizens through self-help literature. *Cultural Studies, 14*, 61-78.

Rincover, A., & Ducharme, J. M. (1987). Variables influencing stimulus overselectivity and "tunnel vision" in developmentally delayed children. *American Journal of Mental Deficiency, 91*, 422-430.

Rivara, F. P., Thompson, D. C., Patterson, M. Q., & Thompson, R. S. (1998). Prevention of bicycle-related injuries: Helmets, education, and legislation. *Annual Review of Public Health, 19*, 293-318.

Roberts, M. (1997). *Mediation in family disputes: Principles of practice.* Aldershot, England: Arena.

Robertson, J., Wendiggensen, P., & Kaplan, I. (1983). Towards a comprehensive treatment for obsessional thoughts. *Behaviour Research and Therapy, 21*, 347-356.

Robertson, N. (1999). Stopping violence programmes: Enhancing the safety of battered women or producing better-educated batterers? *New Zealand Journal of Psychology, 28*, 68-78.

Rogers, E. M., Vaughan, P. W., Swalehe, R. M. A., Rao, N., Svenkerund, P., & Sood, S. (1999). Effects of an entertainment-education radio soap opera on family planning behavior in Tanzania. *Studies in Family Planning, 30*, 193-211.

Rokke, P. D., Tomhave, J. A., & Jocie, Z. (2000). Self-management therapy and educational group therapy for depressed elders. *Cognitive Therapy and Research, 24*, 99-119.

Ronen, T., & Rosenbaum, M. (1998). Beyond direct verbal instructions in cognitive behavioral supervision. *Cognitive and Behavioral Practice, 5*, 7-23.

Rose, N. (1996). *Inventing our selves: Psychology, power, and personhood.* Cambridge: Cambridge University Press.

Rose, N. (1999). *Governing the soul: The shaping of the private self* (2nd Ed.). London: Free Association Books.

Rosen, G. M. (2003). Bibliotherapy. In W. O'Donohue, J. E. Fisher & S. C. Hayes (Eds.), *Cognitive behavior therapy: Applying empirically supported techniques in your practice* (pp. 46-55). New York: Wiley.

Rosen, S. (Ed.). (1982). *My voice will go with you: The teaching tales of Milton H. Erickson, M.D.* London: Norton.

Rosenfarb, I. S. (1992). A behavior analytic interpretation of the therapeutic relationship. The Psychological Record, 42, 341-355.

Rosnow, R. L. (1991). Inside rumor: A personal journal. *American Psychologist, 46*, 484-496.

Rosnow, R. L., & Georgoudi, M. (1985). "Killed by idle gossip": The psychology of small talk. In B. Rubin (Ed.), *When information counts: Grading the media* (pp. 59-73). Lexington, MA: Lexington Books.

Ross, J. A., & Frankenberg, E. (1993). *Findings from two decades of family planning research.* New York: The Population Council.

Ross, J. A., & Mauldin, W. P. (1996). Family planning programs: Efforts and results, 1972-1994. *Studies in Family Planning, 27*, 137-147.

Ross, P. C. (1982). Training: Behavior change and the improvement of business performance. In L. W. Frederiksen. (Ed.), *Handbook of organizational behavior management* (pp. 181-217). New York: Wiley.

Rothschild, M. L. (1979, Spring). Marketing communications in nonbusiness situations or why it's so hard to sell brotherhood like soap. *Journal of Marketing, 43*, 11-20.

Roussos, S. T., & Fawcett, S. B. (2000). A review of collaborative partnerships as a strategy for improving community health. *Annual Review of Public Health, 21*, 369-402.

Rowley, K. G., Daniel, M., Skinner, K., Skinner, M., White, G. A., & O'Dea, K. (2000). Effectiveness of a community-directed 'healthy lifestyle' program in a remote Australian Aboriginal community. *Australian and New Zealand Journal of Public Health, 24*, 136-144.

Rumar, K. (1997). The Swedish National Road Safety Programme—A new approach to road safety work. In H. von Holst, A. Nygren & R. Thord (Eds.), *Transportation, traffic safety and health: The new mobility* (pp. 73-86). New York: Springer.

Rusch, F. P., & Keller, K. (2003). Generalization promotion. In W. O'Donohue, J. E. Fisher & S. C. Hayes (Eds.), *Cognitive behavior therapy: Applying empirically supported techniques in your practice* (pp. 183-188). New York: Wiley.

Russell, W. D., Dzewaltowski, D. A., & Ryan, G. J. (1999). The effectiveness of a point-of-decision prompt in deterring sedentary behavior. *American Journal of Health Promotion, 13*, 257-259.

Russos, S., Fawcett, S. B., Francisco, V. T., Berkley, J. Y., & Lopez, C. M. (1997). A behavioral analysis of collaborative partnerships for community health. In P. A. Lamal (Ed.), *Cultural contingencies: Behavior analytic perspectives on cultural practices* (pp. 87-106). London: Praeger.

Rutenberg, N., & Watkins, S. C. (1997). The buzz outside the clinics: Conversations and contraception in Nyanza Province, Kenya. *Studies in Family Planning, 28*, 290-307.

Sabatier, P. A. (1986). What can we learn from implementation research? In F. X. Kaufmann, G. Majone & V. Ostrom (Eds.), *Guidance, control, and evaluation in the public sector* (pp. 313-325). Berlin: De Gruyter.

Sai, F. T. (1993). Obstacles to family planning. In F. Graham-Smith (Ed.), Population—the complex reality: A report of the Population Summit of the world's scientific academies (pp. 303-312). London: The Royal Society

Sajwaj, T., Libet, J., & Agras, S. (1974). Lemon-juice therapy: The control of life-threatening rumination in a six-month old infant. *Journal of Applied Behavior Analysis, 7*, 557-563.

Salmon, P. W. (1981). *On-line computer applications in research into attitude change: Applications in farm management education.* ERDC Report No. 31. Canberra: Australian Government Publishing Service.

Sampson, E. E. (1993). *Celebrating the other: A dialogic account of human nature.* Boudler, CO: Westview Press.

Sanders, M. R. (1992). New directions in behavioral family intervention with children: From clinical management to prevention. *New Zealand Journal of Psychology, 21*, 25-35.

Schein, E. (1969). *Process consultation: Its role in organizational development.* Reading, MA: Addison-Wesley.

Schensul, S. L. (1974). Skills needed in action anthropology: Lessons from El Centro de la Causa. *Human Organization, 33*, 203-209.

Schensul, S. L. (2001). Advocacy in anthropology. In *International Encyclopedia of the Social & Behavioral Sciences* (pp. 204-206). New York: Elsevier.

Schiffrin, D. (1984). Jewish argument as sociability. *Language in Society, 13*, 311-335.

Schinke, S. P., Forgey, M. A., & Orlandi, M. (1996). Teenage sexuality. In M. A. Mattaini & B. A. Thyer (Eds.), *Finding solutions to social problems: Behavioral strategies for change* (pp. 267-288). Washington, DC: American Psychological Association.

Schinke, S. P., Tepavac, L., & Cole, K. C. (2000). Preventing substance use among Native American youth: Three-year results. *Addictive Behaviors, 25*, 387-397.

Schorr, L. B. (1991). Effective programs for children growing up in concentrated poverty. In A. C. Huston (Ed.), *Children in poverty: Child development and public policy* (pp. 260-281). NY: Cambridge University Press.

Schwartz, C. E. (1999). Teaching coping skills enhances quality of life more than peer support: Results of a randomized trial with multiple sclerosis patients. *Health Psychology, 18*, 211-220.

Schwartz, N. B., Molnar, J. J., & Lovshin, L. L. (1988). Cooperatively managed projects and rapid assessments: Suggestions from a Panamanian case. *Human Organization, 47*, 1-14.

Scott, D., Scott, L. M., & Goldwater, B. (1997). A performance improvement program for an international-level track and field athlete. *Journal of Applied Behavior Analysis, 30*, 573-575.

Scott, W. D., & Cervone, D. (2003). Enhancing perceived self-efficacy: Guided mastery therapy. In W. O'Donohue, J. E. Fisher & S. C. Hayes (Eds.), *Cognitive behavior therapy: Applying empirically supported techniques in your practice* (pp. 288-293). New York: Wiley.

Scotti, J. R., Evans, I. M., Meyer, L. H., & Walker, P. (1991). A meta-analysis of intervention research with problem behavior: Treatment validity and standards of practice. *American Journal on Mental Retardation, 96*, 233-256.

Searle, J. R. (1995). *The construction of social reality.* New York: The Free Press.

Segal, E. A., Gerdes, K. E., & Steiner, S. (2003). *Social work: An introduction to the profession*. London: Thomson, Brooks Cole.

Segan, C. J., Borland, R., & Hill, D. J. (1999). Development and evaluation of a brochure on sun protection and sun exposure for tourists. *Health Education Journal, 58*, 177-191.

Segrin, C. (2003). Social skills training. In W. O'Donohue, J. E. Fisher & S. C. Hayes (Eds.), *Cognitive behavior therapy: Applying empirically supported techniques in your practice* (pp. 384-390). New York: Wiley.

Seitz, V., Rosenbaum, L. K., & Apfel, N. H. (1985). Effects of family support intervention: A ten-year follow-up. *Child Development, 56*, 376-391.

Selby, J., & Bradley, B. (2003). Action research intervention with young people: A city council's response. *Australasian Psychiatry, 11*, S122-S126.

Selener, D. (1997). *Participatory action research and social change*. Ithaca, NY: Cornell University.

Severy, L. J. (1999). Acceptability as a critical component of clinical trials. In L. J. Severy & W. B. Miller (Eds.), *Advances in population: Psychosocial perspectives* (Vol. 3, pp. 103-122). London: Jessica Kingsley.

Shafer, E. (1994). A review of interventions to teach a mand repertoire. *The Analysis of Verbal Behavior, 12*, 53-66.

Sharp, G. (1973). *The politics of non-violent action*. Boston, MA: Porter Sargent Publishers.

Shawcross, W. (2000). *Deliver us from evil: Warlords & peacekeepers in a world of endless conflict*. NY: Bloomsbury.

Sheehan, P. W., & Tilden, J. (1983). Effects of suggestibility and hypnosis on accurate and distorted retrieval from memory. *Journal of Experimental Psychology: Learning, Memory and Cognition, 9*, 283-293.

Shiffman, S., Mason, K. M., & Henningfield, J. E. (1998). Tobacco dependence treatments: Review and prospectus. *Annual Review of Public Health, 19*, 335-358.

Shipherd, J. C., & Beck, J. G. (1999). The effects of suppressing trauma-related thoughts on women with rape-related posttraumatic stress disorder. *Behaviour Research and Therapy, 37*, 99-112.

Shipper, F., & White, C. S. (1999). Mastery, frequency, and interaction of managerial behaviors relative to subunit effectiveness. *Human Relations, 52*, 49-66.

Shuey, D. A., Babishangire, B. B., Omiat, S., & Bagarukayo, H. (1999). Increased sexual abstinence among in-school adolescents as a result of school health education in Soroti district, Uganda. *Health Education Research, 14*, 411-419.

Sievert, A. L., Cuvo, A. J., & Davis, P. K. (1988). Training self-advocacy skills to adults with mild handicaps. *Journal of Applied Behavior Analysis, 21*, 299-309.

Simmons, R., Baqee, L., Koenig, M. A., & Phillips, J. F. (1988). Beyond supply: The importance of female family planning workers in rural Bangladesh. *Studies in Family Planning,19*, 29-38.

Simmons, R., Hall. P., Díaz, J., Díaz, M., Fajans, P., & Satia, J. (1997). The strategic approach to contraceptive introduction. *Studies in Family Planning, 28*, 79-94.

Simon, S. J., & Werner, J. M. (1996). Computer training through behavior modeling, self-paced, and instructional approaches: A field experiment. *Journal of Applied Psychology, 81*, 648-659.

Simons, H. W. (2001). *Persuasion in society*. London: Sage.

Simpson, G. E., & Yeager, J. M. (1973). Techniques for reducing prejudice: Changing the situation. In P. Watson (Ed.), *Psychology and race* (pp. 145-174). Harmondsworth, Middlesex: Penguin.

Singh, J. (1990). Voice, exit, and negative word-of-mouth behaviors: An investigation across three service categories. *Journal of the Academy of Marketing Science, 18*, 1-15.

Skinner, B. F. (1957). *Verbal behavior*. Englewood Cliffs: Prentice Hall.

Skinner, B. F. (1968). *The technology of teaching*. New York: Appleton-Century-Crofts.

Skinner, B. F. (1983). Intellectual self-management in old age. *American Psychologist, 38*, 239-244.

Skinner, B. F., & Vaughan, M. (1983). *Enjoy old age*. New York: Norton.

Smedley, B. D., & Syme, S. L. (2001). Promoting health: Intervention strategies from social and behavioral research. *American Journal of Health Promotion, 15*, 149-166.

Smith, C. D. (1996). Competing constraints in alternative dispute resolution: The interactional achievement of formality and informality in mediation. *Australian Review of Applied Linguistics, 19* (2), 79-114.

Smith, L. T. (1999). *Decolonizing methodologies: Research and indigenous peoples.* London: Zed Books.

Smith, S. L. (1997). The effective use of fear appeals in persuasive immunization: An analysis of national immunization intervention messages. *Journal of Applied Communication Research, 25,* 264-292.

Snell-Johns, J., Imm, P., Wandersman, A., & Claypoole, J. (2003). Roles assumed by a community coalition when creating environmental and policy-level changes. *Journal of Community Psychology, 31,* 661-670.

Society for the Experimental Analysis of Behavior. (1987). *Behavior analysis in developmental disabilities.* Lawrence, Kansas: Department of Human Development, University of Kansas.

Society for the Experimental Analysis of Behavior. (1987). *Behavior analysis in the community 1968-1986.* Lawrence, Kansas: Society for the Experimental Analysis of Behavior, Inc.

Sogoric, S., Middleton, J., Lang, S., Ivankovic, D., & Kern, J. (2005). A naturalistic inquiry on the impact of interventions aiming to improve health and the quality of life in the community. *Social Science & Medicine, 60,* 153-164.

Sohn, D-W, & Wall, J. A. (1993). Community mediation in South Korea: A city-village comparison. *Journal of Conflict Resolution, 37,* 536-543.

Sorcher, M., & Spence, R. (1982). The Interface Project: Behavior modeling as social technology in South Africa. *Personnel Psychology, 35,* 557-581.

Spanier, J. (1972). *Games nations play: Analyzing international politics.* New York: Praeger Publishers.

Spence, S. H., Donovan, C., & Brechman-Toussaint, M. (2000). The treatment of childhood social phobia: The effectiveness of a social skills training-based, cognitive-behavioural intervention, with and without parental involvement. *Journal of Child Psychology and Psychiatry, 41,* 713-726.

Spicer, P. (1997). Toward a (dys)functional anthropology of drinking: Ambivalence and the American Indian experience with alcohol. *Medical Anthropology Quarterly, 11,* 306-323.

Stash, S. (1999). Explanations of unmet need for contraception in Chitwan, Nepal. *Studies in Family Planning, 30,* 267-287.

Staske, S. A. (1999). Creating relational ties in talk: The collaborative construction of relational jealousy. *Symbolic Interaction, 22,* 213-246.

Stevens, J. R., & Stevens, C. M. (1992). Introductory small cash incentives to promote child spacing in India. *Studies in Family Planning, 23,* 171-186.

Stevens, R. J., Slavin, R. E., & Farnish, A. M. (1991). The effects of cooperative learning and direct instruction in reading comprehension strategies on main idea identification. *Journal of Educational Psychology, 83,* 8-16.

Stokes, T. F., & Baer, D. M. (1977). An implicit technology of generalization. *Journal of Applied Behavior Analysis, 10,* 349-367.

Stokes, T. F., & Osnes, P. G. (1988). The developing applied technology of generalization and maintenance. In R. H. Horner, G. Dunlap, and R. L. Koegel (Eds.), *Generalization and maintenance: Life-style changes in applied settings* (pp. 5-19). Baltimore, MD: Paul Brookes.

Stokes, T. F., & Osnes, P. G. (1989). An operant pursuit of generalization. *Behavior Therapy, 20,* 337-355.

Stokes, T. F., Fowler, S. A., & Baer, D. M. (1978). Training preschool children to recruit natural communities of reinforcement. *Journal of Applied Behavior Analysis, 11,* 285-303.

Stolz, S. B. (1981). Adoption of innovations from applied behavioral research: "Does anybody care?" *Journal of Applied Behavior Analysis, 14,* 491-506.

Storey, K., Danko, C. D., Ashworth, R., & Strain, P. S. (1994). Generalization of social skills intervention for preschoolers with social delays. *Education and Treatment of Children, 17,* 29-51.

Stromer, R. (1991). Stimulus equivalence: Implications for teaching. In W. Ishaq (Ed.), *Human behavior in today's world* (pp.109-122). New York: Praeger.

Stromer, R., & Mackay, H. A. (1992). Spelling and emergent picture-printed word relations established with delayed identity matching to complex samples. *Journal of Applied Behavior Analysis, 25,* 893-904.

Stromer, R., Mackay, H. A., & Stoddard, L. T. (1992). Classroom applications of stimulus equivalence technology. *Journal of Behavioral Education, 2,* 225-256.

Stuart, R. B. (Ed.). (1982). *Adherence, compliance and generalization in behavioral medicine.* NY: Brunner/Mazel.

Stull, D. D., & Schensul, J. J. (Eds.). (1987). *Collaborative research and social change.* London: Westview Press.

Sullivan, C. M., & Bybee, D. I. (1999). Reducing violence using community-based advocacy for women with abusive partners. *Journal of Consulting and Clinical Psychology, 67,* 43-53.

Sullivan, S., Arroll, B., Coster, G., Abbott, M., & Adams, P. (2000). Problem gamblers: Do GPs want to intervene? *New Zealand Medical Journal, 113,* 204-207.

Sulzer-Azaroff, B. (1982). Behavioral approaches to occupational health and safety. In L. W. Frederiksen. (Ed.), *Handbook of organizational behavior management* (pp. 505-538). New York: Wiley.

Sulzer-Azaroff, B. (1990). Strategies for maintaining change over time. *Behaviour Change, 7,* 3-15.

Sulzer-Azaroff, B., & Mayer G. R. (1977). *Applying behavior-analysis procedures with children and youth.* New York: Holt, Rinehart & Winston.

Sulzer-Azaroff, B., Pollack, M. J., & Fleming, R. K. (1992). Organizational behavior management within cultural constraints: An example from the human service sector. *Journal of Organizational Behavior Management, 12,* 117-137.

Sulzer-Azaroff, B., & Santamaria, M. C. de. (1980). Industrial safety hazard reduction through performance feedback. *Journal of Applied Behavior Analysis, 13,* 287-295.

Sunil, T. S., Pillai, V. K., & Pandey, A. (1999). Do incentives matter? Evaluation of a family planning program in India. *Population Research and Policy Review, 18,* 563-577.

Surratt, H. L., & Inciardi, J. A. (1996). Drug use, HIV risks, and prevention/intervention strategies among street youths in Rio De Janeiro, Brazil. In C. B. McCoy, L. R. Metsch, & J. A. Inciardi (Eds.), *Intervening with drug-involved youth* (pp. 173-190). London: Sage.

Tajfel, H., & Wilkes, A. L. (1963). Classification and quantitative judgement. *British Journal of Psychology, 54,* 101-114.

Tambiah, S. J. (1997). Friends, neighbors, enemies, strangers: Aggressor and victim in civilian ethnic riots. *Social Science and Medicine, 45,* 1177-1188.

Tarbox, J., & Hayes, L. J. (2003). Differential reinforcement of low-rate behavior. In W. O'Donohue, J. E. Fisher & S. C. Hayes (Eds.), *Cognitive behavior therapy: Applying empirically supported techniques in your practice* (pp. 129-135). New York: Wiley.

Tardy, R. W., & Hale, C. L. (1998). Getting "plugged in": A network analysis of health-information seeking among "stay-at-home Moms". *Communication Monographs, 65,* 226-357.

Taylor, I., & O'Reilly, M. F. (1997). Toward a functional analysis of private verbal self-regulation. *Journal of Applied Behavior Analysis, 30,* 43-50.

Taylor, P. J. (1998). Training. In M. Pool & M. Warner (Eds.), *Handbook of human resource management* (pp. 643-654). London: International Thomson Publishing.

Taylor, P. J., O'Driscoll, M. P., & Binning, J. (1998). A new integrated model for training needs analysis. *Human Resource Management Journal, 8* (2), 29-50.

Teaching Tolerance. (1989). *Free at last: A history of the civil rights movement and those who died in the struggle.* Montgomery, AL: The Southern Poverty Law Center.

Teasdale, J. D., Taylor, M. J., Cooper, Z., Hayhurst, H., & Paykel, E. S. (1995). Depressive thinking: Shifts in construct accessibility or in schematic mental models? *Journal of Abnormal Psychology, 104,* 500-507.

Thelwell, R. C., & Greenlees, I. A. (2001). The effects of a mental skills training package on gymnasium triathlon performance. *The Sports Psychologist, 15,* 127-141.

Theodorakis, Y., Weinberg, R., Natsis, P., Douma, I., & Kazakas, P. (2000). The effects of motivational versus instructional self-talk on improving motor performance. *The Sports Psychologist, 14,* 253-272.

Thomas, D. R., & Robertson, N. R. (1990). A conceptual framework for the analysis of social policies. *Journal of Community Psychology, 18,* 194-209.

Thomas, J. (2004). *Guide to managerial persuasion and influence.* Upper Saddle River, NJ: Pearson.

Thyer, B. A. (1983). Behavior modification and social work practice. In M. Hersen, P. Miller & R. Eisler, R. (Eds.), *Progress in behavior modification* (Vol. 15, pp. 172-226). New York: Academic Press.

Thyer, B. A. (1987). Can behavior analysis rescue social work? *Journal of Applied Behavior Analysis, 20,* 207-211.

Thyer, B. A., & Himle, J. (1986). Applied behavior analysis in social and community action: A bibliography. *Behavior Analysis and Social Action, 5,* 14-16.

Timberlake, W., & Farmer-Dougan, V. A. (1991). Reinforcement in applied settings: Figuring out ahead of time what will work. *Psychological Bulletin, 110,* 379-391.

Tishkov, V. (1995). 'Don't kill me, I'm a Krygyz!': An anthropological analysis of violence in the Osh ethnic conflict. *Journal of Peace Research, 32,* 133-149.

Tjosvold, D. (1998). Cooperative and competitive goal approach to conflict: Accomplishments and challenges. *Applied Psychology: An International Review, 47,* 285-342.

Tom, T. L., & Cronan, T. A. (1998). The effects of ethnic similarity on tutor-tutee interactions. *Journal of Community Psychology, 26,* 119-129.

Topper, M. D. (1987). FJUA relocation: Applying clinical anthropology in a troubled situation. In R. M. Wulff & S. J. Fiske (Eds.), *Anthropological praxis: Translating knowledge into action* (pp. 135-145). Boulder, CO: Westview Press.

Towner, E., & Dowswell, T. (2002). Community-based childhood injury prevention interventions: What works? *Health Promotion International. 17,* 273-284.

Tracey, J. B., Tannenbaum, S. I., & Kavanagh, M. J. (1995). Applying trained skills on the job: The importance of work environment. *Journal of Applied Psychology, 80,* 239-252.

Treasure, J. L., Katzman, M., Schmidt, U., Troop, N., Todd, G., & de Silva, P. (1999). Engagement and outcome in the treatment of bulimia nervosa: First phase of a sequential design comparing motivation enhancement therapy and cognitive behavioural therapy. *Behaviour Research and Therapy, 37,* 405-418.

Trinch, S. L. (2001). The advocate as gatekeeper: The limits of politeness in protective order interviews with Latina survivors of domestic abuse. *Journal of Sociolinguistics, 5,* 475-506.

Trout, J., Dokecki, P. R., Newbrough, J. R., & O'Gorman, R. T. (2003). Action research on leadership for community development in West Africa and North America: A joining of liberation theology and community psychology. *Journal of Community Psychology, 31,* 129-148.

Tsey, K., & Every, A. (2000). Evaluating Aboriginal empowerment programs: The case of Family WellBeing. *Australian and New Zealand Journal of Public Health, 24,* 509-514.

Tudiver, F., Bass, M. J., Dunn, E. V., Norton, P. G., & Stewart, M. (Eds.). (1992). *Assessing interventions: Traditional and innovative methods.* London: Sage.

Tunnecliffe, M., & Roy, O. (1993). *Emergency support: A handbook for peer supporters.* Palmyra, Western Australia: Bayside Books.

Twanley, E. W., Jeste, D. V., & Bellack, A. S. (2003). A review of cognitive training in schizophrenia. *Schizophrenia Bulletin, 29,* 359-382.

Underwager, R., & Wakefield, H. (1992). False confessions and police deception. *American Journal of Forensic Psychology, 13,* 49-66.

Valach, L., Young, R. A., & Lynam, M. J. (1996). Family health-promotion projects: An action-theoretical perspective. *Journal of Health Psychology, 1,* 49-63.

Valdez-Menchaca, M. C., & Whitehurst, G. J. (1992). Accelerating language development through picture book reading: A systematic extension to Mexican day care. *Developmental Psychology, 28,* 1106-1114.

Valverde, M., & White-Mair, K. (1999). 'One day at a time' and other slogans for everyday life: The ethical practices of Alcoholics Anonymous. *Sociology, 33,* 393-410.

Vanclay, F. (2002). Conceptualizing social impacts. *Environmental Impact Assessment Review, 22,* 183-211.

Van Hasselt, V. B., Sisson, L. A., & Aach, S. R. (1987). Parent training to increase compliance in a young multihandicapped child. *Journal of Behavior Therapy and Experimental Psychiatry, 18,* 275-283.

Van Houten, R., Nau, P. A., MacKenzie-Keating, S. E., Sameoto, D., & Colavecchia, B. (1982). An analysis of some variables influencing the effectiveness of reprimands. *Journal of Applied Behavior Analysis, 15*, 65-83.

Van Meter, D. S., & Van Horn, C. E. (1975). The policy implementation process: A conceptual framework. *Administration and Society, 6*, 445-488.

Van Raalte, J. L., Cornelius, A. E., Hatten, S. J., & Brewer, B. W. (2000). The antecedents and consequences of self-talk in competitive tennis. *Journal of Sports and Exercise Psychology, 22*, 345-356.

Van Willigen, J., & Finan, T. L. (1991). *Soundings: Rapid and reliable research methods for practicing anthropologists.* Washington, DC: American Anthropological Association.

Vargas, J. S. (1972). *Writing worthwhile behavioral objectives.* New York: Harper & Row.

Vellutino, F. R., Scanlon, D. M., Pratt, A., Sipay, E. R., Small, S. G., Chen, R., & Denckla, M. B. (1996). Cognitive profiles of difficult-to-remediate and readily remediated poor readers: Early intervention as a vehicle for distinguishing between cognitive and experiential deficits as basic causes of specific reading disabilities. *Journal of Educational Psychology, 88*, 601-638.

Vernon, R., Ojeda, G., & Townsend, M. C. (1988). Contraceptive social marketing and community-based distribution systems in Colombia. *Studies in Family Planning, 19*, 354-360.

Vine, B. (2004). *Getting things done at work: The discourse of power in workplace interaction.* Philadelphia, PA: Johns Benjamins.

Viswesvaran, C., & Schmidt, F. L. (1992). A meta-analytic comparison of the effectiveness of smoking cessation methods. *Journal of Applied Psychology, 77*, 554-561.

Vrij, A., & Smith, B. J. (1999). Reducing ethnic prejudice by public campaigns: An evaluation of a present and a new campaign. *Journal of Community & Applied Social Psychology, 9*, 195-215.

Wacker, D. P., Harding, J., Berg, W., Cooper-Brown, L. J., & Barretto, A. (2003). Punishment. In W. O'Donohue, J. E. Fisher & S. C. Hayes (Eds.), *Cognitive behavior therapy: Applying empirically supported techniques in your practice* (pp. 308-313). New York: Wiley.

Waitangi Tribunal. (1988). *Muriwhenua fishing report, WAI 22.* Wellington: Government Printers.

Waitangi Tribunal. (1998a). *Te Whanau o Waipareira report, WAI 84.* Wellington: Government Printers.

Waitangi Tribunal. (1998b). *The Turangi Township remedies report, WAI 414.* Wellington: Government Printers.

Walker, I., & Crogan, M. (1998). Academic performance, prejudice, and the Jigsaw Classroom: New pieces to the puzzle. *Journal of Community & Applied Social Psychology, 8*, 381-393.

Wall, J. A. (1981). Mediation: An analysis, review, and proposed research. *Journal of Conflict Resolution, 25*, 157-180.

Wall, J. A. (1985). *Negotiation: Theory and practice.* Glenview, IL: Scott, Foresman and Company.

Wall, J. A., & Callister, R. R. (1999). Malaysian community mediation. *Journal of Conflict Resolution, 43*, 343-365.

Wall, J. A., & Lynn, A. (1993). Mediation: A current review. *Journal of Conflict Resolution, 37*, 160-194.

Wall, J. A., Stark, J. B., & Standifer, R. L. (2001). Mediation: A current review and theory development. *Journal of Conflict Resolution, 45*, 370-391.

Wallace, M. D., & Robles, A. C. (2003). Differential reinforcement of other behavior and differential reinforcement of alternative behavior. In W. O'Donohue, J. E. Fisher & S. C. Hayes (Eds.), *Cognitive behavior therapy: Applying empirically supported techniques in your practice* (pp. 136-143). New York: Wiley.

Waller, A. L. (1988). *Feud: Hatfields, McCoys, and social change in Appalachia, 1860-1900.* London: University of North Carolina Press.

Wallis, W. D. (1925). The independence of social psychology. *Journal of Abnormal and Social Psychology, 20*, 147-150.

Wang, C. M., & Chen, S. Y. (1973). Evaluation of the first year of the educational saving program in Taiwan. *Studies in Family Planning, 4*, 157-161.

Ward, A. (1993). Historical claims under the Treaty of Waitangi: Avenue of reconciliation or source of new divisions? *The Journal of Pacific History, 28*, 181-203.

Watkins, S. C., & Danzi, A. D. (1995). Women's gossip and social change: Childbirth and fertility control among Italian and Jewish women in the United States, 1920-1940. *Gender & Society, 9*, 469-490.

Webster-Stratton, C. (2001). The Incredible Years: Parents, teachers, and children training series. In S. I. Pfeiffer & L. A. Reddy (Eds.), *Innovative mental health interventions for children: Programs that work* (pp. 31-45). London: The Haworth Press.

Weick, K. E. (1984). Small wins: Redefining the scale of social problems. *American Psychologist, 39*, 40-49.

Weisenberg, M., Schwarzwald, J., Waysman, M., Solomon, Z., & Klingman, A. (1993). Coping of school-age children in the sealed room during Scud Missile bombardment and postwar stress reactions. *Journal of Consulting and Clinical Psychology, 61*, 462-467.

Weiss, T. G. (1999). Sanctions as a foreign policy tool: Weighing humanitarian impulses. *Journal of Peace Research, 36*, 499-509.

Weissberg, R. P., Barton, H. A., & Shriver, T. P. (1997). The Social-Competence Promotion Program for Young Adolescents. In G. W. Albee & T. P. Gullotta (Eds.), *Primary prevention works* (pp. 268-290). London: Sage.

Weissberg, R. P., Kumpfer, K. L., & Seligman, M. E. P. (2003). Prevention that works for children and youth. *American Psychologist, 58*, 425-432.

Welford, A. T. (1968). *Fundamentals of skill.* London: Methuen.

Wexley, K. N. (1984). Personnel training. *Annual Review of Psychology, 35*, 519-551.

Wheeler, D. D., & Janis, I. L. (1980). *A practical guide for making decisions.* New York: The Free Press.

White, T. (1994). Two kinds of production: The evolution of China's family planning policy in the 1980s. In J. L. Finkle & C. A. McIntosh (Eds.), *The new politics of population: Conflict and consensus in family planning* (pp. 137-158). New York: Oxford University Press.

Whitehurst, G. J., Falco, F. L., Lonigan, C. J., Fischel, J. E., DeBaryshe, B. D., Valdez-Menchaca, M. C., & Caufield, M. (1988). Accelerating language development through picture book reading. *Developmental Psychology, 24*, 552-559.

Wilkinson, S., & Kitzinger, C. (2000). Thinking differently about thinking positive: A discursive approach to cancer patients' talk. *Social Science & Medicine, 45*, 797-811.

Williams, A. F., & Preusser, D. F. (1997). Night driving restrictions for youthful drivers: A literature review and commentary. *Journal of Public Health Policy, 18*, 334-345.

Williams, J. A. (1969). *Politics of the New Zealand Maori: Protest and cooperation, 1891-1909.* Oxford: Oxford University Press.

Wilson, K. G., Hayes, S. C., & Byrd, M. R. (2000). Exploring compatibilities between Acceptance and Commitment Therapy and 12-Step treatment for substance abuse. *Journal of Rational-Emotive & Cognitive-Behavior Therapy, 18*, 209-234.

Wilson, K. A., & Chambless, D. L. (1999). Inflated perceptions of responsibility and obsessive-compulsive symptoms. *Behaviour Research and Therapy, 37*, 325-335.

Wilson, R. P. (1998). The role of anthropologists as short-term consultants. *Human Organization, 57*, 245-252.

Winett, R. A. (1993). Media-based behavior change approaches to prevention. In D. S. Glenwick & L. A. Jason (Eds.), *Promoting health and mental health in children, youth, and families* (pp. 181-203). NY: Springer.

Winett, R. A. (1995). A framework for health promotion and disease prevention programs. *American Psychologist, 50*, 341-350.

Winett, R. A., Cleaveland, B. L., Tate, D. F., Lombard, D. N., Lombard, T. N., Russ, C. R., & Galper, D. (1997). The effects of the Safe-Sun program on patrons' and lifeguards' skin cancer risk-reduction behaviors at swimming pools. *Journal of Health Psychology, 2*, 85-95.

Winett, R. A., Leckliter, I. N., Chinn, D. E., & Stahl, B. (1984). Reducing energy consumption: The long-term effects of a single TV program. *Journal of Communications, 34*, 37-51.

Withers, B., & Lewis, K. D. (2003). *The conflict and communication activity book: 30 high-impact training exercises for adult learners.* NY: AMACOM.

Wolf, E. R. (1982). *Europe and the people without history.* Berkeley, CA: University of California Press.

Wolf, M. M. (1978). Social validity: The case for subjective measurement or how behavior analysis is finding its heart. *Journal of Applied Behavior Analysis, 11*, 203-214.

Wolf, M.M., Braukman, C.J., & Ramp, K.A. (1987). Serious delinquent behavior as part of a significantly handicapping condition: Cues and supportive environments. *Journal of Applied Behavior Analysis, 20*, 347-359.

Wolkon, G. H., & Moriwaki, S. (1977). The ombudsman: A serendipitous mental health intervention. *Community Mental Health Journal, 13*, 229-238.

Woodward, G. C., & Denton, R. E. (1996). *Persuasion & influence in American life.* Prospect Heights, IL: Waveland Press.

Wurtele, S. K. (1990). Teaching personal safety skills to four-year-old children. *Behavior Therapy, 21*, 25-32.

Wurtele, S. K. (1995). Health promotion. In M. C. Roberts (Ed.), *Handbook of pediatric psychology* (pp. 200-216). London: Guilford Press.

Yasumaro, S., Silva, M. E., Andrighetti, M. T. M., Macoris, M. L. G., Mazine, C. A. B., & Winch, P. J. (1998). Community involvement in a dengue prevention project in Marília, Sao Paulo State, Brazil. *Human Organization, 57*, 209-214.

Yeager, J. M., & Simpson, G. E. (1973). Techniques for reducing prejudice: Changing the prejudiced person. In P. Watson (Ed.), *Psychology and race* (pp. 96-144). Harmondsworth, Middlesex: Penguin.

Yee, T. T., & Lee, R. H. (1977). Based on cultural strengths, a school primary prevention program for Asian-American youth. *Community Mental Health Journal, 13*, 239-248.

Young, D. S., & Le, D. N. (1987). Training children in road crossing skills using a roadside simulation. *Accident Analysis and Prevention, 19*, 327-341.

Young, G. (1998). Educational interventions: The lions roar. In M. L. Hecht (Ed.), *Communicating prejudice* (pp. 311-325). London: Sage.

Young, J. M., Krantz, P. J., McClannahan, L. E., & Poulson, C. L. (1994). Generalized imitation and response-class formation in children with autism. *Journal of Applied Behavior Analysis, 27*, 685-697.

Zartman, I. W., & Berman, M. R. (1982). *The practical negotiator.* London: Yale University Press.

Zartman, I. W., & Rasmussen, J. L. (Eds.). (1997). *Peacemaking in international conflict: Methods & techniques* (pp. 51-77). Washington, DC: United States Institute of Peace Press.

Zigler, E. F., & Muenchow, S. (1992). *Head Start: The inside story of America's most successful educational experiment.* NY: Basic Books.

Zimmerman, M. et al. (1990). Assessing the acceptability of NORPLANT® implants in four countries: Findings from focus group research. *Studies in Family Planning, 21*, 92-103.

Zitter, R. E., & Fremouw, W. J. (1978). Individual versus partner consequation for weight loss. *Behavior Therapy, 9*, 808-813.

Index